HEMINGWAY
DIRECT AND OBLIQUE

by

RICHARD K. PETERSON

1969
MOUTON
THE HAGUE · PARIS

PS
3515
.E37
Z753

Printed in The Netherlands by Mouton & Co., Printers, The Hague.

STUDIES IN AMERICAN LITERATURE

Volume XIV

☆☆☆☆☆☆☆☆☆☆☆☆☆☆☆☆☆☆☆☆☆☆☆☆☆☆☆☆☆☆☆☆☆

FOR JOANNE

ACKNOWLEDGMENT

CONTENTS

I

THE "MEANING" OF STYLE

A favorite pastime of literary critics in these critical times is the intellectual equivalent of reading character from a man's handwriting or his appearance: it is the game of interpreting a writer's "meaning" from his style. If it is slightly unfair to make sport of critics in this manner, it is probably harmless enough, since critics tend to disparage "critics" in a way which suggests that they do not consider themselves part of that rather disreputable crowd. Critics of Hemingway are perhaps especially prone to the self-flattering gambit of identifying themselves with the writer and sharing his low opinion of critics, whom he has described variously as camp-following eunuchs of literature and as coyotes yipping pleasantly outside in the snow on a cold night when "you are in your own cabin that you have built or paid for with your work".[1] Assuming, however, that criticism is occasionally necessary and serious (which should not mean solemn), it is still somewhat unfair to gibe at efforts to explain the "meaning" of a style, since that is plainly the goal of stylistic description. Mere description is of little value without some conclusion about the significance of the traits described. Having said so much and, moreover, embarking myself on an explanation of the "meaning" of traits which I consider central in Hemingway's style, I yet must find fault with the vast majority of the present interpretations of his style. In

[1] The first description is from a letter to Sherwood Anderson, May 23 (1925?), which is in the Anderson manuscript collection of The Newberry Library, Chicago. The second is from "Old Newsman Writes", *Esquire*, December 1934, p. 26; the cabin sounds very much like Hemingway's "good place" where nothing can touch you, the critics being both outsiders and one of the inferior animals in Hemingway's imagistic value system.

general, their failing is concentrating on too few traits – often only one – with the foreseeable consequence of their being over-simplifications.

Before examining some specific examples of interpretations of Hemingway's style, I should explain that I employ *style* not just in the strict sense of the smaller elements of language – the choice and arrangement of words – but at times to refer to the larger elements of technique or method. For example, the habit of deflation is a trait of Hemingway's style which can be observed both in the use of a single "tough" word to spike the potentially precious or pompous (as in the combination *damned beautiful*) and in deflating progressions like deliberate anticlimax or a self-mocking turn at the end of an expansive passage. I think that such broad traits of manner are best seen by examination of the larger units of method, even by examination of recurrent themes, values and imagery, as well as by close examination of the smaller elements of prose diction.

To avoid an oversimplified interpretation of Hemingway's style, it is important to recognize that it is not all of a piece, a point which Malcolm Cowley makes well:

... it always makes me angry to hear people speaking of his "lean, hard, athletic prose". Sometimes his prose is beautiful, poetic in the best sense, in its exact evocations of landscapes and emotions. Sometimes it is terse and efficient. Sometimes, with its piling up of very short words, it gives the effect of a man stammering, getting his tongue twisted, talking too much but eventually making us understand just what he wants to say.[2]

Moreover, it is possible to speak generally of an early and a later style, of a change beginning somewhere in the 1930's toward greater expansiveness. Such a division is partly a critical convenience, since of course there are many traits which persist from the early to the later style and traits of the later style which are present in embryo in the earlier. Perhaps the difference is best described as a shift in emphasis – a movement away from the severe understatement of much of the early work.

[2] "Hemingway: Work in Progress", *The New Republic*, October 20, 1937, p. 305.

Philip Young notes the change in Hemingway's style by 1940 in *For Whom the Bell Tolls*, but his interpretation of the style's meaning is based on the earlier style, specifically on its being a direct result of trauma (the result of Hemingway's "big wound" in World War I) which it both expresses and tries to control:

The strictly disciplined controls which he has exerted over his hero and his "bad nerves" are precise parallels to the strictly disciplined sentences he writes. Understatement, abbreviated statement and lack of statement reflect without the slightest distortion the rigid restraint which the man feels he must practice if he is to survive. The "mindlessness" of the style is the result of a need to "stop thinking", and is the purest reflection of that need. The intense simplicity of the prose is a means by which the man says, Things must be *made* simple, or I am lost, in a way you'll never be.

. . . .

His subject is violence and pain, and their effects, and the recovery from the effects in the face of and partly through more of the same. The style which expresses this subject matter is itself perfectly expressive of these things, and of the message: life, which is the material, must be constantly forced under the most intense and rigorous control, and held in the tightest of rein, for it is savage and can get out of hand.[3]

Plausible as Young's explanation may appear (and certainly it has some truth in it), it is simply too biographical and essentializing – even as an interpretation of Hemingway's early style – and perhaps too sensational. Granted that the style seems both to reflect and try to control fears, pinpointing the fears so exactly is a dubious undertaking which leads too readily to amateur psychiatry or something akin to the analysis of handwriting. One's handwriting (to pursue the comparison a bit) obviously has a meaning or, more likely, several meanings simultaneously; but the

---

[3] *Ernest Hemingway* (New York, Rinehart and Co., Inc., 1952), pp. 177-178. See also pp. 176, 179. Cf. John Atkins, *The Art of Ernest Hemingway: His Work and Personality* (New York, Roy Publishers, 1953), p. 126: "Everyone who knows Hemingway agrees that his wound in Italy marked him for life, spiritually as well as physically. The shock of this wound was so great that he has spent a large part of the rest of his life trying to assure himself that he is not scared. ... The discipline of his writing is perhaps a reflexion of this other discipline in his mental life."

meanings cannot be deduced from the style alone, and the temptation always is to take what we know of a person and read it back into his style (or handwriting), thus "discovering" in the style what we already know. This circular process is a serious drawback of most of the explanations of the "meaning" of Hemingway's style.

Another drawback, besides the tendency to consider too few factors, is a tendency to push conclusions about the style's meaning to untenable extremes. For example, Hemingway employs irony a great deal, and one effect of irony is to detach the writer from his characters and material. This effect fits very neatly with the recurrent theme of isolation in Hemingway's work and with what several critics, borrowing the phrase from Cowley, call Hemingway's "spectatorial attitude".[4] The next step, reversing the usual relation between attitude and style, is to conclude that the style determined the outlook: "Journalism presented him this way of looking at the world when it taught him the use of the bare, detached style." [5] Then one may conclude that an ironic style is appropriate only to the theme of isolation, so that a novel like *To Have and Have Not* (with a different theme?) must be a disaster:

For more than ten years Hemingway had worked at perfecting a detached, ironical style that would dramatize man's isolation in a blind universe and would convey through its terseness the belief that there is no remedy for man's condition but fortitude. As one might expect, it was no easy matter to enlist that style in the service of collective action for social justice.[6]

Deciding (I think correctly) that *For Whom the Bell Tolls* still expresses romantic isolation beneath its official surface message to the contrary, Weeks proceeds in the latter article to draw two untenable conclusions. First, he professes to see Jordan's view of life as "sufficiently ironic to enable him to accommodate himself

[4] See *Exile's Return: A Literary Odyssey of the 1920's*, rev. ed. (New York, The Viking Press, 1951), pp. 43-45.
[5] Robert P. Weeks, "Hemingway and the Spectatorial Attitude", *Western Humanities Review*, XI (Summer 1957), 280.
[6] Robert P. Weeks, "Hemingway and the Uses of Isolation", *The University of Kansas City Review*, XXIV (December 1957), 122-123.

to the idea of sacrificing his life to a hopeless cause" (p. 124) – which is, I submit, the ironic view reduced to absurdity and not true of the novel anyway. Second, Weeks finds the same early "restrained tight-lipped style" in *For Whom the Bell Tolls* – surely an instance of mental set determining perception, since he is already committed to the inseparability of that particular style and an outlook of detachment and isolation, so that he must see a style which echoes the content.

The inseparability of matter and manner, of content and form, is a modern critical dictum often applied too uncritically in the analysis of style. Moreover, the implication is frequently that there is one "right" form for each idea expressed and that the form can successfully express only that idea. Carried to its logical extreme, the dictum becomes nonsensical; and Kenneth Burke disposes of it in his discussion of "significant form":

... we must question a quasi-mystical attempt to explain all formal qualities as "onomatopoetic" (that is, as an adaptation of sound and rhythm to the pecularities of the sense). In most cases we find formal designs or contrivances which impart emphasis regardless of their subject. Whatever the theme may be, they add saliency to this theme, the same design serving to make dismalness more dismal or gladness gladder. ... To realize that there is such absolute stressing, one has but to consider the great variety of emotions which can be intensified by climactic arrangement, such arrangement thus being a mere "coefficient of power" which can heighten the saliency of the emotion regardless of what emotion it may be.[7]

There is something not only quasi-mystical but almost prescriptive and essentially limited about comments on *For Whom the Bell Tolls* which run, "Because it is another story, this story could not have been told at all in the older style", since it is a "nearly poetic realization of man's *collective* virtues", while the earlier style was "an exact transfiguration of Hemingway's moral attitude

[7] *Counter-Statement*, 2nd ed. (Los Altos, Calif., Hermes Publications, 1953), p. 135. John Atkins makes a similar point about the lack of a necessary equivalence between manner and matter when discussing Hemingway's "code": "... there is no relevance between code and object. To enjoy yourself on the physical plane there is no compulsion to deflate language and smother emotion. In fact, many Elizabethans did just the opposite in pursuit of similar ends" (p. 193).

toward a peculiarly violent and chaotic experience" – i.e., the attitude of the self-contained, tightly self-controlled, isolated individual.[8] Pursuing the notion of the inseparability of form and content, Schorer makes *The Sun Also Rises* a consummate work of art because the form is so exactly equivalent with the subject and the style evaluates the subject:

Hemingway's early subject, the exhaustion of value, was perfectly investigated and invested by his bare style, and in story after story, no meaning at all is to be inferred from the fiction except as the style itself suggests that there is no meaning in life. This style, more than that, was the perfect technical substitute for the conventional commentator; it expresses and it measures that peculiar morality of the stiff lip which Hemingway borrowed from athletes. It is an instructive lesson, furthermore, to observe how the style breaks down when Hemingway moves into the less congenial subject matter of social affirmation: how the style breaks down, the effect of verbal economy as mute suffering is lost, the personality of the writer, no longer protected by the objectification of an adequate technique, begins its offensive intrusion, and the entire structural integrity slackens. Inversely, in the stories and the early novels, the technique was the perfect embodiment of the subject and it gave that subject its astonishing largeness of effect and meaning.[9]

Holding such a view of style, it is little wonder that Schorer can say, "When we speak of technique, then, we speak of nearly everything" (p. 190). Yet what he sees in the style is too limited in several ways. In the first place, a method of understatement and irony may posit a detached writer, but all that necessarily means is a writer who wants to be detached from his material – from the feelings expressed in his work, for example. It does not necessarily follow that the author or the characters in his fiction have to want to remain detached from the rest of the world.

The style shows something about the author's attitude toward his material, all right, something overlooked too often in explanations of the "meaning" of Hemingway's style: it shows

---

[8]   Mark Schorer, "The Background of a Style", *Kenyon Review*, III (Winter 1941), 104, 103.
[9]   "Technique as Discovery", in *Essays in Modern Literary Criticism*, ed. Ray B. West, Jr. (New York, Rinehart and Co., Inc., 1952), p. 203.

something about his attitude toward writing. It is an error to equate this attitude with his attitude toward life as reflected by all the characters, incidents and themes of his work, without producing considerable evidence to support such an equation. Hemingway's underlying distrust of words, for example, has a profound effect on the character of his style, seen not only in his "objectivity", understatement, and various forms of indirection but also in some of the forms that his tendency toward expansiveness takes – e.g., the toughness, the increase in the word *true*, the use of foreignism. In addition, his style shows a typical reaction of the times against the effusive emotionalism of earlier literature, a reaction of both the 1920's and our time which might be summed up in the motto, "Don't wear your heart on your sleeve". Since nothing is quite so gauche according to that view, a bare, "objective" style may reflect fear of possible criticism or ridicule if one allows his feelings open expression. Simply equating bareness of style (which is only part of the picture anyway) with the author's idea of the bareness of life is reduction and oversimplification. It is another example of the tendency to read back into the style an idea expressed otherwise in the work and then to make the whole style take on that "meaning".

To say that Hemingway's early style is appropriate to only one kind of content is a dubious assertion. It is much more accurate to say that it is appropriate to authors who share generally a certain kind of attitude toward their material, toward writing, toward words themselves. Hemingway's distrust of words, his fear of sounding pretentious, arty or "literary", has stylistic effects which have not been stressed sufficiently. One effect might be described as the cultivation of deliberate awkwardness, if it were not for the fact that it is not always clear how deliberate the awkwardness is. For example, it is hard to know how deliberate the awkwardness is in this sentence from *Across the River and into the Trees*: "Her voice was so lovely and it always reminded him of Pablo Casals playing the cello that it made him feel as a wound does that you think you cannot bear" (Ch. xi). Hemingway effectively clouds the issue by being self-consciously ungrammatical at times: ". . . she is sleeping so lovely. He said lovely to

himself since his thinking was often ungrammatical" (Ch. xxxiii).
Yet the rather typical lack of parallelism in this sentence is not so
obviously deliberate: ". . . it had the advantage of you moving
while you do it and that you look at the houses . . . while you are
walking" (Ch. xxi).

That the awkwardness is there I think no one will deny, in
spite of Hemingway's somewhat touchy and self-flattering objection during an interview:

I might say that what amateurs call a style is usually only the un-
avoidable awkwardnesses in first trying to make something that has
not heretofore been made. Almost no new classics resemble other
previous classics. At first people can see only the awkwardness.
Then they [sic] are not so perceptible. When they show so very
awkwardly people think these awkwardnesses are the style and many
copy them.[10]

It may be that Hemingway felt sensitive about his limited formal
education, as his habitually disparaging remarks about the literati
suggest.[11] If so, the feeling probably reinforces his determination
to avoid sounding "literary", to make a literary virtue out of a
possible weakness.

Sometimes the awkwardness is combined with or is the effect
of indefiniteness, a preference for the simple or common word or
construction rather than for the more specific and "literary". One
form of indefiniteness which might be mentioned here is the
coordinate clauses, connected by the simplest, common word
– and – which does not specify the relationship between clauses,
juxtaposing apparently unconnected ideas. One example, which
Leon Edel thinks a successful *non sequitur* in its contrasting the
ideas of spring (new life) and guns (death), is from *A Farewell to
Arms*: "There were many more guns in the country around and
the spring had come" (Ch. iii).[12] Less obvious in "meaning",

[10] George Plimpton, "Ernest Hemingway" (The Art of Fiction, XXI),
The Paris Review, XVIII (Spring 1958), 78.
[11] In "Monologue to the Maestro", *Esquire*, October 1935, Hemingway
has "Mice" (the young aspirant writer) object, "That isn't the way they
teach you to write in college." Hemingway answers, "I don't know about
that. I never went to college. If any sonofabitch could write he wouldn't
have to teach writing in college" (p. 174A).
[12] See "The Art of Evasion", *Folio*, XX (Spring 1955), 19.

perhaps, is an example from *The Sun Also Rises*, though it would
be possible to interpret it as the kind of disconnected view one
gets when driving through a town without stopping:

There were signs on the walls of the churches saying it was forbidden
to play pelota against them, and the houses in the villages had red
tiled roofs, and then the road turned off and commenced to climb
and we were going way up close along a hillside, with a valley below
and hills stretched off back toward the sea. (Ch. x)

Yet we must recognize also that the device is a generalized trait
of Hemingway's, which cannot be completely explained by explaining the "meaning" of each individual instance in isolation.

Robert Penn Warren, contending with reason that the style
reflects the sensibility of the author more than that of the characters, yet makes it reflect a view of the world more than an
attitude toward writing: "The short simple rhythms, the succession of coordinate clauses, the general lack of subordination – all
suggest a dislocated and ununified world." [13] While it is no doubt
true that any style has a psychological meaning, that it ultimately
reflects a view of life even if it more immediately reflects an
aesthetic purpose, I think that in this interpretation the "meaning"
of the style is again oversimplified. In a review of O'Neill's *All
God's Chillun Got Wings*, Edmund Wilson once commented that
by eliminating excessive detail O'Neill had gained intensity.[14] I
wonder whether some such purpose is not the reason for a good
deal of Hemingway's indefiniteness, his lack of specificity, since
the highly detailed or particular passage may achieve complexity
at the expense of intensity. One effect of the repetition which
Hemingway uses so much, for example, is a gain in intensity by
stressing a limited number of things, sacrificing "extra-concrete-
ness", analysis, and complexity. When the method succeeds, such
indefiniteness can result in considerable intensity and suggestive-
ness; when it does not succeed, the result may be anything from
monotony to vagueness to evasiveness.

[13] "Hemingway", *The Kenyon Review*, IX (Winter 1947), 18.
[14] *The Shores of Light: A Literary Chronicle of the Twenties and Thirties* (New York, Farrar, Straus and Young, Inc., 1952), p. 103.

It is clear, however, that aesthetic purposes or values cannot be easily divorced from "moral" values or attitudes toward life in Hemingway's work, if only because of his belief that it is the writer's duty to tell the truth and expose the lie. Since he also feels that words are at least potentially lies, the resulting conflict is bound to have profound effects on the kind of writing he does. It results, for example, not only in his penchant for understatement but in his visible uneasiness in the face of his own tendency toward expansive writing – which in turn results in some of the stylistic traits examined later.

At the same time the dedication to truth-telling and giving the lie extends to his presentation of character and incident – e.g., to his handling of those whom he identifies as fakes or phonies. Lionel Trilling makes the further point that Hemingway's emphasis on correct technique is another facet of his desire to replace fine words and grandiose sentiments with truth or "reality":

Another manifestation of the same desire in Hemingway was his devotion to the ideal of technique as an end in itself. A great deal can go down in the tumble but one of the things that stands best is a cleanly done job. ... professional pride is one of the last things to go. Hemingway became a devotee of his own skill and he exploited the ideal of skill in his characters. His admired men always do a good job; and the proper handling of a rod, a gun, an *espada,* or a pen is a thing, so Hemingway seems always to be saying, which can be understood when speech cannot.[15]

The last chapter, then, though it differs in emphasis from the others which are more closely concerned with style and technique, is still connected with the others and with aesthetic values in its investigation of Hemingway's value system or "code" and the way that the value system affects the work. It deals more with the direct expression of some of Hemingway's ideas, perhaps, while the other chapters – especially iii and iv – deal more with the indirect or oblique. I have borrowed the title of Tillyard's little book on poetry, except for the first word, because it is a handy summary of my approach to Hemingway's work: the considera-

---

[15] "Hemingway and His Critics", in *Hemingway and His Critics: An International Anthology*, ed. Carlos Baker (New York, Hill and Wang, 1961), pp. 65-66.

tion of the various forms of indirection that he employs, together with the overt themes and statements which say the same things directly. Through this approach, I hope that Hemingway emerges the clearer in both his matter and his manner, both directly and obliquely.

My estimate of Hemingway's achievement and influence accords pretty well with Malcolm Cowley's in "Hemingway: Work in Progress":

> Partly it has been a bad influence. It has made people copy the hard-boiled manner of "The Killers" and "Fifty Grand". ... Worst of all, it has caused many young writers to take over Hemingway's vocabulary and his manner of seeing the world – thereby making it impossible for them to be as honest as Hemingway. But in general I think that his influence has been excellent. It has freed many writers – not only novelists but poets and essayists and simple reporters – from a burden of erudition and affectation that they thought was part of the writer's equipment. It has encouraged them to write as simply as possible about the things they really feel, instead of the things they think that other people think they ought to feel. (p. 305)

Examination of what is bad in Hemingway's style and technique removes it from the honorific glow of what is good. No writer benefits from indiscriminate praise of his work regardless of its quality – as Hemingway once wrote to Sherwood Anderson in so many words.[16] Moreover, the drawbacks of the ironic method (if not the ironic temper), a method of which Hemingway is so famous a modern example, need pointing out, since the virtues of the ironic method are too unreservedly touted nowadays.

We should be tough-minded enough to see the writer as a human being with a considerable talent – not as a demigod whose clay feet must be glossed over. To see a writer as a whole, we must look at all of his work. Though it is just that he should be renowned for his best work, the less good should not be hidden or dismissed according to the ironic double standard which makes his successes his own but his failures the fault of his characters.

---

[16] Hemingway wrote to Anderson, May 21, 1926, trying to explain his motives in *The Torrents of Spring*. The letter is in the Anderson manuscript collection of The Newberry Library, Chicago.

II

COOL, CLEAN, WELL-LIGHTED ORDER

Indefiniteness, almost a refusal to specify, is a common denominator of many different aspects of Hemingway's style. His penchant for indefiniteness, akin to indirection in statement, can be seen in his preference for the common, unspecific word, avoiding more particularized and "literary" synonyms: in his liking for such general, valuative adjectives as *nice, fine, good* and in his mannered repetition of forms of the verbs *say* and *be.* Likewise, his many unmodified nouns lack the particularity of the modified, while his pronouns and adverbs without referents add to the effect of indefiniteness, as do the awkward, ambiguously placed phrases and clauses used as modifiers. "Personal pronouns frequently get involved in what is stigmatized . . . as faulty reference; there are sentences in which it is hard to tell the hunter from his quarry or the bullfighter from the bull." [1] Thus "The Mother of a Queen" begins, "When his father died he was only a kid and his manager buried him perpetually."

That sounds like deliberate awkward indefiniteness, but it is not clear whether it is deliberate in this ambiguous sentence from Chapter xxiii of *For Whom the Bell Tolls*: "The man who was leading rode along the trail to where Pablo had circled and stopped" (who stopped?). Compare, from *To Have and Have Not*, "I got out the Smith and Wesson thirty-eight special I had when I was on the police force up in Miami from under the mattress" (Ch. iii) or "He had to pretend he wanted to see Juan

---

[1] Harry Levin, "Observations on the Style of Ernest Hemingway", *Contexts of Criticism* (Cambridge, Mass., Harvard University Press, 1957), pp. 154-155.

Rodriguez, who is a poor stinking gallego that would steal from his own mother that Bee-Lips has got indicted again so, he can defend him" (Ch. ix), in which the ambiguously placed modifiers produce the awkward indefiniteness. In "The Killers" we read, "He had propped open the slit that dishes passed through into the kitchen with a catsup bottle."

Such indefiniteness requires that we qualify the frequent description of Hemingway's style as "concrete", a description based in large part on the unquestioning acceptance of Frederic Henry's denunciation of abstract words and fine phrases:

I was always embarrassed by the words sacred, glorious, and sacrifice and the expression in vain. ... I had seen nothing sacred, and the things that were glorious had no glory and the sacrifices were like the stockyards at Chicago if nothing was done with the meat except to bury it. There were many words that you could not stand to hear and finally only the names of places had dignity. Certain numbers were the same way and certain dates and these with the names of the places were all you could say and have them mean anything. Abstract words such as glory, honor, courage, or hallow were obscene beside the concrete names of villages, the numbers of roads, the names of rivers, the numbers of regiments and the dates. (Ch. xxvii)

Philip Young says that Hemingway was influenced by Pound and the Imagists to avoid vague generalities, using ordinary speech and the exact word (p. 155), while John W. Aldridge says that Hemingway and the "lost generation" learned to "hold tight to themselves and to the concrete simplicities (until the simple and concrete seemed to be all there was, all that was worth knowing) when the world around them seemed to be breaking to pieces".[2]

However, as Joseph Warren Beach points out, the simplest word is the most common and undiscriminated word − not the exact or specific word, the *mot précis* − so that comparison of Hemingway to Flaubert in this regard is misleading.[3] As a matter of fact, Hemingway takes pains to avoid the *mot juste*, probably because it sounds too "literary" to him, preferring the general,

[2] *After the Lost Generation: A Critical Study of the Writers of Two Wars* (New York, McGraw-Hill Book Co., Inc., 1951), pp. 10-11.
[3] *American Fiction 1920-1940* (New York, The Macmillan Co., 1941), p. 102.

unspecific word like *and*. In the sense of meaning highly particular, specific or "extra-concrete",[4] the word *concrete* is an inaccurate term to describe Hemingway's style. Baker, among others, has called attention to the general, unspecific nature of many of Hemingway's descriptions, while Levin notes a trick of generalizing the specific episode: "They always picked the finest places to have the quarrels" ("The Snows of Kilimanjaro").[5]

Hemingway maintains his reputation for concreteness by incidental detail, Levin adds, suggesting that the arc light and the tipped-back derby hat were late additions to "The Killers". Other devices which maintain the impression of concreteness are the use of numbers (as in "The Light of the World": "Down at the station there were five whores waiting for the train to come in, and six white men and four Indians") and the catalogues which give a succession of "objective" details. Part of a catalogue from *To Have and Have Not*, detailing what Richard Gordon sees on his walk after the final quarrel with his wife, may serve to illustrate:

... he passed the frame houses with their narrow yards, light coming from the shuttered windows; the unpaved alleys, with their double rows of houses; Conch town, where all was starched, well-shuttered, virtue, failure, grits and boiled grunts, under-nourishment, prejudice, righteousness, interbreeding and the comforts of religion; the open-doored, lighted Cuban bolito houses, shacks whose only romance was their names: The Red House, Chicha's; the pressed stone Church; its steeples sharp, ugly triangles against the moonlight; the big grounds and the long, black-domed bulk of the convent, handsome in the moonlight; a filling station and a sandwich place, bright-lighted beside a vacant lot where a miniature golf course had been taken out; past the brightly lit main street with the three drug stores, the music store, the five Jew stores, three poolrooms, two barber-shops, five beer joints, three ice cream parlors, the five poor and the one good restaurant, two magazine and paper places, four second-hand joints (one of which made keys), a photographer's, an office

[4] W. K. Wimsatt, Jr., with Monroe C. Beardsley, *The Verbal Icon: Studies in the Meaning of Poetry* (Lexington?, University of Kentucky Press, 1954), p. 138. In many respects Hemingway is closer to what Wimsatt calls the minimum concrete or "substantive level".
[5] Carlos Baker, *Hemingway: The Writer as Artist*, 3rd ed. (Princeton, Princeton University Press, 1963), pp. 50-51; Levin, p. 156.

building with four dentists' offices upstairs, the big dime store, a hotel on the corner with taxis opposite. ... (Ch. xxii)

It is obvious that though the description sounds "concrete" and "objective", the incongruous list near the beginning ("virtue, failure, grits", etc.) is actually fairly abstract, while the effect of the catalogue as a whole is decidedly expansive – almost torrential – rather than bare or understated. Even this kind of "concreteness" has more than one side to it, while concreteness in the sense of specificity is primarily an illusion of the style.

When a trait like indefiniteness appears in so many different forms in a writer's work, surely we have reason to look for it in less obvious places – for instance, in his "objective" words and descriptions. Specifically, I refer to Hemingway's trick of making valuative terms of such apparently objective things as the cool, the clean, the clear, the light (and day), and the well-ordered. Evidence should indicate that not only these words but also descriptions that say essentially the same thing are often not realistic details but subjective appraisals – parts, in this case, of a cluster expressing strong approval.

Obviously, in saying this I do not mean that *day* (to take one example) never stands just for itself; every day and every night in Hemingway's fiction and nonfiction is not something more than plain fact (neither is every mountain, though Carlos Baker's chapter on the subject tends to make one forget it).[6] Nor does the day without exception stand for the same thing when it does represent something more: sometimes night is preferred. By and large, however, there is sufficient evidence to warrant the conclusion that the clean, cool, clear, light, and well-ordered are valued things and generally terms of approval.

Hemingway is hardly unique, of course, in his tendency to make less specific, valuative terms out of the "concrete" and apparently "objective". In a study of the major adjectives in English poetry, Josephine Miles has showed a definite historical

---

[6] Chapter v, "The Mountain and the Plain", in *Hemingway: The Writer as Artist*, pp. 94-116.

trend away from the obvious terms of standard and value (*good*, *great*, *true*) in the traditional poets toward what she calls terms of quality (*green*, *dry*, *warm*, *high*, *bright*) in the modern.[7] She describes the course of the epithet as a shift from an ethic to an aesthetic vocabulary: "I say 'vocabulary' rather than 'subject', because, as we have seen for twentieth-century poets, esthetic terminology in context is strongly full of ethic judgment; *bright* for the moderns can be a direct substitute for *good*, as it functions evaluatively" (p. 408). But if Hemingway is not unique in using "objective" terms to express values or attitudes, he is distinctive no doubt in the particular terms that he utilizes. (Note at the same time his reliance on standard terms of value like *good*; his practice is not the use of the one to the exclusion of the other but the addition of "concrete" terms of value to standard ones.) When we have discovered what is *clean*, for example, and what is implied in an emphasis on cleanness and the other items in the cluster, we should be that much closer to an understanding of Hemingway's makeup and its effect on his ethics and aesthetics.

While use of apparently objective words to express values reflects in part a predilection for the nonspecific, general, and simple, it also reflects other tendencies in Hemingway: his show of being "objective", terse, noncommittal (his understatement) while expressing omitted thoughts and feelings indirectly – avoiding the direct and overt. But even more important ultimately may be the question why these particular words, images, image clusters, and themes are preferred – why they recur – what things they express that are so important to Hemingway that he continues to dwell on them. When examined from this point of view, "concrete" and "objective" words and details may tell a different story than the one usually told about Hemingway.

A classic example of the usual story is, perhaps, a passage from Ford Madox Ford's introduction to the Modern Library edition of *A Farewell to Arms*. In the process of praising Hemingway's

---

[7]   *Major Adjectives in English Poetry: From Wyatt to Auden*, University of California Publications in English, XII, No. 3 (Berkeley, University of California Press, 1946), 305-426.

restraint and "discipline" in his choice of words and his new and distinctive way of looking at things, Ford refers to the end of Chapter xxxi where Frederic Henry has hidden under the canvas on a railroad gondola car loaded with guns which "smelled cleanly of oil and grease". Ford praises the description this way:

Hemingway's use of the word "cleanly" is an instance of what I have just been saying. The guns smelled cleanly of oil and grease. Oil and grease are not usually associated in the mind with a clean smell. Yet at the minutest reflection you realise that the oil and grease on the clean metal of big guns are not dirt. So the adverb is just. You have had a moment of surprise and then your knowledge is added to. The word "author" means "someone who adds to your consciousness".[8]

In other words, Ford praises the term *cleanly* for its aptness, accuracy, and realism: the guns really are not dirty. But in the preceding chapter (xxx) Henry says of the barn in which he, Piani, and Bonello hid during the retreat, "I heard the rain on the roof and smelled the hay and, when I went down, the clean smell of dried dung in the stable." In what sense can this be considered an accurate or realistic description? More to the point is the obvious question, *clean* in contrast with what? It seems sure that *clean* here is a term of praise; here and elsewhere it is a valuative, not a realistic, word in Hemingway. Accordingly, such words and details cannot be fully understood in isolated passages. It is necessary to examine together and compare instances of such descriptions, then to infer the meaning of *clean* for Hemingway.

In the same novel we find that a great number of valued things are clean, clear or cool – any one or a combination of them. The times when their opposites are preferred are few, and then it is mainly coldness which is found lacking, as we might expect, since the association between warmth and life or humanity is so common. Thus, when the soldier above Frederic Henry in the

---

[8] *A Farewell to Arms* (New York, The Modern Library, 1932), p. xvii. This is the usual story, at any rate, in the 1920's. With E. M. Halliday, contemporary criticism has returned via irony, indirection, and ambiguity to the general point of Ford's essay: that Hemingway is a great *realist*. See Halliday's "Hemingway's Ambiguity: Symbolism and Irony", *American Literature*, XXVIII (March 1956), 1-22.

ambulance has hemorrhaged to death, the description is cold: "The drops fell very slowly, as they fall from an icicle after the sun has gone. It was cold in the car in the night as the road climbed" (Ch. ix). It is not surprising that coldness should be associated with death and warmth with life. What is surprising is the relatively few examples of this sort that one can find in Hemingway. Inevitably one wonders why cold or coolness is so often associated with valued things, instead of warmth. Why does Hemingway like it cold?

A simple answer would be that Hemingway enjoys coolness by contrast, the way that Frederic Henry savors a drink of cold water dipped from the lake after he has been rowing for hours: "I was thirsty after the brandy and the water was icy cold, so cold it made my teeth ache" (Ch. xxxvii). The last clause is telescoped into "achingly cold" when Robert Jordan enjoys a refreshing drink from a mountain stream:

He sat now by the stream watching the clear water flowing between the rocks and, across the stream, he noticed there was a thick bed of watercress. He crossed the stream, picked a double handful, washed the muddy roots clean in the current and then sat down again beside his pack and ate the clean, cool green leaves and the crisp, peppery-tasting stalks. He knelt by the stream and, pushing his automatic pistol around on his belt to the small of his back so that it would not get wet, he lowered himself with a hand on each of the two boulders and drank from the stream. The water was achingly cold. (*For Whom the Bell Tolls,* Ch. i)

Just as the cold drink is extra-invigorating by contrast with the brandy or the peppery water cress, so the cold air outside gives extra spice to the "lovely" warm bed that Frederic and Catherine occupy in their room at the Guttingen's:

We went to bed in the dark in the big bedroom and when I was undressed I opened the windows and saw the night and the cold stars and the pine trees below the window and then got into bed as fast as I could. It was lovely in bed with the air so cold and clear and the night outside the window. (Ch. xxxviii)

Similarly, Cantwell and Renata feel twice as snug under their blanket in the gondola with the cold wind blowing outside (*Across the River and into the Trees,* Ch. xiii). Recall that Jordan insists on sleeping outside the cave in the snow and it is here that Maria comes to him to share his sleeping robe (Ch. xx).

Even in these examples, however, there is a question whether the enjoyment is simply intensified by combining opposite sensations of coldness and warmth. There seems to be something cleaner about love in a cold, clear atmosphere, something obviously lacking in the kind of affairs Henry had on his first leave in Milan, as he tries to explain winefully to the priest ("we did not do the things we wanted to do; we never did such things"):

I had wanted to go to Abruzzi. I had gone to no place where the roads were frozen and hard as iron, where it was clear cold and dry and the snow was dry and powdery and hare-tracks in the snow and the peasants took off their hats and called you Lord and there was good hunting.

Instead, he had gone to Milan, to smoke and noisy cafés and drunken excitement in the night, "to wake with it sometimes morning and all that had been there gone and everything sharp and hard and clear and sometimes a dispute about the cost" (Ch. iii).

The last passage anticipates a rather odd recurrent figure in later works. For instance, there is the sixty-year-old grain broker, one of the "haves" that Hemingway describes on the various yachts anchored at the Key West yacht basin, who "never wanted a woman in his room. When he wanted one he went to hers, and when he was through he was through, and now that he was through for good his brain had the same clear coldness always that had, in the old days, been an after effect" (*To Have and Have Not*, Ch. xxiv). In *For Whom the Bell Tolls*, after Pablo has run away with the exploder, caps, and fuses, and Jordan in a fit of anger has "mucked" everyone he can think of in Spain, his anger gradually dies down, "his mind now as quiet, empty-calm and sharp, cold-seeing as a man is after he has had sexual intercourse with a woman that he does not love" (Ch. xxxv). The Harry of "The Snows of Kilimanjaro" expresses similar feelings, if not in precisely the same imagery. One of his reminiscences, covering a period of whoring during which he tried to "kill his loneliness" after a quarrel with his true love (apparently), ends with the memory of the "blousy" look in the morning of an Armenian girl for whom he had fought a British soldier. But more revealing perhaps is his outburst to his present companion, who has bought him and to whom he lies to give her her money's worth. When she tells him how he loved it at the places where they stayed in Paris, he says, "Love is a dunghill. . . . And I'm the cock that gets on it to crow." (Dung here is obviously not "clean".)

One is reminded of a bantering passage in *A Farewell to Arms* between Rinaldi and Frederic Henry on the latter's return to the front. Rinaldi says,

"Look, baby, this is your old tooth-brushing glass. I kept it all the time to remind me of you."

"To remind you to brush your teeth."

"No. I have my own too. I kept this to remind me of you trying to brush away the Villa Rossa from your teeth in the morning, swearing and eating aspirin and cursing harlots. Every time I see that glass I think of you trying to clean your conscience with a toothbrush." He came over to the bed. "Kiss me once and tell me you're not serious."

"I never kiss you. You're an ape."

"I know, you are the fine good Anglo-Saxon boy. I know. You are the remorse boy, I know. I will wait till I see the Anglo-Saxon brushing away harlotry with a toothbrush." (Ch. xxv)

It appears that when lovemaking does not take place in a cool, clear, or clean context, the result is a cold, clear emptiness or a cleansing ritual. Something symbolically equivalent occurs in Henry's immersion in the Tagliamento river during the Caporetto retreat, or in Jake's retreat to San Sebastian, on whose cool early-morning freshness he comments repeatedly, where swimming in the cold water he washes away memories of the fiesta at Pamplona (*The Sun Also Rises*, Ch. xix). The martinis Henry drinks at the hotel bar in Stresa after deserting perform a like function: "I had never tasted anything so cool and clean. They made me feel civilized. I had had too much red wine, bread, cheese, bad coffee and grappa. I sat on the high stool before the pleasant mahogany, the brass and the mirrors and did not think at all" (Ch. xxxiv).

In each case we see a reaction to something "dirty". It is almost as if the "purifying" qualities of coolness, clearness or cleanness must accompany an act as attendant conditions or appear afterwards as a kind of bleak sense of guilt or something else "clean". Either way, a strong, almost stern, moral emphasis is apparent.

If we return now to the passage in Chapter iii of *A Farewell to Arms* where Henry is trying to explain his feelings to the priest, we find that he makes further associations:

I tried to tell about the night and the difference between the night and the day and how the night was better unless the day was very clean and cold and I could not tell it; as I cannot tell it now. But if you have had it you know. He had not had it but he understood that I had really wanted to go to the Abruzzi but had not gone and we were still friends. . . .

The difference between the night and the day or the dark and the light is a recurrent theme in Hemingway's work. As we proceed, we will observe a strangely ambivalent attitude toward the night and the things of the night, as in the previous example: the night is better (sometimes) unless the day is very clean and cold. Since day and light are parts of the clean-cold-clear cluster, it is almost inevitable that we ask what other things are associated with dark and night – heat and dirtiness? Eventually we will try to discover what things are dirty and what besides purity and moral strictness is represented by the clean-cool-light cluster. First, let us examine some passages in which the night seems at least partially attractive.

In the example last quoted, Frederic Henry plainly associates the night with sexual excitement. Note his description of his wild and rather dizzying leave in Milan:

I had gone . . . to the smoke of cafés and nights when the room whirled and you needed to look at the wall to make it stop, nights in bed, drunk, when you knew that that was all there was, and the strange excitement of waking and not knowing who it was with you, and the world all unreal in the dark and so exciting that you must resume again unknowing and not caring in the night, sure that this was all and all and all and not caring. Suddenly to care very much and to sleep to wake with it sometimes morning and all that had been there gone and everything sharp and hard and clear and sometimes a dispute about the cost.

The sense of unreality and particularly the whirling sensation described here are significant aspects of the night associations. To anticipate a bit, I suggest that it is these which are both the delights and terrors of the night.

In the following passage, describing a night in the hotel at Stresa, Henry says that with Catherine the night was the better time:

> That night at the hotel, in our room with the long empty hall outside and our shoes outside the door, a thick carpet on the floor of the room, outside the windows the rain falling and in the room light and pleasant and cheerful, then the light out and it exciting with smooth sheets and the bed comfortable, feeling that we had come home, feeling no longer alone, waking in the night to find the other one there, and not gone away; all other things were unreal. ... I know that the night is not the same as the day: that all things are different, that the things of the night cannot be explained in the day, because they do not then exist, and the night can be a dreadful time for lonely people once their loneliness has started. But with Catherine there was almost no difference in the night except that it was an even better time. (Ch. xxxiv)

But here, without any break or transition, occurs one of the oddest juxtapositions in Hemingway. Immediately after this assertion of the delights of the night, there come the terrors:

> If people bring so much courage to this world the world has to kill them to break them, so of course it kills them. The world breaks every one and afterward many are strong at the broken places. But those that will not break it kills. It kills the very good and the very gentle and the very brave impartially. If you are none of these you can be sure it will kill you too but there will be no special hurry.

In this startling juxtaposition we get about as graphic a description of the two sides of the irrational night as can be found anywhere in Hemingway. More often one aspect or the other is emphasized, but the irrationality or sense of unreality remains. In this example, for instance, Jordan is talking to Maria the night before blowing up the bridge about "going to Madrid" (the phrase for their wishful thinking which eventually becomes a euphemism for impending death):

> Then suddenly surrendering to something, to the luxury of going into unreality, he said, "Let us talk of Madrid and of us in Madrid."

. . . .

Then he surrendered again and let himself slip into it, feeling a voluptuousness of surrender into unreality that was like a sexual acceptance of something that could come in the night when there was no understanding, only the delight of acceptance. (Ch. xxxi)

The night, that is, seems to represent the "dark" side of the mind, with the day or light being something like understanding, rationality, reality, and order.

If something associated with the night happens in the day, then one knows that it is real. After hearing from Pilar about the earth-moving aspects of orgasms, Robert Jordan in a mystical moment compares all human beings with gypsies:

Nobody knows what tribes we came from nor what our tribal inheritance is nor what the mysteries were in the woods where the people lived that we came from. All we know is that we do not know. We know nothing about what happens to us in the nights. When it happens in the day though, it *is* something. (Ch. xiii)

In slightly different terms, day is the time of the rational and reasonable, so that on the morning of blowing up the bridge Jordan has lost all confidence in his thoughts of the night before:

... your plan stinks. It stinks, I tell you. It was a night plan and it's morning now. Night plans aren't any good in the morning. . . . So now you know it is no good. (Ch. xxxviii) [9]

It is not a very big step from the idea that night thoughts are no good in the morning to the idea that night thoughts are no good. In other words, the terrors of the irrational tend to overshadow the delights; the sense of unreality is frightening; the disorder is fearful. Jake, who has got very drunk at dinner to drown his feelings of disgust, reads in bed a while to keep the room from going round:

I turned off the light and tried to go to sleep. It was not necessary to read any more. I could shut my eyes without getting the wheeling sensation. But I could not sleep. There is no reason why because it is dark you should look at things differently from when it is light. The hell there isn't!

[9] Cf. *The Fifth Column*, in which Philip tells Dorothy, "Never believe what I say in the night. I lie like hell at night" (III.i).

I figured that all out once, and for six months I never slept with the electric light off. That was another bright idea. (Ch. xiv)

The bad pun, with its suggestion of self-disgust, does not hide the fact, however, that the light represents some kind of control over night thoughts and feelings which are very painful. Or as Jake puts it elsewhere, after his mind has been "jumping around" and he has been crying over Brett, "It is awfully easy to be hard-boiled about everything in the daytime, but at night it is another thing" (Ch. iv). This is what Phil means in his dialogue with the girl who is leaving him to have an affair with another woman ("The Sea Change"):

"I'm sorry", she said, "if you don't understand."
"I understand. That's the trouble. I understand."
"You do", she said. "That makes it worse, of course."
"Sure", he said, looking at her. "I'll understand all the time. All day and all night. Especially all night."

One of the most direct statements in Hemingway of the terrors of the night is, of course, the story "Now I Lay Me", which begins with Nick's explanation,

I myself did not want to sleep because I had been living for a long time with the knowledge that if I ever shut my eyes in the dark and let myself go, my soul would go out of my body. I had been that way for a long time, ever since I had been blown up at night and felt it go out of me and go off and then come back. I tried never to think about it, but it had started to go since, in the nights, just at the moment of going off to sleep, and I could only stop it by a very great effort.

After some description of the ways that he kept himself awake nights, Nick continues, "If I could have a light I was not afraid to sleep, because I knew my soul would only go out of me if it were dark. So, of course, many nights I was where I could have a light and then I slept because I was nearly always tired and often very sleepy."

In "A Way You'll Never Be" Nick tells Captain Paravicini, "I can't sleep without a light of some sort. That's all I have now." He adds, "It's a hell of a nuisance once they've had you certified as nutty. . . . No one ever has any confidence in you again." In

"In Another Country", walking home at night from a café, "trying to keep near the street lights", "I" knows that he could never have done the things his companions did to get their medals, "and I was very much afraid to die, and often lay in bed at night by myself, afraid to die and wondering how I would be when I went back to the front again".

Mr. Frazer of "The Gambler, the Nun, and the Radio", who "had been through this all before", plays the radio all night long, "turned so low he could barely hear it, and he was learning to listen to it without thinking". When he does think – and "usually he avoided thinking all he could" – he shows the same distrust of his night thoughts that Robert Jordan did:

What was the real, the actual, opium of the people? He knew it very well. It was gone just a little way around the corner in that well-lighted part of his mind that was there after two or more drinks in the evening; that he knew was there (it was not really there of course). What was it? He knew very well. What was it? Of course; bread was the opium of the people. Would he remember that and would it make sense in the daylight?

The "well-lighted part of his mind" comes after a couple of drinks; Frazer also calls liquor "the giant killer", as do Robert Wilson in "The Short Happy Life of Francis Macomber" and Robert Jordan in *For Whom the Bell Tolls* (Ch. xliii). For Jordan it takes the place "of all the things he had enjoyed and forgotten and that came back to him when he tasted that opaque, bitter, tongue-numbing, brain-warming, stomach-warming, idea-changing liquid alchemy" (Ch. iv). We might note here that what is a "giant killer" for the heroes and "anaesthetic" for Professor Mac-Walsey in *To Have and Have Not* (Ch. xxii) is just "chemical courage" for the grain broker in that novel, who is quite definitely not a hero (Ch. xxiv). Drink, like the well-lighted (if Hemingway had only said the well-lit), creates a small, safe, secure place where one is temporarily free of fear.

Many of the strands of this cluster come together in the story "A Clean, Well-Lighted Place". Like Nick, the older waiter cannot sleep at night; he sympathizes with the old customer who has recently attempted suicide and who wants to stay up at night:

"I am of those who like to stay late at the café", the old waiter said. "With all those who do not want to go to bed. With all those who need a light for the night."

To the younger waiter, who objects that there are bodegas open all night, he explains, "You do not understand. This is a clean and pleasant café. It is well lighted. The light is very good and also, now, there are shadows of the leaves." Then he continues to himself,

It is the light of course but it is necessary that the place be clean and pleasant. . . . What did he fear? It was not fear or dread. It was a nothing that he knew too well. It was all a nothing and a man was nothing too. It was only that and light was all it needed and a certain cleanness and order. Some lived in it and never felt it but he knew it all was nada y pues nada y nada y pues nada.

Light, cleanness, and order are qualities of what Delmore Schwartz terms the "Arcady" of Hemingway's morality or code, set always against a background of war and despair.[10] Carlos Baker, associating the clean, well-lighted and -ordered with what he calls the "Home-concept" in Hemingway, suggests that the *nada* to which it is opposed is something more than mere nothingness, but something "so huge, terrible,, overbearing, inevitable, and omnipresent that, once experienced, it can never be forgotten" (p. 124). Philip Young has a tendency to confirm Schwartz's view that the war, or more specifically Hemingway's wounding, is the explanation for the terrors that the clean, well-lighted and orderly try to banish or control.[11] Frederick J. Hoffman also makes a great deal of the "unreasonable wound" and its effect on Hemingway's work.[12] The emphasis on order or rationality as a reaction to the "unreasonable wound" or to the disorder and irrationality of war is a possible, even a tempting, explanation. So is the emphasis on light, since the "big wound" occurred at night. Even coolness and cleanness may

---

[10] "Ernest Hemingway's Literary Situation", in *Ernest Hemingway: The Man and His Work*, ed. John K. M. McCaffery (Cleveland, The World Publishing Co., 1950), p. 119.

[11] See especially pp. 12-13, 17-19, 25, 28-29, 178-180, 214-215.

[12] *The Twenties: American Writing in the Postwar Decade* (New York, The Viking Press, 1955), pp. 67-75. See also Hoffman's "No Beginning and No End: Hemingway and Death", *Essays in Criticism*, III (January 1953), 75-80.

be included as reactions to the violent passions, disorder and filth of war.

Such an explanation is probably correct in part – but only in part. Whatever is represented by the opposites of coolness, cleanness, light, and order seems to be more complicated. When Baker goes on to refer to the *nada* as a "besieging horror of the limitless, the hallucinatory, the heartland of darkness, [which] bulks like a Jungian Shadow behind the lives of many of the protagonists" (p. 132), he indulges himself in trying to make something mythic and archetypal out of the irrational, in my opinion. But he does suggest the possibility that the "trauma" which haunts Hemingway and his heroes is more involved than the other theories make it. The closest he comes to defining the "Jungian Shadow" is when he calls *nada* "this beast in the jungle" (p. 125).

May we add "this beast in the bullring"? What did Hemingway mean in this third-person account of himself?

Since he was a young boy he has cared greatly for fishing and shooting. If he had not spent so much time at them, at skiing, at the bull ring, and in a boat, he might have written much more. On the other hand, he might have shot himself.[13]

What does the well-ordered ceremony of the bullfight mean to Hemingway and to his heroes who get "that disturbed emotional feeling that always comes after a bull-fight, and the feeling of elation that comes after a good bull-fight" (*The Sun Also Rises*, Ch. xv)?

There has been a good deal of discussion of the bullfight as an expression of the "code" or as a substitute religion.[14] Then Melvin Backman points out the opposition between Pedro Romero and Robert Cohn who is "woman-dominated, . . . without the vital maleness which Hemingway . . . deems absolutely essential to the true man".[15] But Backman seemingly misses the sex symbolism of the bull in *The Sun Also Rises*: Mike's equating Cohn with the steers, while the others identify themselves with the bull

[13] Georges Schreiber, *Portraits and Self-Portraits* (Boston, Houghton Mifflin Co., 1936), p. 57.
[14] See, for example, Young, pp. 67-68, and Hoffman, pp. 73, 83.
[15] "Hemingway: the Matador and the Crucified", *Modern Fiction Studies*, I (August 1955), 4.

(Ch. xiii). We know that Hemingway's attitude toward the things of the night is at least ambivalent. Now, what is it that Hemingway enjoys seeing killed at the climax of an extremely ritualistic ceremony whose predetermined maneuvers are called *suertes*? There is a kind of security (the English equivalent of *suerte*) and order maintained by methodically killing the animal which obviously represents something more than a male bovine to the spectators who feel a sense of purgation at its death. Is it not the beast in himself – rather than the beast in the ring or in the jungle – which the spectator is relieved to see killed (temporarily)? As the climax to a systematic, ordered, repressive ceremony, one's irrational or animal-like impulses are symbolically destroyed, and one is symbolically cleansed.

Young tends to take this preoccupation with death too literally, I think, explaining it in terms of a "traumatic neurosis" and "death wish" (pp. 138-139). Kenneth Burke seems closer to the truth in his explanation of symbolic killing.[16] Briefly, he regards symbolic killing as an inferior idiom of a process in forming one's identity: the rejection of an unwanted aspect of the self by projecting it on something else – a scapegoat. There is more than a chance, of course, that the process will not be understood by the person employing it, a result being the kind of *mystique* of killing that we find in *Death in the Afternoon*. But considering the fact that the "heroes" of *The Sun Also Rises* both identify themselves with the bulls and get an almost ecstatic sense of release at seeing them killed, it appears likely that the psychological process is akin to the one Burke describes. The *aficionado* of the bullfight feels symbolically cleansed by the death of the bull. Some recognition of this is probably the reason for Hemingway's insistence on calling the bullfight a tragedy throughout *Death in the Afternoon*: purgation is the result of the animal's death. As Sherwood Anderson observes in *Dark Laughter*, "In war or in peace we do not kill the man we hate. We try to kill the thing we hate in ourselves" (Ch. xxv).

[16] "The Philosophy of Literary Form", *The Philosophy of Literary Form: Studies in Symbolic Action* (Baton Rouge, Louisiana State University Press, 1941), pp. 38-42, 45-46.

To see what support there is for this theory, let us examine what in Hemingway's terms is dirty. The distinction that Jordan makes between the excitement of a snowstorm and the excitement of battle is fairly well in accord with the war and trauma theories of Hemingway's work. Jordan's rage against the unseasonable storm and against Pablo's pleasure in it disappears:

> Now that his rage was gone he was excited by this storm as he was always by all storms. In a blizzard, a gale, a sudden line squall, a tropical storm, or a summer thunder shower in the mountains there was an excitement that came to him from no other thing. It was like the excitement of battle except that it was clean. There is a wind that blows through battle but that was a hot wind; hot and dry as your mouth; and it blew heavily; hot and dirtily; and it rose and died away with the fortunes of the day. He knew that wind well.
>
> But a snowstorm was the opposite of all that. ... In a snowstorm it always seemed, for a time, as though there were no enemies. In a snowstorm the wind could blow a gale; but it blew a white cleanness and the air was full of a driving whiteness and all things were changed and when the wind stopped there would be the stillness. (Ch. xiv)

There is something almost cleansing about the storm in contrast with Jordan's rage. It gives "clean" excitement in contrast with the hot, dry, dirty rage and fear of battle. Similarly, it is obvious why Frederic Henry after escaping from the front can call oil and grease and even cow dung clean. But there is more to the contrast: the dirty is something human, while the clean is nonhuman.

In *Green Hills of Africa*, in one of the longest sentences he ever wrote, Hemingway makes this contrast between the Gulf Stream and the "stench of comrades" (it is remarkable how often Hemingway's celebrated sense of smell is concerned with the clean and the dirty – the latter usually human):

> If you serve time for society, democracy, and the other things quite young, and declining any further enlistment make yourself responsible only to yourself, you exchange the pleasant, comforting stench of comrades for something you can never feel in any other way than by yourself. That something I cannot yet define completely but the feeling comes when you write well and truly of something and know impersonally you have written in that way and those who are paid to read it and report on it do not like the subject so they say it is all a fake, yet you know its value absolutely; or when you do

something which people do not consider a serious occupation and yet you know, truly, that it is as important and has always been as important as all the things that are in fashion, and when, on the sea, you are alone with it and know that this Gulf Stream you are living with, knowing, learning about, and loving, has moved, as it moves, since before man, and that it has gone by the shoreline of that long, beautiful, unhappy island since before Columbus sighted it and that the things you find out about it, and those that have always lived in it are permanent and of value because that stream will flow, as it has flowed, after the Indians, after the Spaniards, after the British, after the Americans and after all the Cubans and all the systems of governments, the richness, the poverty, the martyrdom, the sacrifice and the venality and the cruelty are all gone as the high-piled scow of garbage, bright-colored, white-flecked, ill-smelling, now tilted on its side, spills off its load into the blue water, turning it a pale green to a depth of four or five fathoms as the load spreads across the surface, the sinkable part going down and the flotsam of palm fronds, corks, bottles, and used electric light globes, seasoned with an occasional condom or a deep floating corset, the torn leaves of a student's exercise book, a well-inflated dog, the occasional rat, the no-longer-distinguished cat; all this well shepherded by the boats of the garbage pickers who pluck their prizes with long poles, as interested, as intelligent, and as accurate as historians; they have the viewpoint; the stream, with no visible flow, takes five loads of this a day when things are going well in La Habana and in ten miles along the coast it is as clear and blue and unimpressed as it was ever before the tug hauled out the scow; and the palm fronds of our victories, the worn light bulbs of our discoveries and the empty condoms of our great loves float with no significance against one single, lasting thing – the stream. (Ch. viii)

"Vanity of vanities, saith the Preacher, vanity of vanities; all *is* vanity", says the passage from Ecclesiastes from which Hemingway took the title and one of the introductory quotations for *The Sun Also Rises*. Hemingway, I think, is much closer to T. S. Eliot in spirit and content (perhaps also in technique) than has often been recognized.

With this picture of pungent disgust with things human in mind, one can question the supposed major shift in social outlook in *For Whom the Bell Tolls*. People still stink. When Pilar describes for Jordan what death smells like, she mentions the smell of "the brass handle of a screwed-tight porthole on a rolling ship that is swaying under you so that you are faint and hollow in the stomach" and the odor of a refuse pail with dead flowers in it; but her longest and most vivid descriptions are given to the nauseating stench of human things:

". . . you must go down the hill in Madrid to the Puente de Toledo early in the morning to the *matadero* and stand there on the wet paving when there is a fog from the Manzanares and wait for the old women who go before daylight to drink the blood of the beasts that are slaughtered. When such an old woman comes out of the *matadero,* holding her shawl around her, with her face gray and her eyes hollow, and the whiskers of age on her chin, and on her cheeks, set in the waxen white of her face as the sprouts grow from the seed of a bean, not bristles, but pale sprouts in the death of her face; put your arms tight around her, *Inglés,* and hold her to you and kiss her on the mouth and you will know the second part that odor is made of."

. . . .

". . . it is important that the day be in autumn with rain, or at least some fog, or early winter even and now thou shouldst continue to walk through the city and down the Calle de Salud smelling what thou wilt smell where they are sweeping out the *casas de putas* and emptying the slop jars into the drains and, with this odor of love's labor lost mixed sweetly with soapy water and cigarette butts only faintly reaching thy nostrils, thou shouldst go on to the Jardín Botánico where at night those girls who can no longer work in the houses do their work against the iron gates of the park and the iron picketed fences and upon the sidewalks. It is there in the shadow of the trees against the iron railings that they will perform all that a man wishes; from the simplest requests at a remuneration of ten centimos up to a peseta for that great act that we are born to and there, on a dead flower bed that has not yet been plucked out and replanted, and so serves to soften the earth that is so much softer than the sidewalk, thou wilt find an abandoned gunny sack with the odor of the wet earth, the dead flowers, and the doings of that night. In this sack will be contained the essence of it all, both the dead earth and the dead stalks of the flowers and their rotted blooms and the smell that is both the death and birth of man. Thou wilt wrap this sack around thy head and try to breathe through it." (Ch. xix)

Jordan's wisecrack at the end of this, that if Kashkin really smelled like that "it is a good thing I shot him", disposes of a critic,[17] but it does not dispose of the fact that the climactic item in the catalogues from both *Green Hills of Africa* and *For Whom the Bell Tolls* is something sexual – as if the ultimate in what is revolting. (In Helen Gordon's denunciation of love in Chapter xxi of *To Have and Have Not*, the word *dirty* occurs three times.)

There seems little doubt that something about human physicality is unclean for Hemingway. Note the simile in "The Capital of the World" when Paco, wounded while playing matador with Enrique the dishwasher, feels "his life go out of him as dirty water empties from a bathtub when the plug is drawn". In *Death in the Afternoon*, explaining why bullfighting is a minor art form, Hemingway says, "If it were permanent it could be one of the major arts, but it is not and so it finishes with whoever makes it, while a major art cannot even be judged until the unimportant physical rottenness of whoever made it is well buried" (Ch. x).

However, it is in "Fathers and Sons" that we get the most direct statement of this theme:

Nick loved his father but hated the smell of him and once when he had to wear a suit of his father's underwear that had gotten too small for his father it made him feel sick and he took it off and put it under two stones in the creek and said that he had lost it. He had told his father how it was when his father had made him put it on but his father had said it was freshly washed. It had been, too. When Nick had asked him to smell of it his father sniffed at it indignantly and said that it was clean and fresh.

After being whipped for lying about losing the underwear, Nick sits inside the woodshed with a cocked shotgun, watching his father sit on the porch and thinking how he could kill him. When the anger subsides, Nick feels sick (and scared?). "Then he had gone to the Indian camp, walking there in the dark, to get rid of the smell. There was only one person in his family that he liked the smell of; one sister. All the others he avoided all contact with." It appears, then, that to some extent this concern with cleanliness and the meaning of the concern antedate the war

---

[17]   See Atkins, p. 145. This was apparently Hemingway's revenge for J. Kashkeen's article, "Ernest Hemingway: A Tragedy of Craftsmanship" (1935), in McCaffery, pp. 76-108.

experiences and the wounding of the Hemingway hero. It seems likely that so does the concern with the cool, well-lighted, and ordered.[18]

Having examined what smells dirty, let us see now what smells clean or good. In the main such things are not human, though in "Fathers and Sons" Nick seems to like the smell of the Indian girl Trudy Gilby and the smell of the Indian camp. To Frederic Henry oil, grease, and dried dung smelled clean. In *Death in the Afternoon* Hemingway says that the valor of the matador Luis Freg did not have the good "smell of smoked leather or the smell of a frozen road or the smell of the sea when the wind rips the top from a wave", but instead "was clotted and heavy and there was a thin part underneath that was unpleasant and oozy" (Ch. xix). Though Hemingway compares the second with syrup, it sounds more like some physical secretion or excretion.

Robert Jordan remarks on the odors of the cave, "the fire smoke and man smell, the tobacco, red-wine and brassy, stale body smell" (Ch. xviii), which he avoids by sleeping outside. The smell of the horses – barely mentioned – is contrasted with "the unwashed and sour slept-in-clothing smell of the new men and the wood-smoky sleep-stale smell of the others who had been in the cave. Pablo was standing close to him and he smelled the brassy, dead-wine smell that came from him like the taste of a copper coin in your mouth" (Ch. xli). That brassy smell, remember, was the first part of the odor of death as Pilar described it.

In another passage Jordan lists the smells that he loves:

The night was clear and his head felt as clear and cold as the air. He smelled the odor of the pine boughs under him, the piney smell of the crushed needles and the sharper odor of the resinous sap from the cut limbs. Pilar, he thought. Pilar and the smell of death. This is the smell I love. This and fresh-cut clover, the crushed sage as you ride after cattle, wood-smoke and the burning leaves of autumn. That

18   I doubt that it is necessary to accept all of Bernard S. Oldsey's explanation, "Hemingway's Old Men", *Modern Fiction Studies*, I (August 1955), 32. Oldsey sees the suicide of Hemingway's father as the traumatic event in Hemingway's life rather than any event of the war, and the throwing away of the underwear as a violent rejection of the father. Undoubtedly, this partly explains the gesture, but the emphasis on cleanliness and smell is not limited to the father even in "Fathers and Sons".

must be the odor of nostalgia, the smell of the smoke from the piles
of raked leaves burning in the streets in the fall in Missoula. Which
would you rather smell? Sweet grass the Indians used in their baskets?
Smoked leather? The odor of the ground in the spring after rain?
The smell of the sea as you walk through the gorse on a headland
in Galicia? Or the wind from the land as you come in toward Cuba
in the dark? That was the odor of the cactus flowers, mimosa and the
sea-grape shrubs. Or would you rather smell frying bacon in the
morning when you are hungry? Or coffee in the morning? Or a
Jonathan apple as you bit into it? Or a cider mill in the grinding, or
bread fresh from the oven? You must be hungry, he thought. . . .
(Ch. xx)

It appears again that as close as any good smell comes to being
human is when it is connected with the Indians. The other odors,
unless one infers a cook for the cooking food, are the odors of
things, especially the odor of the outdoors and the woods. The
wood need not be only pine, either; in fact, two pages earlier when
Jordan cut the boughs for his bed, they were from a spruce tree.

The parklike wood without undergrowth (clean) is one example of
the "good place" in Hemingway – in Baker's terms, the "Home-
concept". In *A Farewell to Arms* it is a pine forest that Catherine
and Frederic walk through, with a soft, carpetlike floor which is
not hardened by the frost: ". . . it was lovely walking in the woods"
(Ch. xxxviii). In *The Sun Also Rises*,

It was a beech wood and the trees were very old. Their roots bulked
above the ground and the branches were twisted. We walked on the
road between the thick trunks of the old beeches and the sunlight
came through the leaves in light patches on the grass. The trees were
big, and the foliage was thick but it was not gloomy. There was no
undergrowth, only the smooth grass, very green and fresh, and the
big gray trees well spaced as though it were a park. (Ch. xii)

For some reason, perhaps because of the cool light, the mixed
shadows of the leaves and patches of light are a detail in other
descriptions of the wood:

Then the plain was behind us and ahead there were big trees and
we were entering a country the loveliest that I had seen in Africa.
The grass was green and smooth, short as a meadow that had been
mown and is newly grown, and the trees were big, high-trunked, and

old with no undergrowth but only the smooth green of the turf like a deer park and we drove on through shade and patches of sunlight. . . . I could not believe we had suddenly come to any such wonderful country. (*Green Hills of Africa*, Ch. xii)

Recall that the old waiter made a point of this in explaining the attractions of the clean, well-lighted café: "The light is very good and also, now, there are shadows of the leaves."

In "Fathers and Sons" it appears that the direct light is too hot, and the "weed-grown slashing" of the present sounds rather disorderly; this is the hemlock wood behind the Indian camp, where Nick learned about sex from Trudy Gilby:

. . . each year there was less forest and more open, hot, shadeless, weed-grown slashing.
But there was still much forest then, virgin forest where the trees grew high before there were any branches and you walked on the brown, clean, springy-needled ground with no undergrowth and it was cool on the hottest days and they three lay against the trunk of a hemlock wider than two beds are long, with the breeze high in the tops and the cool light that came in patches, and Billy said:
"You want Trudy again?"

This period in the hero's life obviously was very important. The foundations of what is clean and dirty seem to be forming, along with what smells like which. The nostalgia of the story is very strong, and a good part of the nostalgia is connected with Nick's feelings about the Indians – particularly the smell of them, "the sweetgrass smell, the smoke smell and that other like a fresh cased marten skin". No jokes about them nor about old squaws, nor the sick smell they get to have, nor the way they ended could take that away, Nick thinks, adding in semi-pidgin English, "Long time ago good. Now no good." [19]

In "Big Two-Hearted River", which seems in some ways an

[19] In *A Farewell to Arms* the nostalgia is also strong in a passage apparently referring to the same woods: " . . . lying in a barn in the hay took away all the years in between. We had lain in hay and talked and shot sparrows with an air-rifle when they perched in the triangle cut high up in the wall of the barn. The barn was gone now and one year they had cut the hemlock woods and there were only stumps, dried tree-tops, branches and fireweed where the woods had been. You could not go back" (Ch. xxx). The barn is another "good place".

attempt to recapture this "long time ago good", Nick, after
walking through a scorched, burned-over land and across an
"uneven, shadeless pine plain", comes to an "island" of pine trees
with a breeze high in their tops and stops for a nap:

There was no underbrush in the island of pine trees. The trunks of
the trees went straight up or slanted toward each other. The trunks
were straight and brown without branches. The branches were high
above. Some interlocked to make a solid shadow on the brown forest
floor. Around the grove of trees was a bare space. It was brown and
soft underfoot as Nick walked on it. This was the over-lapping of
the pine needle floor, extending out beyond the width of the high
branches. The trees had grown tall and the branches moved high,
leaving in the sun this bare space they had once covered with shadow.
Sharp at the edge of this extension of the forest floor commenced
the sweet fern. (Part I)

Lying in the shade of the pine trees, looking up at the sky through
the moving branches, Nick falls asleep. Here, Baker remarks
(p. 127), Nick does not need any light to sleep, since the place
itself represents the same kind of security as a light (though, of
course, it *is* daytime).

The inside of the tent also gives the sense of peace and security,
complete with the pleasant smell and the dim light which comes
through the canvas:

Inside the tent the light came through the brown canvas. It smelled
pleasantly of canvas. Already there was something mysterious and
homelike. Nick was happy as he crawled inside the tent. He had not
been unhappy all day. This was different though. Now things were
done. There had been this to do. Now it was done. It had been a
hard trip. He was very tired. That was done. He had made his camp.
He was settled. Nothing could touch him. It was a good place to
camp. He was there, in the good place. He was in his home where
he had made it.

Without going as far as Young does into the meaning of the
swamp where "fishing was a tragic adventure", we can see that it
is hardly a clean or well-ordered place. In the swamp the trunks
of the cedars grow so close together and their branches are so low
that it would not be possible to walk; the sun does not come
through except in patches; "in the fast deep water, in the half

light, the fishing would be tragic".[20] This is one of the rare times when the patchy or dim light is definitely bad.

Usually the good place or the valued thing has one or more of the qualities associated with the cool, clean, well-lighted place (or the ideal wood). At the beginning of *For Whom the Bell Tolls*, for instance, Robert Jordan seems to be in such a place: "He lay flat on the brown, pine-needled floor of the forest, his chin on his folded arms, and high overhead the wind blew in the tops of the pine trees." The Abruzzi, as the priest describes it to Frederic Henry in the hospital, is another:

It was cool in the summer at night and the spring in Abruzzi was the most beautiful in Italy. But what was lovely was the fall to go hunting through the chestnut woods. The birds were all good because they fed on grapes and you never took a lunch because the peasants were always honored if you would eat with them at their houses. (Ch. xi)

In "Soldier's Home" truth is associated with the cool and clear, while lying or exaggeration produces nausea:

Krebs found that to be listened to at all he had to lie, and after he had done this twice he, too, had a reaction against the war and against talking about it. A distaste for everything that had happened to him in the war set in because of the lies he had told. All of the times that had been able to make him feel cool and clear inside himself when he thought of them; the times so long back when he had done the one thing, the only thing for a man to do, easily and naturally, when he might have done something else, now lost their cool, valuable quality and then were lost themselves.

"Krebs acquired the nausea in regard to experience that is the result of untruth or exaggeration"; it is a short step from this reaction to a feeling that talk or words inevitably distort the truth, that the whole thing is too complicated – that only the simple is likely to be true – that it is probably best not to verbalize at all.

Krebs, who spends "the hottest hours of the day in the cool

---

[20]   "Big Two-Hearted River", Part II. Young thinks that Nick fears the swamp because at its entrance "the river narrowed", a detail which reminds him of the place on the Fossalta where he was first wounded. This, Young tries to connect with Nick's fear of "the different width of the river" in "A Way You'll Never Be" (p. 25).

dark of the pool room", likes to watch the girls but decides that they and the process of getting one of them are too complicated:

> They were too complicated. There was something else. Vaguely he wanted a girl but he did not want to have to work to get her. . . . He did not want to get into the intrigue and the politics. He did not want to have to do any courting. He did not want to tell any more lies.
>
> . .   .   .
> . . . he would have liked a girl if she had come to him and not wanted to talk. But here at home it was all too complicated. . . . That was the thing about French girls and German girls. There was not all this talking. You couldn't talk much and you did not need to talk. It was simple and you were friends.

The association of the true with the simple or reticent, and of verbalization itself with exaggeration or lies, will become more apparent in subsequent chapters. The thing to note here is the connection between the cool-clean-light-orderly and the theme of not talking about it (also, avoiding emotion and not thinking).

In his chapter "The Mountain and the Plain", Baker makes further associations of imagery and themes:

> The Home-concept . . . is associated with the mountains; with dry-cold weather; with peace and quiet; with love, dignity, health, happiness, and the good life; and with worship or at least the consciousness of God. The Not-home concept is associated with low-lying plains; with rain and fog; with obscenity, indignity, disease, suffering, nervousness, war and death; and with irreligion. (p. 102)

These good things to some extent represent the eternal, the non-human, and "rational"; the bad are temporal, human, and "irrational". Looking back to the passage from *Death in the Afternoon* on why bullfighting is a minor art form, we can see that it is in a sense immortality that Hemingway seeks in art: "If it were permanent it could be one of the major arts, but it is not and so it finishes with whoever makes it, while a major art cannot even be judged until the unimportant physical rottenness of whoever made it is well buried."

The weakness of Baker's explanation, as E. M. Halliday points out, is the attempt to force all of Hemingway's work – specifically, all of *A Farewell to Arms* – to fit this symbolic structure.[21] To avoid distortion, any consideration of Hemingway must take into account also exceptions to the prevalent imagistic structure. In *A Farewell to Arms*, for instance, the mountains at times, though "lovely", represent frustrating and insurmountable obstacles to ever winning the war:

... I looked to the north at the two ranges of mountains, green and dark to the snow-line and then white and lovely in the sun. Then, as the road mounted along the ridge, I saw a third range of mountains, higher snow mountains, that looked chalky white and furrowed, with strange planes, and then there were mountains far off beyond all these that you could hardly tell if you really saw. Those were all the Austrians' mountains and we had nothing like them. (Ch. viii)

The ambulance driver Passini makes the same point about the mountains in an argument with Frederic Henry:

"War is not won by victory. What if we take San Gabriele? What if we take the Carso and Monfalcone and Trieste? Where are we then? Did you see all the far mountains to-day? Do you think we could take all them too? Only if the Austrians stop fighting." (Ch. ix)

Later, while recovering in the hospital, Henry repeats Passini's sentiments:

The Italians were using up an awful amount of men. I did not see how it could go on. Even if they took all the Bainsizza and Monte San Gabriele there were plenty of mountains beyond for the Austrians. I had seen them. All the highest mountains were beyond. On the Carso they were going forward but there were marshes and swamps down by the sea. Napoleon would have whipped the Austrians on the plains. He never would have fought them in the mountains. (Ch. xix)

Obviously the mountains here do not represent the good things associated with the "Home-concept".

However, with qualification Baker's explanation can be a helpful key to the imagistic and thematic organization of much of Hemingway's work. In "The Snows of Kilimanjaro" the mountain, like the safari, is associated with clean living and "discipline":

They had made this safari with the minimum of comfort. There was no hardship; but there was no luxury and he had thought that he

---

[21] "Hemingway's Ambiguity", p. 11.

could get back into training that way. That in some way he could work the fat off his soul the way a fighter went into the mountains to work and train in order to burn it out of his body.

(Valued sports seem always to take on some such moral significance for Hemingway.) But the mountain is an ambivalent symbol: it represents the clean, cool, and eternal, but the eternal is nonhuman and nonliving – pure but dead. As several critics have remarked, there is a pointed contrast between the dead but pure, dried and frozen leopard near the western summit of Kilimanjaro ("the House of God") and Harry "with a gangrened leg, who is very mortal, rotting fast away in the heat of the lowlands".[22]

Baker points out some of the same highland-lowland contrast in *The Sun Also Rises* and in *Green Hills of Africa*. In *For Whom the Bell Tolls* there is the ambivalence of the mountain again:

By placing his action among the high slopes of the Sierra de Guadarramas, a clean, well-lighted place where the weather is cold and the air clear, Hemingway has achieved a kind of idyll in the midst of war, an island (like that of Nick Adams in his afternoon grove on the way to the Big Two-Hearted River) surrounded by the sinister. ... This is a mountain fastness like Burguete in *The Sun Also Rises*, or like the priest's homeland of Abruzzi in *A Farewell to Arms*, or like the Alpine sanctuary to which Frederick [sic] and Catherine retire for their short happy life together. One sees again the lowland-versus-highland ·image; on the plain before Madrid the fascists are deployed, but here are high slopes, concealment, and something like the good life, a veritable island in the midst of *nada*. Still, in the words of Donne's devotion, "no man is an island". In this savage war, no mountain can serve as a permanent sanctuary. El Sordo, on his high hilltop position, finds no good life. Fascist cavalry surround it, and three fascist planes destroy it from above. Similarly, when the bridge is blown, Pablo's mountain cave becomes untenable as a refuge. (Baker, p. 257)

The cold wind from the mountains has a similar mixed significance in *Across the River and into the Trees*. On the one hand,

[22] Young, p. 50. See Baker, pp. 195-196n, quoting C. C. Walcutt (*Explicator* 7, April 1949, item 43) and E. W. Tedlock, Jr. (*Explicator* 8, October 1949, item 7).

Cantwell is relieved to get out of the wind (where the twinges of his heart associate it with death) and into Harry's bar – "he had made it again, and was at home" (Ch. ix) – or into the Gritti Palace Hotel, "out of the wind and the cold . . . into the light and warmth of the lobby" (Ch. xi). Out of the wind from the mountains and "from somewhere else", under their blanket in the gondola, Renata says, "We are in our home and I love you." [23] She sounds a familiar note the next morning: "Do you still love me in the cold, hard Venice light of morning? It is really cold and hard isn't it?" (Ch. xxiv). But the love, having occurred the night before in such a cold, clean atmosphere, is not dissipated in (or by) the cold light of morning. Moreover, when Cantwell gets to his hotel room, he makes a point of having the windows opened wide so that the cold air can come in:

> The Canal was grey as steel now in the quick, failing, winter light and the Colonel said, "Arnaldo, open the windows."
> "There is much wind, my Colonel, and the room is badly heated due to the lack of electric power."
> "Due to the lack of rainfall", the Colonel said. "Open the windows. All of them."
> "As you wish, my Colonel."
> The waiter opened the windows and the north wind came into the room. (Ch. viii)

And the cold air enhances the beauty of Venice: "Now, beating up the Canal, against the cold wind off the mountains, and with the houses as clear and sharp as on a winter day, which, of course, it was, they saw the old magic of the city and its beauty" (Ch. vi).

The "Home-concept" needs qualification when Baker opposes it to the cold and clear and eternal, as he does in the preceding examples: it is more relevant to see that the qualities of the cool, clean, lighted, and ordered are themselves ambivalent – that they imply not just the good clean life but also the nonhuman and dead. We have here a characteristic romantic dilemma, just as the mountain-lowland contrast is typical romantic imagery – the mountain being the hero's abode. By identifying himself with

[23] While I have followed some of Baker's examples here (p. 282), my interpretation differs somewhat from his, which tends to explain the cold wind merely as death.

nature, and particularly with the grand or remote or inanimate in nature, the romantic hero raises himself above the human or the ordinary masses. Sooner or later, however, he discovers that the natural is nonhuman or nonliving, and only through death can he really be one with it. (Hemingway's romantic orientation is discussed at greater length in Chapter v.)

The "Home-concept" needs another qualification, too. Baker is probably right when he says that women are closely associated with the "Home-concept" (or the "good place"):

The significance of Maria, when she is seen in the light of such other heroines as Catherine Barkley, Marie Morgan, and even Dorothy Bridges, is finally symbolic. In the lonely alien region of the Guadarramas, she comes to stand as the image of "home". Most of Hemingway's women tend to take on this special symbolic meaning. Dorothy Bridges (a fairly unsympathetic portrait) is explicitly equated with nostalgia. ... Catherine Barkley and Marie Morgan, though in different ways, represent normal domesticity vanquished by war and by the economic struggle for survival. Similarly, Maria stands for the normal in the midst of a terrible abnormality. (p. 256)

However, Baker's choice of terms – "Home-concept' rather than "good place" – leads him to stress an opposition between alternative forms of the same thing:

... the Home-circle has another alternate than that of *nada*. This is the idea of male companionship, rough and friendly camaraderie, an informal brotherhood with by-laws which are not written down but are perfectly understood and rigidly adhered to by the contracting parties. Hemingway summed up the matter in his title Men Without Women. For woman, closely associated with the Home-symbol, stands in opposition, perhaps even in a kind of enmity, to that wholly happy and normal condition which two men, hiking or drinking or talking together, can build like a world of their own. (p. 132)

Whatever opposition exists between the alternatives should not blind us to the fact that both are forms of the "good place". The whole sporting code with its attention to routine, ritual, know-how about details, an almost dedicated and moral "discipline", is part of the cluster of cool, clean, well-lighted and -ordered things. Whatever opposition exists between the men-without-women and men-with-women alternatives (Baker's terms) lies probably in the first's being if anything "cleaner" (the second raises the difficult problem of sex) and in the first's being freer (the second places limitations on the hero's ego). But the desperation of the romantic love affair, a refuge against the world, is qualitatively equivalent to the desperation of the sporting rituals. They mustn't fight, Catherine says, "because there's only us two and in the world there's all the rest of them. If anything comes between us we're gone and then they have us" (Ch. xxi). Compare the almost hysterical attitude toward skiing in "Cross-Country Snow" (or recall Hemingway's words about hunting, fishing, bullfighting, skiing, and boating in *Portraits and Self-Portraits*); when George says that perhaps they will never go skiing again, Nick answers, "We've got to. . . . It isn't worth while if you can't." Each is an almost obsessive ritual, a kind of "code", which provides temporary security in a world of terrible uncertainty.

The connection between the cool, clean, well-lighted, and ordered and the ritual-like code should now be apparent. Rituals and sanitation are primary defenses against anxiety:

An obsessive urge toward cleanness, order, and light is common to most of the protagonists of Hemingway's short stories and to the admirable characters of all his longer works, fiction and nonfiction. . . . In brief the locales of Hemingway's works are quite tidy and clean. These locales which the protagonists and heroes either find or make become a clear symbol. They become the primary indicators of the defensive insecurity which is the bottom nature of all the Hemingway protagonists and heroes. They also become the primary emblems of the hero's obsessively motivated sanitary code.[24]

Allen goes on to point out the abundance of cleansing water imagery in Hemingway's work, the "variety of sparkling streams, rivers, lakes, and oceans (not to mention purifying sweats and tasty drinks)". So much one may reasonably say. Attempting to account for the genesis of the attitudes reflected is another matter. While it seems likely that they began forming early, it is at best speculation to trace them back to feelings of inadequacy and worthlessness and childhood fears of being unwanted and un-

[24]   Charles A. Allen, "Ernest Hemingway's Clean, Well-Lighted Heroes", *The Pacific Spectator*, IX (Autumn 1955), 387.

loved, as Allen tries to do (p. 385). Such exactness must be left to psychiatry, if it is possible at all. It is sufficient for our purposes to note the imagistic structure of Hemingway's work and from the evidence at hand to analyze as far as possible the attitudes implied in what is present.

One thing we may obviously conclude is that words like *cool, clean*, and the like are terms of value in Hemingway, undoubtedly related to the whole complex of attitudes examined so far. When fishing boats are praised in *Across the River and into the Trees*, they are called clean:

> They made the left turn and came along the canal where the fishing boats tied up, and the Colonel looked at them and his heart was happy because of the brown nets and the wicker fish traps and the clean, beautiful lines of the boats. It's not that they are picturesque. The hell with picturesque. They are just damned beautiful. (Ch. v)

They may be "damned beautiful", but they are also *cleanly* beautiful. Compare the "purity of line" of the matador Romero in *The Sun Also Rises*:

> Romero never made any contortions, always it was straight and pure and natural in line. The others twisted themselves like corkscrews, their elbows raised, and leaned against the flanks of the bull after his horns had passed, to give a faked look of danger. Afterward, all that was faked turned bad and gave an unpleasant feeling. Romero's bull-fighting gave real emotion, because he kept the absolute purity of line in his movements and always quietly and calmly let the horns pass him close each time. ... Brett saw how something that was beautiful done close to the bull was ridiculous if it were done a little way off. (Ch. xv)

Note the association here between purity, beauty, danger, and truth – and Romero's simplicity and restraint of action – so like the association in "Soldier's Home" between coolness, truth, simplicity and restraint in speech. Truth, beauty, "discipline", and the cool-clean-light-orderly are closely linked.

As Hemingway puts it otherwise in *Death in the Afternoon*, with a terrible pun on *execution*, what amateur spectators like first about the bullfight is the "picturesque", "useless and romantic things", but "when they have learned to appreciate values through experience what they seek is honesty and true, not tricked, emotion and always classicism and purity of execution of all the suertes . . ." (Ch. i). In another passage he says, "Killing cleanly and in a way which gives you aesthetic pleasure and pride has always been one of the greatest enjoyments of a part of the human race." (The moment of killing the bull is called, of course, the "moment of truth".) The further explanation, I suspect, has sometimes been taken too literally:

One of its greatest pleasures, aside from the purely aesthetic ones . . . is the feeling of rebellion against death which comes from its administering. . . . when a man is still in rebellion against death he has pleasure in taking to himself one of the Godlike attributes; that of giving it. (Ch. xix)

From the emphasis on killing *cleanly* and the odd word *administering* (one administers punishment or medicine – but *death?*), which is repeated in the book, it seems likely that something unclean is being done away with. (The desire to be god or demigod, superhuman, is characteristic of the romantic hero. The means, suggested earlier, may be the symbolical killing of the too human parts of oneself.) On the other hand, it reflects poorly on the killer if he kills so ineptly that the victim suffers messily before dying; together with some conscience-salving, this is most of the point of the following passage from *Green Hills of Africa:*

I felt a son of a bitch to have hit him and not killed him. I did not mind killing anything, any animal [afterthought?], if I killed it cleanly, they all had to die and my interference with the nightly and seasonal killing that went on all the time was very minute and I had no guilty feeling at all. . . . I was a son of a bitch to have gut-shot him. (Ch. xiii)

What is clean is good, true, and beautiful, and vice versa. To understand Hemingway's aesthetic one must realize that these things are practically interchangeable.

III

"DISCIPLINE"

1

The word "discipline" is commonly used to describe Hemingway's style, especially the style of his earlier work (that written before 1932 and *Death in the Afternoon*). At the same time, it is used to describe Hemingway's concern with rules of behavior, controls over random impulses – his rituals or "code". The two interests are so closely linked as to be almost one and the same. Therefore although the main emphasis in this chapter will be on "discipline" or its lack in Hemingway's style, it may prove not only necessary but instructive occasionally to examine parts of the "code" as well. A more detailed consideration of the "code" and the hero is the subject of Chapter v.

When Hemingway is setting forth in Chapter i of *Green Hills of Africa* the requirements for a would-be writer of a prose having a fourth and fifth dimension, he insists that "there must be discipline. The discipline of Flaubert". By and large critics have agreed with him, assessing his work by whether it reflects more or less "discipline". It is obvious from their doing so that "discipline" is an honorific word – and, in fact, among some contemporary critics it is hardly more than a term of praise. It seems desirable to determine as far as possible what this "discipline" consists of, to see what attitudes and aesthetic ideals it involves, and from this to try to evaluate it. Until this is done, "discipline" will remain a vague term of approval.

As in behavior, "discipline" in style apparently refers to a system of controls – not merely to selection but to verbal restraint, even reticence, to "objectivity", "simplicity", understatement and "irony". (The quotation marks indicate, first of all, that these are honorific terms: *objectivity*, for example, might be described dyslogistically as *inhibition*. Secondly, I think that some of these terms are not really accurate descriptions: *simplicity*, for example, cannot be applied without considerable qualification to a sophisticated style which aims at the roundabout suggestion of feelings and effects which are explicitly omitted.) That is, "discipline" seems to refer to a method of indirection which we have already seen operating in Hemingway's use of certain supposedly objective words and details to suggest attitudes that he avoids stating directly.

A basic question, then, is whether indirection is *ipso facto* a literary virtue, and another is what the quality of Hemingway's indirection may be. Even more than *discipline*, *irony* and *understatement* have been used too automatically as critical terms of praise, as though irony were not capable of being poorly handled like any other rhetorical device. The time is past due for closer evaluation of the quality of some of Hemingway's irony and understatement, including that of the earlier style which many critics agree shows more "discipline" than the later.

For several reasons *Death in the Afternoon* seems to me a pivotal book in examining this aspect of Hemingway's style. It marks a convenient point (some may think it too early) for a change in Hemingway's style often felt to have occurred during the 1930's. Moreover it states most overtly Hemingway's theories about and his preoccupation with the question of degree of statement – i.e., understatement and overstatement. The preoccupation with understatement is not the same thing, however, as either the theory or its practice. As a matter of fact, Hemingway states contradictory theories in *Death in the Afternoon*: one theory virtually equating understatement and truth, the other defending "flowery" writing as sometimes necessary. Not surprisingly, theory and practice frequently do not coincide, so that attempts to describe Hemingway's style as an illustration of his theory sometimes obscure more than they illuminate. Instead, it is Hemingway's *preoccupation* with understatement and his apparent feeling that the true is the understated which shed the most light on his practice. Regardless of theory or practice, understatement remains for him an important aesthetic problem.

On the second page of *Death in the Afternoon* Hemingway sets forth a theory of understatement and "objectivity" which closely resembles T. S. Eliot's theory of the "objective correlative". Eliot says, "The only way of expressing emotion in the form of art is by finding an 'objective correlative'; in other words, a set of objects, a situation, a chain of events which shall be the formula of that *particular* emotion; such that when the external facts . . . are given, the emotion is immediately evoked." [1] Hemingway says of the period in the early 1920's when he was trying to write, beginning with the "simplest" things (like violent death), "I found the greatest difficulty, aside from knowing truly what you really felt, rather than what you were supposed to feel, and had been taught to feel, was to put down what really happened in action; what the actual things were which produced the emotion that you experienced", "the real thing, the sequence of motion and fact which made the emotion and which would be as valid in a year or in ten years or, with luck and if you stated it purely enough, always. . . ." At the end of Chapter xvi he restates the theory figuratively:

If a writer of prose knows enough about what he is writing about he may omit things that he knows and the reader, if the writer is writing truly enough, will have a feeling of those things as strongly as though the writer had stated them. The dignity of movement of an ice-berg is due to only one-eighth of it being above water.

What we have here is a theory of significant omission, omission particularly of emotion which, in turn, is to be suggested by the right selection of objective facts – the implication being that this process somehow makes it "truer" than if it were directly stated. But Hemingway's iceberg figure introduces another element, *dignity*, which adds a new dimension to the strange association between understatement and truth. Perhaps truth as such matters less in the roundabout presentation of emotion than dignity of

[1] "Hamlet and His Problems", *The Sacred Wood* (London, Methuen and Co., Ltd., 1950), p. 100.

appearance. (Cf. one of the elder waiter's reasons for preferring a clean, well-lighted café to a bar: "Nor can you stand before a bar with dignity although that is all that is provided for these hours.") In his aside on how he was always embarrassed by abstract words like glory, honor, courage and hallow, which he thinks "obscene" in comparison with concrete names and dates, Frederic Henry also stresses the dignity of the "objective": "There were many words that you could not stand to hear and finally only the names of places had dignity" (Ch. xxvii).

The distrust of words that we see here is something Hemingway shares with many of his contemporaries. Like them, he

is shy of everything that smacks of what seems to him sophistication, because of the element of inflation and pretense which he has been led to connect with it in his mind. He has had an unfortunate experience with cultivated writers and has learned to suspect them wherever found. He is the burned child that fears the fire. And he is one of a large class. He is one of the war generation, who have learned to dislike big words because they were so much abused both during the War and in the age that prepared the War.[2]

Distrust of words runs like a refrain through their work: through E. E. Cummings' *The Enormous Room*, for instance, with its exposé of "those unspeakable foundations upon which are builded with infinite care such at once ornate and comfortable structures as *La Gloire* and *Le Patriotisme*" (Ch. vi), a book which Hemingway wrote Edmund Wilson in 1923 was "the best book published last year that I read".[3] It appears in John Andrews' reflections after talking to the "Y" man in *Three Soldiers*:

Men were more humane when they were killing each other than when they were talking about it. So was civilization nothing but a vast edifice of sham, and the war, instead of its crumbling, was its fullest and most ultimate expression. ... Were they all shams, too, these gigantic phrases that floated like gaudy kites high above mankind? Kites, that was it, contraptions of tissue paper held at the end of a string, ornaments not to be taken seriously. (IV.i)

Dos Passos' later hero Jimmy Herf echoes the distrust in the more

---

[2] Beach, p. 110.
[3] Quoted in *The Shores of Light*, p. 118.

"objective" manner of *Manhattan Transfer*: "His mind unreeling
phrases, he walks on doggedly. ... If only I still had faith in
words" (III. iv).

When Paul Bäumer, the hero of *All Quiet on the Western
Front*, tries to explain why he cannot talk to his father or to
others about his war experiences, his deepest experiences, he
sounds much like Krebs in "Soldier's Home":

> He wants me to tell him about the front; he is curious in a way that
> I find stupid and distressing; I no longer have any real contact with
> him. There is nothing he likes more than just hearing about it. I
> realize he does not know that a man cannot talk of such things; I
> would do it willingly, but it is too dangerous for me to put these
> things into words. I am afraid they might then become gigantic and
> I be no longer able to master them. What would become of us if
> everything that happens out there were quite clear to us?
> . . . .
> They talk to me too much. They have worries, aims, desires, that I
> cannot comprehend. I often sit with one of them in the little beer-
> garden and try to explain to him that this is really the only thing: just
> to sit quietly, like this. They understand of course, they agree, they
> may even feel it so too, but only with words, only with words, yes,
> that is it – they feel it, but always with only half of themselves. . . .[4]

Krebs has the same inability to communicate his deepest feelings
and finds that to express them he must so distort them that they
"lost their cool, valuable quality and then were lost themselves";
thus he acquires "the nausea in regard to experience that is the
result of untruth or exaggeration, and when he occasionally met
another man who had really been a soldier ... he fell into the
easy pose of the old soldier among other soldiers: that he had
been badly, sickeningly frightened all the time. In this way he
lost everything." The idea, surely not limited to Krebs the character, is clear: that words will falsify, that words are lies and talk
cheapens. And there is perhaps the further idea that Paul Bäumer
mentioned – that it is dangerous to put deep feelings into words,
whether because one may lose control over them (as Paul fears)
or because one will just lose them (as Krebs does).

[4]   Erich Maria Remarque, *All Quiet on the Western Front*, tr. A. W.
Wheen (Boston, Little, Brown and Co., 1958), pp. 166-167, 170 (Ch. vii).

Macomber, having lost his fear and (accordingly) become a man, asks Robert Wilson, the professional hunter, if he has a feeling of happiness about action to come:

"You're not supposed to mention it", Wilson said, looking in the other's face. "Much more fashionable to say you're scared. Mind you, you'll be scared too, plenty of times."
"But you *have* a feeling of happiness about action to come?"
"Yes", said Wilson. "There's that. Doesn't do to talk too much about all this. Talk the whole thing away. No pleasure in anything if you mouth it up too much."

In "Cross-Country Snow" we get this exchange:

"There's nothing really can touch skiing, is there?" Nick said. "The way it feels when you first drop off on a long run."
"Huh", said George. "It's too swell to talk about."

Brett expresses the idea more succinctly in Chapter vii of *The Sun Also Rises* as she and Jake are talking over the hopelessness of their love:

"Isn't it rotten? There isn't any use my telling you I love you."
"You know I love you."
"Let's not talk. Talking's all bilge. I'm going away from you, and then Michael's coming back."

What this distrust of verbalizing feelings may result in is suggested later in the novel when Brett, after saying that she is never going to talk about her affair with Pedro Romero, starts talking about it anyway. Jake says,

"I thought you weren't going to ever talk about it."
"How can I help it?"
"You'll lose it if you talk about it."
"I just talk around it. You know I feel rather damned good, Jake." (Ch. xix)

It is plain that both agree on the bad effects of talking about what matters most; talking "around" it is safer. How much of Hemingway's "objectivity", one wonders, is akin to stylized small talk about safe or unimportant topics, avoiding what is emotionally charged and suggesting it very obliquely? Beach calls Jake's warning to Brett a deep saying and one to which any man must respond who cares more for actual states of the spirit than for their verbal equivalents. States of the spirit are fragile and tenuous affairs; and in general we feel that the less said about them the better, lest they be cheapened and lost. Man is given to spiritual vanity; and words are liars. This saying of Jake's is as good a clue as we can find to Hemingway's distrust of verbalism, and his reticence on the subject of spiritual states. (p. 112)

But when we have allowed that feelings are difficult to express in words and that words can become empty and meaningless, we must wonder how far such a fundamental distrust of verbalization is consistent with the practice of a verbal art. Shying away from feelings as something too fragile or delicate for examination (or perhaps as too crude and messy?) is subject to a less favorable interpretation than Beach's. James T. Farrell, for instance, in describing the characters of *The Sun Also Rises* comments, "Their conversation is reduced to enthusiastic small talk about their escapades. And this talk, as well as their actions, is largely a matter of pose and gesture." [5]

Isaac Rosenfeld makes a similar observation about *A Farewell to Arms*, contending that Hemingway's style covers up emotional starvation with "honorific leanness".[6] The hero's title to manliness being emotional restraint, the restraint increases as the emotion increases, the attempt being to suggest that " 'still waters run deep', and similar over-evaluations of standard Anglo-Saxon behavior" (p. 150). Rosenfeld cites the following passage as a description of Frederic Henry's love for Catherine while he is riding the railroad gondola away from the front:

I could remember Catherine but I knew I would get crazy if I thought about her when I was not sure yet I would see her, so I would not think about her, only about her a little, only about her with the car going slowly and clickingly, and some light through the canvas and my lying with Catherine on the floor of the car. Hard as the floor of the car to lie not thinking only feeling, having been away too long, the clothes wet and the floor moving only a little each

---

[5] "*The Sun Also Rises*", in McCaffery, p. 222.
[6] "A Farewell to Hemingway", *The Kenyon Review*, XIII (Winter 1951), 151.

time and lonesome inside and alone with wet clothing and hard floor for a wife. (Ch. xxxii)

Rosenfeld is correct in one sense in saying that this presents us with a blank, a suppression of longing, instead of longing itself. However, in context what seems intended is more the cold emptiness of feeling, intensified by the expansive, rather Steinish repetition of the last sentence in which the suggestion of the motion of the gondola car and his fantasy about lying with Catherine add strongly to the impression of Henry's bleak feelings. There is actually considerable feeling conveyed in the passage, partly by contrast (a typical device of Hemingway's); it seems to me an example of the successful use of indirection. I think the same is true of the ending of the novel, rain and all, with its increase in understatement and "objectivity" as the emotional intensity increases:

It seems she had one hemorrhage after another. They couldn't stop it. I went into the room and stayed with Catherine until she died. She was unconscious all the time, and it did not take her very long to die.

. . . .

... after I had got them out and shut the door and turned off the light it wasn't any good. It was like saying good-by to a statue. After a while I went out and left the hospital and walked back to the hotel in the rain.

This is a characteristic Hemingway low-key ending, a device that is not always so successful. Ideally, one should give a proportionate balance of successful and unsuccessful examples of the use of understatement, "irony", and "objectivity". But since space is limited and since the devices are so often praised as "discipline", perhaps it will do to look at some instances where they appear less than successful. Such instances frequently bear out Rosenfeld's assertion that "it is only the trivial feeling that one can afford to let out freely" (p. 150) or J. Kashkeen's observation, "Whole stories are nothing but a euphemism, the entire story 'Hills Like White Elephants' for instance, pivoting on one unspoken word" (p. 99). Kashkeen was rather hasty about writing Hemingway off (1935), but the fact is that many of Hemingway's

indirect effects which once, apparently, sounded just the note to
catch the ear of his audience now seem less happy.

2

The most striking qualities of Hemingway's early work were, in
Philip Young's words, "the rigorous objectivity with which they
were told, their complete lack of 'thinking', and the unbelievably
sharp and simple prose" (pp. 150-151). Although this description
leaves out of account such traits of Hemingway's early style as the
experiments with repetition and rigidity of syntax (e.g., "Up in
Michigan") and with colloquialism and foreignism (e.g., "Chapters" iv and ix of *In Our Time*), it does give much of the flavor
of the early work. Not thinking is not yet the explicit and recurrent
theme which it becomes from *The Sun Also Rises* on, except for
an occasional comment about Nick in Part I of "Big Two-
Hearted River": "He felt he had left everything behind, the need
for thinking, the need to write, other needs. It was all back of
him"; "His mind was starting to work. He knew he could choke
it because he was tired enough." But it is obvious throughout
"Big Two-Hearted River", as it is in so much of the early work,
that the abundance of "objective" detail substitutes for and
vaguely suggests something else, some very strong but unmen-
tioned feeling, which the hero pointedly does not think about. It
is as though his attention, and the reader's, were being continually
directed to everything and anything else – to the small detail,
even to the trivial – while knowing all the time that there is
something much more important in the background which is only
hinted at.

The effect of this early work is frequently one of emotional
numbness, emptiness, or bleakness and not infrequently one of
mystification. The description of Liz at the end of "Up in
Michigan", even to the cold mist from the bay, foreshadows
Frederic Henry's bleakness of feeling in the examples above
(where rain replaces the mist): "There was a mist coming up from
the bay. She was cold and miserable and everything felt gone.

. . . A cold mist was coming up through the woods from the bay"
(cf. the end of "My Old Man": "Seems like when they get started
they don't leave a guy nothing").

Similar in both effect and imagery, while even more "objective"
and rigidly simple in syntax, is "Chapter" v of *In Our Time*, the
description of six cabinet ministers shot in the rain in the early
morning against the wall of a hospital with its shutters nailed shut,
its courtyard full of pools of water. One of the ministers is too
sick from typhoid to stand up, so that when the soldiers fire the
first volley he is "sitting down in the water with his head on his
knees". One might describe the tone of this sketch as "the mono-
tone of terror" [7] or find especial horror in the detail of the sick
minister who is shot or in the ironic detail that the shooting occurs
against the wall of a hospital with its shutters nailed shut, but the
bleakness is suggested again mainly by the rain imagery which
Hemingway used also in "Chapter" ii ("Minarets stuck up in the
rain"). Hemingway's dependence on such "objective" details to
give the attitude he has omitted is clear in his earliest work.

But the implied in such cases generally lacks the specificity of
the direct. It is here that the theory of the "objective correlative"
breaks down. It is all very well to talk about leaving the emotion
to the reader, who will become impatient if the writer emphasizes
it – "Dickens's great fault" [8] – but it is much easier to show the
writer trying to achieve the correct sequence of "objective fact"
which will arouse a particular emotion than it is to show that he
actually does so.[9] Suppression of emotion is just as likely to

[7] Maxwell Geismar, "Ernest Hemingway: You Could Always Come
Back", in McCaffery, p. 148.
[8] Atkins, p. 181.
[9] See, for example, Aldridge, pp. 30-32. Aldridge finds in the Caporetto
retreat "an exact equivalent in action for the unreality, the abstractness,
which the war had assumed in Frederick [*sic*] Henry's mind" (p. 30);
he sees in the Pamplona fiesta "the key or parallel in action for the
animal savagery which [the visitors] loose upon one another" (p. 31). But
his subsequent "parallels" show best how far afield one can go with the
"objective correlative": "A moment after a steer is gored in the bull ring,
Robert Cohn, the man who behaved badly by daring to admit his feelings,
is publicly humiliated in a café. As the Spaniard later in the story is
accidentally killed by a bull, Cohn is socially and spiritually murdered by
the unfeeling Brett; and while Jake watches the Spaniard's funeral proces-

produce an impression of emotional numbness, and bareness of
presentation to suggest lack of emotion. It is hard to be very
critical of readers who do not see the point of stories like "Big
Two-Hearted River", "The Killers", or "The End of Something"
("'What's the matter, Nick?, Marjory asked. 'I don't know', Nick
said, getting wood for a fire. . . . 'I feel as though everything was
gone to hell inside me. I don't know, Marge. I don't know what to
say' ").

Like any other device, "objectivity" can become a mannerism
or trick. The reason, perhaps, that this truism has eluded many of
Hemingway's critics is that they have shared in his overreaction
against the emotional exaggeration of so much late nineteenth-
century writing. But there is a limit to the effectiveness of this
kind of procedure: "If you describe really outrageous events as
though they happen daily in your back yard you get a critical
impact which Woe Woe and Cry Havoc do not impart" (Atkins,
p. 79). That result is possible, but far from inevitable, and as
Atkins also remarks, the effect of the flat statement may well be to
convey emotional inhibition (hardness or caution). When he finds
greater force in the indirect, Atkins is close to E. M. W. Tillyard's
conviction that no direct statement of the commonplace is likely
to carry the weight of the oblique.[10] Such a view is typical when
obliquity is fashionable – which it is today, as Tillyard also points
out (p. 32). However, the opposite may be contended: that the
indirect often lacks the force of the direct because it is vaguer, and

---

sion go down the street, Cohn, equally dead, leaves Pamplona. . . . In each
case the inner drama of the characters has found an object in the events
which surround them" (pp. 31-32).

[10] *Poetry Direct and Oblique* (London, Chatto and Windus, 1948), p. 43.
Cf. Robert L. Lair, "Hemingway and Cézanne: An Indebtedness", *Modern Fiction Studies*, VI (Summer 1960), 165: both artists, says Lair, share
an aversion to "that nineteenth-century romanticism which they believed
had deteriorated into mere sentimentality. That is not to say that either
of them is without sentiment or genuine emotion, but each fears above
all else the direct expression of naked or unrestrained emotion." But in
the twinkling of an eye, what sounds like a possible failing becomes
certain literary virtue: "One need only note the behavior of the widowered
major of 'In Another Country' to see how calm, classical restraint can be
made to convey a torment of bereavement and bewildered outrage. . . .
Hemingway does not need to tell us how to *feel*; he makes us *experience*."

the indirect expression can rarely give the exactness of the direct. What, for example, is one to make of "Chapter" x of *In Our Time*, an "objective" description of a gored horse in a bullfight?

They whack-whacked the white horse on the legs and he kneed himself up. The picador twisted the stirrups straight and pulled and hauled up into the saddle. The horse's entrails hung down in a blue bunch and swung backward and forward as he began to canter, the *monos* whacking him on the back of his legs with the rods. He cantered jerkily along the barrera. He stopped stiff and one of the *monos* held his bridle and walked him forward. The picador kicked in his spurs, leaned forward and shook his lance at the bull. Blood pumped regularly from between the horse's front legs. He was nervously wobbly. The bull could not make up his mind to charge.

What is the emotional effect of this – horror? anger at brutality? fascination with bloodletting? emotional numbness? Carlos Baker admires the "clean" prose, free of literary tricks except for the repetition of the word *forward* "which adds to the intensity of the account because 'forward' is where the bull stands with one wet horn" (p. 61). In the selection of details he professes to find the author's attitude: pity for the horse and enmity toward the picador and the ring-servants in such details as the horse's exposed entrails, the pumping of his blood, the *monos*' whacking the horse, and the picador's kicking in his spurs. But is this an accurate description of the author's attitude, the correlative emotion to the "objective" facts? It seems unlikely, unless the attitude of Hemingway and his heroes altered a good deal, later on.

In *The Sun Also Rises* Bill and Jake advise Cohn and Brett to watch the bullfight selectively: "There's nothing but that horse part that will bother you", Jake says, "and they're only in for a few minutes with each bull. Just don't watch when it's bad." But of course Brett cannot stop looking at the horses, while Cohn turns green at the sight (" 'She couldn't take her eyes off them', Mike said. 'She's an extraordinary wench' "):

"I wish they didn't have the horse part", Cohn said.
"They're not important", Bill said. "After a while you never notice anything disgusting." (Ch. xv)

Hemingway says pretty much the same thing in his own person in *Death in the Afternoon:*

I belief that the tragedy of the bullfight is so well ordered and so strongly disciplined by ritual that a person feeling the whole tragedy cannot separate the minor comic-tragedy of the horse so as to feel it emotionally. If they sense the meaning and end of the whole thing even when they know nothing about it; feel that this thing they do not understand is going on, the business of the horses is nothing more than an incident. If they get no feeling of the whole tragedy naturally they will react emotionally to the most picturesque incident. . . .

The aficionado, or lover of the bullfight, may be said, broadly, then, to be one who has this sense of the tragedy and ritual of the fight so that the minor aspects are not important except as they relate to the whole. (Ch. i)

This is not an aside, either, but the conclusion to an eight-page explanation of the difficulty of knowing what you really feel rather than what you are supposed to feel or were taught to feel.

Referring to the incident described in "On the Quai at Smyrna" (the Introduction to *In Our Time*, 1930), the Greeks' breaking the forelegs of their baggage animals and dumping them into shallow water to drown, Hemingway says that he was sure in advance that he would not like the bullfight because of the horses. He thought the bullfight would be simple and barbarous and cruel, "but the bullfight was so far from simple and I liked it so much that it was much too complicated for my then equipment for writing to deal with and, aside from four very short sketches, I was not able to write anything about it for five years – and I wish I would have waited ten". Whether one ought to feel that way or not, the horses seem funny in their loss of dignity:

There is certainly nothing comic by our standards in seeing an animal emptied of its visceral content, but if this animal instead of doing something tragic, that is, dignified, gallops in a stiff old-maidish fashion around a ring trailing the opposite of clouds of glory it is as comic when what it is trailing is real as when the Fratellinis give a burlesque of it in which the viscera are represented by rolls of bandages, sausages and other things. . . . I have seen it, people running, horse emptying, one dignity after another being destroyed in the spattering, and trailing of its innermost values, in a complete burlesque of tragedy. I have seen these, call them dis-embowellings, that is the worst word, when, due to their timing, they were very funny.

You *ought* to be horrified and disgusted at what happens to these "parodies of horses", Hemingway says, but there is no way to be sure that you will be unless you make up your mind to be no matter what your feelings are. In their lack of dignity ("discipline"?), the horses become, by an interesting psychological shift in the observer Hemingway, hardly even real:

They are so unlike horses; in some ways they are like birds, any of the awkward birds such as the adjutants or the wide-billed storks, and when, lifted by the thrust of the bull's neck and shoulder muscles their legs hang, big hoofs dangling, neck drooping, the worn-out body lifted on the horn, they are not comic; but I swear they are not tragic. . . . They look a little as a dead pelican does. A live pelican is an interesting, amusing, and sympathetic bird . . . but a dead pelican looks very silly.

This happens to be a rare case when we can check one of Hemingway's "objective" indirect descriptions against his explicit attitude elsewhere – not for the purpose of claiming that the attitude given at length in *Death in the Afternoon* is the necessary correlative to the "Chapter" x sketch, but instead to show how indefinite the suggestions of such rigorous objectivity are. When it requires an explanation as long as *Death in the Afternoon* to make clear what the author does feel, one must remain dubious about explications of the intensity of feeling in a nine-sentence "objective" sketch: it is difficult to believe that anyone can assess the intensity of the feeling (except by the intensity with which it is repressed) very accurately until he is fairly sure what the feeling is.[11] It may be, on the other hand, that the feeling is excluded because it is too difficult or "dangerous" to express, just as talking and even thinking are frequently threatening occupations for Hemingway's heroes.

[11] Cf. the contrary and more typical view which Baker expounds: "At café tables, in quiet rooms, or in the compartments of trains, men and women talk together with a concentrated diffidence which almost conceals the intensity of their feelings. Upon examination, it turns out to be this very intensity, this intensity very close to the intensity of poetry, which has deceived some of his critics into supposing that Hemingway is an exponent of violence for its own sake. . . . He is after intensity, and his brand of intensity is to be achieved not by physical exercise but only through the exercise of the utmost restraint" (p. 142).

3

"Discipline" and "objectivity" are subject to widely divergent interpretations. Rosenfeld, for instance, talks about Hemingway's caution and his "careful style" (p. 155), while Beach sees a laudable experiment in economy:

Our artists in fiction have tried to see how far they can go with a mere notation of objective facts. And they have rediscovered the important esthetic principle of economy. They have found that, other things being equal, the best effect is that achieved with the greatest economy of means. There is, for one thing, the great gain of avoiding the obvious. The sentiment is not wanting in Hemingway. But he finds that he can give more point to his sentiment if he does not dress it out in fine language. And all the more so because this method requires more skill than that which depends on fine language for making its point. It requires that the facts shall be so rightly ordered that they will speak for themselves. (p. 111)

There are certain questions to raise about this method, which, as Beach adds, is a limited one. The first is how far it is actually more economical to give an indirect "objective" description to suggest the emotions than it is to describe emotions directly. Another is when the method is primarily a means of avoidance – whether of the obvious, the inflated, or the crude. One thing is certain: it is much more difficult with the indirect than with the direct to scrutinize it closely and to criticize the quality of the feeling (the author can always object that he never actually *said* any such thing). It is this aspect of Hemingway's "objectivity" which I will try to examine next.

A distinction should be made first about so-called objective descriptions. The "behavioristic" description of feelings in terms of physical reactions is frequently not objective at all: "My old man sat there and sort of smiled at me, but his face was white and he looked sick as hell and I was scared and felt sick inside because I knew something had happened and I didn't see how anybody could call my old man a son of a bitch and get away with it." [12] Such description is not really objective any more than is

[12]   "My Old Man." See Beach, p. 98.

Joe's reaction to the horse Kzar: "I never saw such a horse. He was being led around the paddocks with his head down and when he went by me I felt all hollow inside he was so beautiful." The description is scarcely more objective (though considerably less definite) when Nick's father's anger is referred to how his back looks: "The doctor chewed the beard on his lower lip and looked at Dick Boulton. Then he turned away and walked up the hill to the cottage. They could see from his back how angry he was" ("The Doctor and the Doctor's Wife").

In these cases the objective and subjective are presented together; the objective seems to serve mainly to direct the reader's attention away from the feeling just enough so that the feeling will not appear exaggerated (the purpose, I think, is to deflate). The method and effect are about the same in the scene where Frederic Henry first kisses Catherine Barkley:

I kissed her hard and held her tight and tried to open her lips; they were closed tight. I was still angry and as I held her suddenly she shivered. I held her close against me and could feel her heart beating and her lips opened and her head went back against my hand and then she was crying on my shoulder. (Ch. v)

In other "objective" descriptions, the purpose of deflation, of avoiding the possibly grandiose or crude or "messy" feeling, is still present, but the feeling itself is much more rigidly suppressed. What is suggested, however, is sometimes such an excess of emotion that to mention it at all would be apparently to risk loss of control. Beneath the bitter "facts" of the ending of "A Very Short Story", for instance, there seems to be a torrent of feeling that is only safe to hint at.

The situation at first is that of Frederic Henry and Catherine Barkley: Luz, a nurse, takes night duty for three months so that she can come to the wounded soldier's bed. They want to get married so that everyone will know, "so they could not lose it", but there are too many legal technicalities. Here the parallel ends: after the armistice he returns to Chicago to get a job and send for her, but in the meantime she falls in love with a major of arditi; she writes to America that theirs was only "a boy and girl affair" and that she expects to be married in the spring. The very short story ("Chapter" x of *in our time*, 1924) ends with the "facts" that the major never married her, that Luz never got an answer to her letter to America, and that shortly afterward he contracted gonorrhea from a department store salesgirl "while riding in a taxicab through Lincoln Park". The form may be "objective" and understated, but the ending communicates outrage, hurt, and sorrow, the cruelty of life and love, and the pathetic victim they make of one. The feeling seems disproportionate and the "objectivity" a way of suggesting but never actually stating it.[13]

A good deal of Hemingway's "objectivity" suggests one or more of the following feelings, in such a way that one suspects they are too excessive to state openly: bitterness, outrage, hurt, and shock, or a bleakness which accompanies or follows the others. Perhaps this quality of some of Hemingway's "objective epitomes" will be clearer if we look first at a few obvious examples before the less obvious.[14]

The first is a typical anticlimactic chapter ending in *The Sun Also Rises*. Jake, acting as pander, has arranged to bring Brett and Pedro Romero together in a café; he pointedly gets up to leave them alone:

> I stood up. Romero rose, too.
> "Sit down", I said. "I must go and find our friends and bring them here."

[13] The changes made in the ending of *A Farewell to Arms* may be considered partly as an effort to provide more adequate foundation for this feeling of being the victim of life, wounded in war, wounded in love. Catherine's death gives a more "dignified" reason for this feeling than Luz's faithlessness does: the hero is a victim of the cruelty and indifference of the universe instead of a mere failure in personal relations. Kenneth Burke makes a similar point in *A Rhetoric of Motives* (New York, George Braziller, Inc., 1955) when discussing the end of *A Farewell to Arms*: " . . . a novelist, ending on the death of his heroine, might picture the hero walking silently in the rain. No weeping here. Rather stark 'understatement'. Or look again, and do you not find that the very heavens are weeping in his behalf? . . . There is even a certain covert apotheosis of the emotion here, making it 'heavenly' thus roundabout" (p. 326).

[14] E. M. Halliday uses the term "objective epitome" in "Hemingway's Ambiguity" and in "Hemingway's Narrative Perspective", *The Sewanee Review*, LX (Spring 1952), 208-218. In the former article Halliday cites the next two passages as examples of the device (pp. 6-7).

He looked at me. It was a final look to ask if it were understood. It was understood all right.

"Sit down", Brett said to him. "You must teach me Spanish."

He sat down and looked at her across the table. I went out. The hard-eyed people at the bull-fighter table watched me go. It was not pleasant. When I came back and looked in the café, twenty minutes later, Brett and Pedro Romero were gone. The coffee-glasses and our three empty cognac-glasses were on the table. A waiter came with a cloth and picked up the glasses and mopped off the table. (Ch. xvi)

The "objectivity" hardly conceals the excessive feeling of hurt and pathos; in its lack of subtlety it seems a mere mannerism to avoid stating openly the kind of feeling that it suggests.

The pathos is if anything more strained in this example from *A Farewell to Arms*. Worried about Catherine's difficult labor, Frederic Henry is on his way back to the hospital after a quick breakfast:

Outside along the street were the refuse cans from the houses waiting for the collector. A dog was nosing at one of the cans.

"What do you want?" I asked and looked in the can to see if there was anything I could pull out for him; there was nothing on top but coffee-grounds, dust and some dead flowers.

"There isn't anything, dog", I said. The dog crossed the street. I went up the stairs in the hospital to the floor Catherine was on and down the hall to her room. I knocked on the door. There was no answer. I opened the door; the room was empty, except for Catherine's bag on a chair and her dressing-gown hanging on a hook on the wall. (Ch. xli)

Such is life, the "objective" parallel suggests, a dog's life, heartless and heartbreaking as an empty garbage can or an empty room.

The passage has obvious similarities to the overwrought description of the Gulf Stream and catalogue of the refuse of human endeavor in Chapter viii of *Green Hills of Africa*. And it seems to me to look forward to the description in *The Old Man and the Sea* of the collapse of the old man followed by the passing of an indifferent cat:

He started to climb again and at the top he fell and lay for some time with the mast across his shoulder. He tried to get up. But it was too difficult and he sat there with the mast on his shoulder and looked at the road. A cat passed on the far side going about its business and the old man watched it. Then he just watched the road. (pp. 133-134)

The unasked question seems to be, does no one care?

If the old man violated his luck by failing to observe limits, by going out too far, and paid by having his fish eaten by sharks, Paco, the boy waiter of "The Capital of the World", pays with his life for his lack of knowledge of the details of bullfighting while playing matador with the dishwasher Enrique: ". . . he stepped his left foot two inches too far forward and the knife did not pass, but had slipped in as easily as into a wineskin". As Paco is bleeding to death on the diningroom floor of the Pension Luarca, "feeling his life go out of him as dirty water empties from a bathtub when the plug is drawn", Hemingway turns to a bitterly "objective" description of what the other inhabitants of the Pension are doing at the moment, continuing the ironic contrast that he employs throughout the story:

. . . the two sisters of Paco were still in the moving-picture palace of the Gran Via, where they were intensely disappointed in the Garbo film, which showed the great star in miserable low surroundings when they had been accustomed to see her surrounded by great luxury and brilliance. . . . All the other people from the hotel were doing almost what they had been doing when the accident happened, except that the two priests had finished their devotions and were preparing for sleep, and the gray-haired picador had moved his drink over to the table with the two houseworn prostitutes. A little later he went out of the café with one of them. It was the one for whom the matador who had lost his nerve had been buying drinks.

What is the purpose of this account here if not to point up the grand indifference of the rest of the world, absorbed in its own trivial and sordid affairs, during Paco's moment of agony? The story ends with a final bitter, low-key twist of the knife:

The boy Paco had never known about any of this nor about what all these people would be doing on the next day and on other days to come. He had no idea how they really lived nor how they ended. He did not even realize they ended. He died, as the Spanish phrase has it, full of illusions. He had not had time in his life to lose any of them, nor even, at the end, to complete an act of contrition.

He had not even had time to be disappointed in the Garbo picture which disappointed all Madrid for a week.

Is the tone of bitterness and outrage justified? It is pathetic that Paco should die for his foolishness, but how could anyone else know about it and why should the others not be interested in their own affairs? The tone, suggested by the simile that life is like dirty water, seems illegitimate in the circumstances, but the whole is dignified by the "objective", "disciplined" presentation.

Comparison of the story with W. H. Auden's poem "Musée des Beaux Arts", which treats the same general theme as pictured in Breughel's *The Fall of Icarus*, focuses very well the difference in underlying feeling. The world is still indifferent, but the poem does not share the questionable outrage of the story:

> About suffering they were never wrong,
> The Old Masters: how well they understood
> Its human position; how it takes place
> While someone else is eating or opening a
>   window or just walking dully along;
> . . . .
> They never forgot
> That even the dreadful martyrdom must run
>   its course
> Anyhow in a corner, some untidy spot
> Where the dogs go on with their doggy life
>   and the torturer's horse
> Scratches its innocent behind on a tree.
> . . . .
> ... the expensive delicate ship that must
>   have seen
> Something amazing, a boy falling out of the
>   sky,
> Had somewhere to get to and sailed calmly on.

Here also are irony and ironic contrast, but how different their quality is in the poem.

Having examined some comparatively obvious examples of "objectivity" and the underlying feeling, we may be able to discern more in other "objective" passages. For example, the description of the place where Frederic and Catherine could not go because of his jaundice, though "objective" and even understated, is thoroughly pathetic in effect:

The whites of the eyes were yellow and it was the jaundice. I was sick for two weeks with it. For that reason we did not spend a convalescent leave together. We had planned to go to Pallanza on Lago Maggiore. It is nice there in the fall when the leaves turn. There are walks you can take and you can troll for trout in the lake. It would have been better than Stresa because there are fewer people at Pallanza. Stresa is so easy to get to from Milan that there are always people you know. There is a nice village at Pallanza and you can row out to the islands where the fishermen live and there is a restaurant on the biggest island. But we did not go. (Ch. xxii)

That is not to say that the pathos here is necessarily excessive or illegitimate but that an effort has been made to conceal it – Hemingway perhaps feeling uneasy about expressing it openly.

In *The Sun Also Rises* we get this dry, newspaperlike account of the end of the bull which had killed an *aficionado* named Vicente Girones when the bulls were running through the street to the bullring:

The bull who killed Vicente Girones was named Bocanegra, was Number 118 of the bull-breeding establishment of Sanchez Taberno, and was killed by Pedro Romero as the third bull of that same afternoon. His ear was cut by popular acclamation and given to Pedro Romero, who, in turn, gave it to Brett, who wrapped it in a handkerchief belonging to myself, and left both ear and handkerchief, along with a number of Muratti cigarette-stubs, shoved far back in the drawer of the bed-table that stood beside her bed in the Hotel Montoya, in Pamplona. (Ch. xvii)

Again the point seems to be the indifference of others; the passage is tinged with a rather gratuitous bitterness at the indifference, also echoed in the typical low-key ending of the chapter:

"Was anybody killed in the ring?"
"I don't think so. Just badly hurt."
"A man was killed outside in the runway."
"Was there?" said Bill.

It does not take much of this mannerism to incline one toward the view of the "old lady" in *Death in the Afternoon* who complains about the lack of a "wow" at the end of a story that the author tells her. "Ah, Madame", he responds, "it is years since I added the wow to the end of a story. Are you sure you are unhappy if the wow is omitted?" (Ch. xv). It is true that one gets tired of exclamation marks and "wows", but their emphasized omission can also become a trick of no more subtlety than an exclamation mark (unwritten). A steady diet of indirection and understatement palls after a while as much as overstatement, especially in passages where one suspects that what is omitted is excessive feeling which the author then hints at.

4

The Greeks were nice chaps too. When they evacuated they had all their baggage animals they couldn't take off with them so they just broke their forelegs and dumped them into the shallow water. . . . It was all a pleasant business. My word yes a most pleasant business.

The ending of "On the Quai at Smyrna" is fairly typical of the verbal irony of Hemingway's early work.[15] The bitterness and shock shows transparently enough through the rather facile inversion, and the preceding paragraph removes any possible doubt on that score: "You remember the harbor. There were plenty of nice things floating around in it. That was the only time in my life I got so I dreamed about things." This is the war and perhaps one of the incidents that Harry in "The Snows of Kilimanjaro" could not stand to think about or talk about:

That was the day he'd first seen dead men wearing white ballet skirts and upturned shoes with pompons on them. The Turks had come steadily and lumpily and he had seen the skirted men running and the officers shooting into them and running then themselves and he and the British observer had run too until his lungs ached and his mouth was full of the taste of pennies and they stopped behind some rocks and there were the Turks coming as lumpily as ever. Later he had seen the things that he could never think of and later still he had seen much worse. So when he got back to Paris that time he could not talk about it or stand to have it mentioned.

[15] " . . . in the weaker sections of Hemingway's new craft we may see more clearly what in its perfection we suspect. In his over-emphasis, sometimes flippant or ostentatiously virile, or with a sort of disdainful bravado, Hemingway shows us his defenses. 'It was a pleasant business. My word yes a most pleasant business.' This is just a little too jolly" (Geismar, p. 149).

(Hemingway returns to the memory of the horrors at Smyrna not only in Chapter i of *Death in the Afternoon* but also in Chapter xii when relating "A Natural History of the Dead" to the "old lady", who reminds him, "You wrote about those mules before.")

"My word yes a most pleasant business." To the elementary inversion, Hemingway added an occasional Briticism, apparently to get a final ironic twist. The same device is used in "Chapter" iv of *In Our Time*:

It was a frightfully hot day. We'd jammed an absolutely perfect barricade across the bridge. . . . It was absolutely topping. They tried to get over it, and we potted them from forty yards. . . . We were frightfully put out when we heard the flank had gone, and we had to fall back.

Such "irony" has been pretty consistently overpraised, as has the use of *only* in the final paragraph of Chapter i of *A Farewell to Arms*: "At the start of the winter came the permanent rain and with the rain came the cholera. But it was checked and in the end only seven thousand died of it in the army."

A general critical predilection for irony, understatement and indirection has resulted in such facility being valued much too highly. Yet it is not much more profound than Jake's comment in *The Sun Also Rises* about introducing a pickup to a group of his acquaintances (she has very bad teeth): "Georgette smiled that wonderful smile, and we shook hands all round" (Ch. iii). The same kind of "irony", only at greater length, pervades the description of Mrs. Laughton, one of the awful tourists (a writer's wife) at Freddy's bar in *To Have and Have Not*. She is first described as having "blonde curly hair cut short like a man's, a bad complexion, and the face and build of a lady wrestler. She wore shorts, too." She has been saying "nerts to you" to Professor MacWalsey, who remarks, "How charming." Then comes the following "ironic" description: " 'Nerts, nerts, double nerts to you', said the lady wrestler in a sudden access of charm, giving him the benefit of her pimpled profile" (Ch. xv).

Irony provides no saving grace when Hemingway is dealing with those he considers fakes, phonies, or outsiders. An example like the next one shows very clearly how little subtlety irony may have. In Chapter xxv of *To Have and Have Not* we get an ironic contrast between two women whose husbands have been shot by Cuban gunmen – Marie Morgan and Mrs. Albert Tracy. Marie Morgan, numb with grief, "hadn't been able to cry since about noon". Mrs. Tracy, on the other hand, makes a messy spectacle of herself, screaming to provide sound effects for the morbidly curious crowd on the dock, craning their necks to see the dead men on Freddy's boat.

Eventually the crowd pushes so hard that Mrs. Tracy, "still screaming, fell into the green water, the scream becoming a splash and bubble". Two Coast Guard men dive in and fish her out, and the following passage ensues, capped by the author's "ironic" comment:

No one in the crowd had made a move to aid her, and, as she stood dripping on the stern, she looked up at them, shook both her fists at them and shouted, "Basards! Bishes!" Then as she looked into the cockpit she wailed, "Alber. Whersh Alber?"

"He's not on board, Mrs. Tracy", the sheriff said, taking up a blanket to put around her. "Try to be calm, Mrs. Tracy. Try to be brave."

"My plate", said Mrs. Tracy tragically. "Losht my plate."

. . . .

"Are you all right, Mrs. Tracy?" the sheriff said, putting the blanket around her.

"All rie?" said Mrs. Tracy. "All rie?" then clenched both her hands and put back her head to really scream. Mrs. Tracy's grief was greater than she could bear.

Without a doubt, *To Have and Have Not* is a poor novel. But that fact does not alter another: bad writing sometimes shows as clearly as good (sometimes more clearly) what a writer's characteristic methods and procedures are (which should not be taken to mean, of course, that the successful passages are therefore suspect too). The treatment meted out here to Mrs. Tracy is after all pretty much the same treatment given Robert Cohn in *The Sun Also Rises*, though his rough handling comes via the other characters instead of straight from the author. Mrs. Tracy doesn't know how to behave any more than Cohn did; she doesn't know how to "take it" like Marie Morgan; and she bears the brunt of this "satire" and "irony" as a result. What a passage like this suggests, I think, is that the irony or understatement of some (not all) more subdued passages may conceal feelings of similarly dubious quality.

In *A Farewell to Arms* there is something roughly equivalent though not so outspoken in Henry's "ironic" wisecrack to one of the incompetent doctors who says that they must wait at least six months before operating on his knee. Henry replies that he does not believe it, and this exchange takes place:

> "Do you want to keep your knee, young man?"
> "No", I said.
> "What?"
> "I want it cut off", I said, "so I can wear a hook on it."
> "What do you mean? A hook?"
> "He is joking", said the house doctor. He patted my shoulder very delicately. "He wants to keep his knee. This is a very brave young man." (Ch. xv)

It is somehow inevitable that this doctor who is not competent to do his job without holding a consultation first and who is capable of asking stupid rhetorical questions should not be able to understand irony when he encounters it. This is simply part of an elaborate system by which fakes and phonies are identified (see Chapter v). The fact to note here is that they are fair game and that the writing itself (reflecting underlying feelings) seems to undergo distortion when they make an appearance.

There is too much evidence to the contrary to permit us to refer all such attitudes and "irony" just to the characters (in effect making the author twice as ironic). While no one will argue nowadays for an exact equation between a character and the author, the diametrically opposed view that there is no correspondence between them can be as seriously misleading. It is a grave mistake to suppose that the irony can be confined to Frederic Henry as narrator when we are told that "only" seven thousand died of the cholera. One cannot have it both ways at once: if Hemingway deserves praise for the excellence of his characters and their speech, he is at times involved in their lapses too.

The bitter, understated ending of *The Sun Also Rises* no longer has the telling impact it once had on readers (is not much of the detachment of the novel mainly a matter of surface?):

"Oh, Jake", Brett said, "we could have had such a damned good time together."
Ahead was a mounted policeman in khaki directing traffic. He raised his baton. The car slowed suddenly pressing Brett against me.
"Yes", I said. "Isn't it pretty to think so?"

The crushing understatement or irony at the end where one expects the "wow" is a device characteristic of a lot of Hemingway's work. Thus "Now I Lay Me", after its long account of Nick's night thoughts with which he occupies himself "because I had been living for a long time with the knowledge that if I ever shut my eyes in the dark and let myself go, my soul would go out of my body", ends with the banal sentiment of his orderly: "He was going back to America and he was very certain about marriage and knew it would fix up everything." This seems to me a successful use of the device, like "A Clean, Well-Lighted Place" ending on a similar note after the older waiter has reviewed the horrors of *nada* which make him one of "those who need a light for the night":

Now, without thinking further, he would go home to his room. He would lie in the bed and finally, with daylight, he would go to sleep. After all, he said to himself, it is probably only insomnia. Many must have it.

"The Sea Change" has at least two other characteristic forms of irony/understatement besides the low-key ending. The end of the story comes after the girl has left the young man, Phil, for a lesbian affair, and he tells the barman that he is now a changed man:

"I'm a different man, James", he said to the barman. "You see in me quite a different man."
"Yes, sir?" said James.
"Vice", said the brown young man, "is a very strange thing, James." . . . As he looked in the glass, he saw he was really quite a different-looking man.
. . . .
"I said I was a different man, James", he said. Looking into the mirror he saw that this was quite true.

"You look very well, sir", James said. "You must have had a very good summer."

The title of the story is an allusion, as are so many of Hemingway's titles (e.g., "Up in Michigan", "In Another Country", "Fathers and Sons", *In Our Time, The Sun Also Rises, A Farewell to Arms, For Whom the Bell Tolls, Across the River and into the Trees*).[16] Like Eliot, Hemingway resorts a great deal to allusion to suggest or replace attitudes that have been omitted in the interests of "objectivity" – often but not always with ironic effect. Eliot may depend more on the literary allusion, as Baker says (pp. 56-57), but Hemingway uses the device more than is frequently recognized; and in Chapter xii of *Death in the Afternoon*, while telling the "old lady" "A Natural History of the Dead" and his desire to see the death of a few Humanists, he says he learned the device from Eliot:

... regardless of how they started I hope to see the finish of a few, and speculate how worms will try that long preserved sterility; with their quaint pamphlets gone to bust and into foot-notes all their lust.

Old lady: That's a very nice line about lust.

Author: I know it. It came from Andrew Marvell. I learned how to do that by reading T. S. Eliot.

The title of "The Sea Change" is of course an ironic allusion to Ariel's song in *The Tempest* (I. ii. 396-401):

Full fathom five thy father lies;
Of his bones are coral made;
Those are pearls that were his eyes;
Nothing of him that doth fade
But doth suffer a sea-change
Into something rich and strange.

But in the course of the story there is a different allusion – to Pope's *An Essay on Man*, II, ll. 217-220 – which is doubly ironic because the young man cannot remember the part which describes his own reaction to vice:

" 'Vice is a monster of such fearful mien' ", the young man said bitterly, "that to be something or other needs but to be seen. Then we

16 For more information see Young, especially pp. 31, 60, 87-88, 154, 234, 236-237.

something, something, then embrace." He could not remember the words. "I can't quote", he said.

"Let's not say vice", she said. "That's not very polite."

"Perversion", he said.

The passage which the young man cannot recall goes as follows:

> Vice is a monster of so frightful mien,
> As, to be hated, needs but to be seen;
> Yet seen too oft, familiar with her face,
> We first endure, then pity, then embrace.

This inability to quote accurately is, incidentally, a trait which Phil shares with Scripps O'Neil in *The Torrents of Spring* and with Robert Jordan in *For Whom the Bell Tolls* (Ch. xiv):

But to snow! Now in this month. Cut it out, he said to himself. Cut it out and take it. It's that cup, you know. How did it go about that cup? He'd either have to improve his memory or else never think of quotations because when you missed one it hung in your mind like a name you had forgotten and you could not get rid of it. How did it go about that cup? [17]

Young suggests that Hemingway perhaps learned from Eliot also which poems to allude to. In spite of its obvious exaggeration, his suggestion appears to contain some truth. "The lines from Marlowe which gave Hemingway his much-worked phrase 'in another country' had been quoted by Eliot in his 'Portrait of a Lady'." [18] Moreover, in *The Waste Land* Eliot had already used an allusion to lines from "To His Coy Mistress" in the same context in which Hemingway uses it in *A Farewell to Arms*. Lines 196-198 of *The Waste Land* read,

> But at my back from time to time I hear
> The sounds of horns and motors, which shall bring
> Sweeney to Mrs. Porter in the spring.

[17] So many of Hemingway's heroes are compared to the crucified Christ and his ability to "take it" (cf. "Today Is Friday") that I suspect the allusion here has to do with the same thing – perhaps with the cup Christ had to drink (Matthew 26:39, 42). Jordan's train of thought leads him, somewhat ironically, to ask for a cup of wine.

[18] Young, p. 237. See Phyllis Bartlett, "Other Countries, Other Wenches", *Modern Fiction Studies*, III (Winter 1957-58), 345-349, for a discussion of Marlowe's lines in Eliot, Hemingway, Faulkner, and elsewhere.

The passage in *A Farewell to Arms* has the same association between motor horns and the lines from Marvell:

> Down below on the street a motor car honked.
> > "'But at my back I always hear
> > Time's winged chariot hurrying near'",
> I said.
> "I know that poem", Catherine said. "It's by Marvell. But it's about a girl who wouldn't live with a man." (Ch. xxiii)

Twenty-one years later Colonel Cantwell alludes to Marlowe and to *The Waste Land* as he explains to Renata how dreadful his wife was. "She had more ambition than Napoleon and about the talent of the average High School Valedictorian", he says, adding that she was a woman journalist:

> "But they are dreadful", the girl said.
> "I agree."
> . . . .
> "You wouldn't tell her about us, so she could write about it?"
> "No. I told her about things once, and she wrote about them. But that was in another country and besides the wench is dead."
> "Is she really dead?"
> "Deader than Phoebus the Phoenician. But she doesn't know it yet." [19]

While such examples hardly prove that Hemingway learned from Eliot which allusions to use, they do suggest that there was considerable influence and that the techniques of the two have similarities. For example, this passage from *A Farewell to Arms*, giving Frederic Henry's stream of consciousness as he is falling asleep, bears comparison with the techniques of both Joyce and Eliot:

> If there were no war we would probably all be in bed. In bed I lay me down my head. Bed and board. Stiff as a board in bed. Catherine was in bed now between two sheets, over her and under her. Which side did she sleep on? Maybe she wasn't asleep. Maybe she was lying thinking about me. Blow, blow, ye western wind. Well, it blew and it wasn't the small rain but the big rain down that rained. It rained all night. You knew it rained down that rained. Look at it.

[19] Ch. xxvii. Cantwell's memory is also faulty in reproducing quotations: line 312 of *The Waste Land* reads, "Phlebas the Phoenician".

Christ, that my love were in my arms and I in my bed again. That my love Catherine. That my sweet love Catherine down might rain. Blow her again to me. (Ch. xxviii)

The allusion is to the anonymous Elizabethan lyric:

> O western wind, when wilt thou blow,
> That the small rain down can rain?
> Christ, if my love were in my arms
> And I in my bed again!

Such experiments as this indicate Hemingway's keen awareness of the stylistic experiments of the writers slightly antedating him. Whether or not he was directly influenced by Eliot, as he says, his use of allusions reflects a device which Eliot "popularized" in *The Waste Land*.

Allusions abound especially in *For Whom the Bell Tolls* and *Across the River and into the Trees*, where they seem part of a relaxing of "discipline" and understatement. In *For Whom the Bell Tolls*, for instance, we find such improbabilities as El Sordo's echoing Lady Macbeth: "We must think much about the manner of our going" (Ch. xi; *Macbeth*, III. iv. 119-120); and Pilar's referring to *Love's Labour's Lost* in her description of the odor of death (Ch. xix) and to *All's Well That Ends Well* as she tells Jordan not to worry (Ch. xxxviii). Moreover, the joking between Agustín and Jordan about onions seems to serve mainly as a peg to hang another allusion on:

"What hast thou against the onion?"
"The odor. Nothing more. Otherwise it is like the rose."
Robert Jordan grinned at him with his mouth full.
"Like the rose", he said. "Mighty like the rose. A rose is a rose is an onion."
"Thy onions are affecting thy brain", Agustín said. "Take care."
"An onion is an onion is an onion", Robert Jordan said cheerily and, he thought, a stone is a stein is a rock is a boulder is a pebble. (Ch. xxiv)

But *Across the River and into the Trees* is even fuller of improbable allusions, among them allusions to Blake: "Why have I never seen a gondola before? What hand or eye framed that dark-ed symmetry?" (Ch. xiii); to "The Pearl": " 'All I can tell

you is that Mister Tito has plenty problems.' 'Well I know that
now truly', the night porter who was really only a boy said. 'I
hope you do. . . . I wouldn't call it, as knowledge, any pearl of
great price' " (Ch. xx); to Dante: " 'You sound like Dante', she
said sleepily. 'I am Mister Dante', he said. 'For the moment.' And
for a while he was and he drew all the circles. They were as un-
just as Dante's but he drew them" (Ch. xxxii); and to an obscure
line from Edgar Quinet which James Joyce once quoted to
Hemingway: "He went out from the bathroom into the other
room, and he was as young as at his first attack" (Ch. xi), " 'Let's
be *fraîche et rose comme au jour de bataille.*' 'Who said that?' 'I
haven't the slightest idea' " (Ch. xxxviii).[20]

Another allusion looks backward to "The Short Happy Life of
Francis Macomber", as the *Gran Maestro* and Cantwell remember
"the men who decided that they did not wish to die; not thinking
that he who dies on Thursday does not have to die on Friday"
(Ch. vii):

"You know, I'd like to try another lion", Macomber said. "I'm
really not afraid of them now. After all, what can they do to you?"
"That's it", said Wilson. "Worst one can do is kill you. How does
it go? Shakespeare. Damned good. See if I can remember. Oh,
damned good. Used to quote it to myself at one time. Let's see. 'By
my troth, I care not; a man can die but once; we owe God a death
and let it go which way it will he that dies this year is quit for the
next.' Damned fine, eh?"
He was very embarrassed, having brought out this thing he had
lived by. . . .[21]

---

[20] See *Green Hills of Africa*, Ch. iv, and Baker, p. 284n.
[21] In his introduction to *Men at War* (New York, Crown Publishers,
1942), Hemingway explains where he got the quotation and what it means
to him: "After being severely wounded two weeks before my nineteenth
birthday I had a bad time until I figured it out that nothing could happen
to me that had not happened to all men before me. . . . I was very
ignorant at nineteen and had read little and I remember the sudden
happiness and the feeling of having a permanent protecting talisman when
a young British officer I met when in the hospital first wrote out for me,
so that I could remember them, these lines: '*By my troth, I care not: a
man can die but once; we owe God a death . . . and let it go which way
it will, he that dies this year is quit for the next.*' That is probably the
best thing that is written in this book and, with nothing else, a man can
get along all right on that" (pp. xiii-xiv).

The allusion is to a speech by the soldier Feeble (unintentional irony?) in *Henry IV, 2*, III. ii. 250-255. At least two things seem significant about Wilson's reciting his credo: the explicit statement of the high-sounding sentiment he lives by, and his embarrassment at stating it and attempt to puncture the pretentious sound with *damns.*

Something similar occurs when Harry accuses himself in "The Snows of Kilimanjaro":

He had destroyed his talent by not using it, by betrayals of himself and what he believed in, by drinking so much that he blunted the edge of his perceptions, by laziness, by sloth, and by snobbery, by pride and by prejudice, by hook and by crook. What was this? A catalogue of old books?

What happens here, I think, is that Hemingway allows his "discipline" to relax, but becomes uneasy at the lack of understatement (that is, he feels even in the process of abandoning understatement that the understated is truer and more dignified); the result, which is fairly typical of one reaction in his later works, is to try to deflate the high-flown with tough talk or with a wisecrack turned against the self.

Just as the literature of the 1920's shows a marked preoccupation with indirection and irony,[22] so in its effort to be "objective" and emotionless it relies heavily on allusion to replace the subjective and keep it at one remove from the writer. In this respect, Eliot and Hemingway are typical rather than exceptional. The

[22] Part II, Chapter iii of *This Side of Paradise* is titled "Young Irony" – only one of many references by Fitzgerald, not to consider his manner. On the first page of *The Beautiful and Damned* we read, "In 1913, when Anthony Patch was twenty-five, two years were already gone since irony, the Holy Ghost of this later day, had, theoretically at least, descended upon him. Irony was the final polish of the shoe, the ultimate dab of the clothesbrush, a sort of intellectual 'There!' ... " Recall the fun that Jake and Bill have in Chapter xii of *The Sun Also Rises* with Mencken's phrase "irony and pity". In "Essay in Pedagogy", *Prejudices: Fifth Series*, Mencken advises American novelists to write, among other figures, about the typical American journalist: "Let him be done ironically, as Lewis did Babbitt, but let him be done also with pity" (New York, Alfred A. Knopf, 1926, p. 235). While irony neither began nor ended with the 1920's (witness today), it obviously suited the temper of the time as if made to measure for it.

practice of Ezra Pound comes to mind at once, and so does that of Dos Passos. The following passage from *Manhattan Transfer*, for example, is typical of Dos Passos' method in this novel; here is Ellen (Elaine) Oglethorpe "thinking":

> A walk'll make me feel better. She sits at her dressingtable and shakes her hair down about her shoulders. "It's such a hellish nuisance, I'd like to cut it all off . . . spreads apace. The shadow of white Death. . . . Oughtnt to stay up so late, those dark circles under my eyes. . . . And at the door, Invisible Corruption. . . . If I could only cry. . . .
> Far from the shore, far from the trembling throng
> Whose sails were never to the tempest given
> Gosh it's six o'clock already. She starts walking up and down the room again. I am borne darkly fearfully afar. . . . The phone rings. (II.viii)

The passage is built around allusions to stanzas viii and lv of "Adonais", conveying indirectly the romantic concern with mutability and the audacity and trepidation of the romantic voyager; yet the passage itself is very pointedly "objective" and non-romantic. Such use of indirection makes the author extremely hard to pin down, which is very likely one of its purposes. Yet from other knowledge of Dos Passos' work, as from other knowledge of Hemingway's, it is difficult to believe that either is as detached from the romantic as his "irony" might suggest. On the contrary, the irony has a strong aroma of concealment.

It is not only allusion but other kinds of indirection too which make me agree with Atkins that Hemingway's is very much "an esoteric literature".[23] Atkins illustrates with "Hills Like White Elephants", the story which Kashkeen describes less graciously as "a euphemism . . . pivoting on one unspoken word". Atkins argues, "People very often do not name the most important things in their lives, though they may refer to them continually" (pp. 59-60) – i.e., a justification in terms of realism. But in reality, of course, the people know what they are referring to from

---

[23] P. 59. Atkins goes on at once to defend the procedure for the pleasure it gives him once he grasps the key and is able to make a meaningful whole out of what seemed at first disconnected fragments. Is this not precisely the esoteric appeal of a great deal of irony and indirection, rather than the more honorific claims to greater truth or realism?

previous communication, while in a story the effect is something else – ideally, mystification followed by the pleasure of discovery.

Also, Kashkeen's criticism cannot be so lightly dismissed by arguments from reality. When does understatement become euphemism? When what is omitted is something tabu or unpleasant or something that the writer appears to dread stating, the two begin to merge. For instance, as close as we get to a statement of the unnamed topic of the quarrel (abortion) in "Hills Like White Elephants" is in the following passage:

"It's really an awfully simple operation, Jig", the man said. "It's not really an operation at all."

The girl looked at the ground the table legs rested on.

"I know you wouldn't mind it, Jig. It's really not anything. It's just to let the air in."

The girl did not say anything.

"I'll go with you and I'll stay with you all the time. They just let the air in and then it's all perfectly natural."

Baker, attempting to follow up Hemingway's praise of Henry James in *Green Hills of Africa* and to find similarities between them, remarks on each writer's habit of establishing the subject of a conversation by hint and allusion rather than by direct statement (p. 185n). Such parallels are interesting perhaps, but relatively uninformative until the purposes and effects of the practice are clarified. Examples of this method abound in Hemingway. In "The Sea Change", for example, the only indication of what is wrong is a number of indirect hints – the young man's references to vice and perversion and these two exchanges:

The man looked at her.

"I'll kill her", he said.

"Please don't", the girl said.

. . . .

"I'm sorry", she said.

"If it was a man – "

"Don't say that. It wouldn't be a man. You know that. Don't you trust me?"

Is this understatement or euphemism? Is the effect of this kind of indirection the pleasure of referring to the tabu without ever

naming it? In the same story there are even vaguer references to
something else, which allow the reader's imagination to wander to
practically any forbidden ground that it will. The girl objects to
the young man's use of the words *vice* and *perversion*, and he
retorts,

> "That's the name for it."
> "No", she said. "We're made up of all sorts of things. You've
> known that. You've used it well enough."
> "You don't have to say that again."
> "Because that explains it to you."
> "All right", he said. "All right."

So he sends her off. But what is the conversation about? It seems
to me that Kashkeen's charge of euphemism finds considerable
support in this kind of thing.

On the one hand, the use of pronouns and adverbs without
referents can be viewed as part of Hemingway's indefiniteness,
which sounds colloquial yet may be more expressive than anything
explicit could be. That is, it is related to his penchant for the
common, undiscriminated, or unspecific word, which is pointedly
not literary or high-flown. On the other hand, it can be looked at
as part of his general predilection for understatement and indirection. Both are aspects of a fear of pretentiousness or sentimentality – ultimately a distrust of words. But like any other
device, the "colloquial" or indirect word without a referent may
become itself a somewhat pretentious mannerism, which seems
more coy than truthful or dignified.

It is difficult to avoid the suspicion that Hemingway would
dread having to state plainly what *it* refers to in these passages:

> Don't lie to yourself about Pilar pushing her into your sleeping robe
> and try to make it nothing or to make it lousy. You were gone when
> you first saw her. When she first opened her mouth and spoke to
> you it was there already and you know it. Since you have it and
> you never thought you would have it, there is no sense throwing dirt
> at it, when you know what it is and you know it came the first time
> you looked at her as she came out bent over carrying that iron
> cooking platter.
> It hit you then and you know it and so why lie about it? (*For
> Whom the Bell Tolls*, Ch. xiii)

... he thought without intention, trying to find what had made it at the first. He knew he did not deserve it and he accepted it and he lived by it, but he sought, always, to understand it. (*Across the River and into the Trees,* Ch. xl)

It refers in each case to an intensely romantic love which might be very hard to deal with explicitly without risking unfavorable critical reactions.

In *Across the River and into the Trees* there is this explanation why Renata loves Cantwell:

He did not know, among other things, that the girl loved him because he had never been sad one waking morning of his life. ...
They make almost none like that, and the girl, although she was a young girl, knew one when she saw one. (Ch. xli)

In *For Whom the Bell Tolls*, the night before the bridge is to be blown up Maria apologizes to Robert Jordan for having failed him (she is too sore for lovemaking), and there follows a mixture of euphemism and allusion:

"Thou canst talk with me of Madrid", he said and thought: I'll keep any oversupply of that for tomorrow. I'll need all of that there is tomorrow. There are no pine needles that need that now as I will need it tomorrow. Who was it cast his seed upon the ground in the Bible? Onan. How did Onan turn out? he thought. I don't remember ever hearing any more about Onan. (Ch. xxxi)

At other times, though euphemistic, the indefinite pronoun appears more a habit or mannerism. For example, there seems to be little other reason for using *it* instead of *blood* in Chapter xviii of *To Have and Have Not* in the description of Harry looking at Albert Tracy, who has been shot by a Cuban gunman: "As he swung her out, spinning the wheel with his good arm, he looked astern to watch the clearance past the piling, and saw Albert on his knees in the stern, his head slipped sidewise now, in a pool of it."

The same thing is true of Chapter x where Harry is wondering whether the Cubans, who plan to rob the bank, will kill the lawyer Bee-lips and later Albert and him; however, none of this is stated – or very clear – at this point, as Harry thinks only in terms of *that* and *it*:

There's Bee-lips that will know about everything. Still they must
have thought about that. They must figure on that. Do you suppose
Bee-lips is so dumb he won't know that's what they will do? I
wonder. Of course maybe that isn't what they figure to do. Maybe
they aren't going to do any such thing. But it's natural that's what
they would do and I heard that word. If they do it they'll have to do
it just when it closes or they'll have the coast guard plane down
from Miami. . . . Bee-lips can help me get the boat out tonight. Bee-
lips is the one. Because sure as hell they've figured about Bee-lips. . . .
Suppose they figure about me and Albert. Did any of them look like
sailors? . . . I have to find out about that because if they figure on
doing without Albert or me from the start there's no way.

This is nearly understatement for its own sake; and the main
effect of it, when read without the benefit of later knowledge, is
mystification.

Of course, Hemingway is not responsible for the tabus and
censorship problems that he encounters as a writer, but his means
of circumventing them are sometimes rather coy and distracting:
e.g., the plethora of *obscenities* and *unprintables* in *For Whom
the Bell Tolls* which make the characters themselves self-conscious (reflecting, no doubt, a like feeling in the author). While
the following passages are quite funny, they seem to indicate that
Hemingway feels he may be overdoing the euphemisms (i.e.,
sounding pretentious), with the result that the characters joke
about them – taking the sting out of possible criticism by antici-
pating it. In the first example, Jordan's refusal to divulge any
information brings a torrent of obscenities from Agustín:

"Tell me this. Is it true about the bridge?"
"What about the bridge?"
"That we blow up an obscene bridge and then have to obscenely
well obscenity ourselves off out of these mountains?"
"I know not."

. . . .

"Go to the unprintable", Agustín said. "And unprint thyself. But do
you want me to tell you something of service to you?"
"Yes", said Robert Jordan. "If it is not unprintable", naming the
principal obscenity that had larded the conversation. . . . Agustín
laughed in the dark when he heard the word. (Ch. iii)

In the next example, even Pilar shows self-consciousness about
the string of obscenities, which are again turned into a joke:

"Where the un-nameable is this vileness that I am to guard?"

"In the cave", Pilar said. "In two sacks. And I am tired of thy obscenity."

"I obscenity in the milk of thy tiredness", Agustín said.

"Then go and befoul thyself", Pilar said to him without heat.

"Thy mother", Agustín replied.

"Thou never had one", Pilar told him, the insults having reached the ultimate formalism in Spanish in which the acts are never stated but only implied.

"What are they doing in there?" Agustín now asked confidentially.

"Nothing", Pilar told him. "*Nada*. We are, after all, in the spring, animal."

"Animal", said Agustín, relishing the word. "Animal. And thou. Daughter of the great whore of whores. I befoul myself in the milk of the springtime."

. . . .

"You", she said, and laughed that booming laugh. "You lack variety in your cursing. But you have force. Did you see the planes?"

"I un-name in the milk of their motors", Agustín said, nodding his head and biting his lower lip.

"That's something", Pilar said. "That is really something. But really difficult of execution."

"At that altitude, yes", Agustín grinned. "*Desde luego*. But it is better to joke." (Ch. ix)

The joking is supposedly about the actual obscenities or about the planes which they all fear. All the same, it functions to prevent a mannerism from sounding too mannered − or at least to show that Hemingway himself knows that it has its funny side.

One of Hemingway's recurrent images seems slightly euphemistic as well. In "Fathers and Sons" Nick thinks what he cannot tell his son about the Indian girl Trudy Gilby:

Could you say she did first what no one has ever done better and mention plump brown legs, flat belly, hard little breasts, well holding arms, quick searching tongue, the flat eyes, the good taste of mouth, then uncomfortably, tightly, sweetly, moistly, lovely, tightly, achingly, fully, finally, unendingly, never-endingly, never-to-endingly, suddenly ended, the great bird flown like an owl in the twilight, only it daylight in the woods and hemlock needles stuck against your belly.

Rafael uses the same bird figure with the same meaning when he asks Jordan why he didn't kill Pablo:

"Three or four times we waited for you to kill him. Pablo has no friends."

"I had the idea", Robert Jordan said. "But I left it."

"Surely all could see that. Every one noted your preparations. Why didn't you do it?"

"I thought it might molest you others or the woman."

"*Qué va.* And the woman waiting as a whore waits for the flight of the big bird. Thou art younger than thou appearest." (Ch. v)

In *Across the River and into the Trees* the figure is repeated in the account of Cantwell's and Renata's lovemaking in a gondola:

She said nothing, and neither did he, and when the great bird had flown far out of the closed window of the gondola, and was lost and gone, neither of them said anything. He held her head lightly with his good arm and the other arm held the high ground now. (Ch. xiii)

The topographical metaphors which Hemingway uses in this chapter and in Chapter xxxi of *For Whom the Bell Tolls* are also sexual euphemisms, common in Elizabethan poetry.[24] They are (indefinite) literary allusions, to be sure, but they serve the purposes of understatement and euphemism as well.

5

Another part of Hemingway's technique which is usually praised as irony is his employment of "ironic contrast" or juxtaposition. Beach, for example, tries to find the "fifth dimension" of prose which Hemingway talks about in Chapter i of *Green Hills of Africa* in his ironic and indirect handling of situations:

There is something at work here in the author's imagination which we might call irony, if that were not a word and faculty so much abused that it suggests an effect cliché and banal. Let us call it finesse. This author generally manages to give to his situation what James calls a "turn of the screw" – a turn of the imagination that reveals some unsuspected aspect of human nature and raises the subject to a higher pitch of interest and poignancy. (p. 108)

[24] See, for example, "geography and topography, metaphors from", in the general index to the essay in Eric Partridge, *Shakespeare's Bawdy: A Literary and Psychological Essay and a Comprehensive Glossary*, rev. ed. (London, Routledge and Kegan Paul, Ltd., 1955), p. 57.

Beach illustrates what he means by reference to the turn of events at the end of "Fifty Grand" and to the absence of comment in "My Old Man" about the tenderness of the relations between Joe and his father, with all the values presented through the boy's point of view: "The beauty of it is in the indirection of the approach – the achievement of the effect without recourse to the obvious devices of rhetoric." This is a fairly typical modern critical attitude in its high regard for indirection, (because of?) its dislike of open and effusive emotional display and (because of?) an excess of that in earlier literature. However, I cannot share Beach's admiration for the theatrical reversal of expectations in "Fifty Grand", nor its pointed low-key ending: " 'You're some boy, Jack', John says. 'No', Jack says. 'It was nothing.' " (The effect is to suggest "heroic" attitudes and qualities. It is precisely the effects of these contrasts and ironies which need scrutiny.)

Similarly, Brooks and Warren find much of the point of "The Killers" in the contrasted reactions of George, Nick, and the cook Sam, and in the ironical contrast between the world of normality represented by Mrs. Bell and the unreal, brutal, mechanical code of the killers.[25] But what is the point of the extra little irony when Nick leaves Hirsch's rooming-house?

"Well, good-night, Mrs. Hirsch", Nick said.
"I'm not Mrs. Hirsch", the woman said. "She owns the place. I just look after it for her. I'm Mrs. Bell."
'Well, good-night, Mrs. Bell", Nick said.

Brooks and Warren attempt to explain this exchange as some more of Mrs. Bell's representing normality:

Even if the unreal horror of the movie thriller has become real, even if the hunted man lies upstairs on his bed trying to make up his mind to go out, Mrs. Bell is still Mrs. Bell. She is not Mrs. Hirsch. Mrs. Hirsch owns the place, she just looks after it for Mrs. Hirsch. She is Mrs. Bell. (p. 319)

However, it strikes me that this is one of life's little ironies, so exploited later in "The Capital of the World": that during the awful moment of trial others are busy with their trivial mixups

---

[25] Cleanth Brooks, Jr., and Robert Penn Warren, *Understanding Fiction* (New York, Appleton-Century-Crofts, Inc., 1943), pp. 317-319.

– they don't even know whom they are talking to. But it also smacks of a mannerism, irony tending to become an end in itself once it has been established as the dominant mode of expression.

Compare the mixup between Cantwell and his driver in *Across the River and into the Trees* (Cantwell has been expounding on painters and the driver asks if he knows a lot about them):

"Painters?" he answered the driver. "I know quite a little about them, Burnham."

"I'm Jackson, sir. Burnham's up at the rest center at Cortina. That's a fine place, sir."

"I'm getting stupid", the Colonel said. (Ch. iii)

Cantwell then proceeds to give him some more information about art. If this passage serves any further purpose, I think it is one of deflation – not so much of Cantwell the officer as of Cantwell the pontificator – one of many reactions to the high-sounding in the novel.

Ironic contrast is a device that Hemingway began using early, both in individual stories and in the arrangement of his first volume of stories, *In Our Time*, in which the short stories are juxtaposed with "chapter" sketches – e.g., "Chapter" xv, the hanging of Sam Cardinella, inserted between the parts of "Big Two-Hearted River". It is a dubious statement to say that the "impersonal death and destruction" of the "chapters" could have no meaning save what it gains from juxtaposition with "the comforts and the excitements of Nick Adams' life in the northern Michigan woods",[26] since the "chapters" originally stood alone in the earlier *in our time*, and the "chapters" and stories are hardly the opposites that this statement implies. Nevertheless, we have Hemingway's word for it that the juxtaposition was no accident:

Finished the book of 14 stories with a chapter on *In Our Time* between each story – that is the way they were meant to go – to give the picture of the whole between examining it in detail. Like looking with your eyes at something, say a passing coast line, and then

---

[26] Frederick J. Hoffman, *The Modern Novel in America 1900-1950* (Chicago, Henry Regnery Co., 1951), p. 93. But very many of the stories are introductions to the unpleasant, violent or evil, as Young points out (p. 3), or hint at something similar in the background (e.g., "Big Two-Hearted River").

looking at it with 15X binoculars. Or rather, maybe, looking at it and then going in and living in it – and then coming out and looking at it again.[27]

The individual stories frequently center around such contrasts as that between Nick's father and mother in "The Doctor and the Doctor's Wife" – the Christian Scientist mother who cannot believe that anyone would intentionally pick a fight to avoid paying his bill, the angry father whom Nick prefers. "Indian Camp" ends with Nick, who has just witnessed the bloody suicide of an Indian husband, feeling "quite sure that he would never die". In "Cross-Country Snow" the contrast is between "the fellowship and freedom of the slopes and the mixed blessings of the United States and parenthood".[28]

The device has been regarded not only as a basic method of Hemingway's but as a reflection of his basic theme:

The ironic gap between expectation and fulfillment, pretense and fact, intention and action, the message sent and the message received, the way things are thought or ought to be and the way things are – this has been Hemingway's great theme from the beginning; and it has called for an ironic method to do it artistic justice.[29]

Harry Levin describes it (perhaps more accurately) as the "romantic preconception exploded by contact with harsh reality" (p. 150). It is a frequent, bitter point of such contrast that things are not as they should be – the point of many an angry, disillusioned idealist or romantic, whether or not he poses as a realist or naturalist or an "objective" recorder of events (cf. Dos Passos). In its purest form, perhaps, it is stated by Pilar as the difference between beautiful appearances and rotten reality:

[27] Letter to Edmund Wilson, from Paris, October 18, 1924, quoted in *The Shores of Light*, pp. 122-123. In the letter Hemingway agrees with Wilson that the lack of capital letters of *in our time* was a silly affectation. In general, Hemingway avoided the more radical literary experiments of his contemporaries.
[28] Young, pp. 14-15. Young points out the further "irony" that many of the stories have not been understood because they seem not to be about Nick Adams at all but about other people: Nick just happens to be around (p. 3).
[29] Halliday, "Hemingway's Ambiguity", p. 15.

... the three of them sat down under a pine tree and looked across the mountain meadow to where the tops of the peaks seemed to jut out from the roll of the high country with snow shining bright on them now in the early afternoon sun.

"What rotten stuff is the snow and how beautiful it looks", Pilar said. "What an illusion is the snow." (Ch. xii)

But we may be more specific yet about the uses to which the contrast is put. While the following is by no means an exhaustive list, I would say that these are some of the main effects of Hemingway's contrasts (the categories obviously overlap):

(1) to show the dirtiness of things human, particularly as compared to nature. This is the point of the description of the Gulf Stream and the human garbage in it in Chapter viii of *Green Hills of Africa*. And according to his letter to Maxwell Perkins, November 19, 1926, Hemingway meant *The Sun Also Rises* to be "a damn tragedy with the earth abiding forever as the hero", for he had "a great deal of fondness and admiration for the earth, and not a hell of a lot for my generation"; [30]

(2) to show people's ignorance, their lack of awareness of or sympathy for or sensitivity to another's suffering (this is closely related to the first category, but without the nature contrast). "The Capital of the World" exemplifies this use, pushed to its dubious if not illegitimate extreme. A more successful use (in general) is the series of contrasts toward the end of *A Farewell to Arms* between the everyday activities Henry encounters on each trip to the café to eat and the ordeal he sees Catherine undergoing at the hospital; these contrasts are surely meant to increase the emotional intensity of the ending. This category is closely related to the third;

(3) to show who the hero is and what the "heroic" attitudes and qualities are by contrast with the "phony". Hemingway is especially liable to distortion here – as in the contrast between Mrs. Tracy who loses her dental plate, falls into the water and makes a messy display of her grief, and Marie Morgan who shows how to take it like a "man". In one of the less successful contrasts near the end of *A Farewell to Arms*, while Henry lingers outside

[30]   Quoted by Baker, p. 81.

the operating amphitheater where Catherine has been taken, this incident occurs:

> Two nurses were hurrying toward the entrance to the gallery.
> "It's a Caesarean", one said. "They're going to do a Caesarean."
> The other one laughed. "We're just in time. Aren't we lucky?"
> They went in the door that led to the gallery.

The laughter is like a blow in Henry's face: one person's suffering is another's entertainment. It is a typical incident in that only the hero recognizes the import of what is happening, while the ill-assorted fakes, phonies, and tourists in Hemingway never realize or appreciate it.

The difference between the second and third categories can be made plainer by reference to Henry's reflections on the universal lack of concern:

> Once in camp I put a log on top of the fire and it was full of ants. As it commenced to burn, the ants swarmed out and went first toward the centre where the fire was; then turned back and ran toward the end. When there were enough on the end they fell off into the fire. ... I remember thinking at the time that it was the end of the world and a splendid chance to be a messiah and lift the log off the fire and throw it out where the ants could get off onto the ground. But I did not do anything but throw a tin cup of water on the log, so that I would have the cup empty to put whiskey in before I added water to it. I think the cup of water on the burning log only steamed the ants.
> So now I sat out in the hall and waited to hear how Catherine was.

The hero recognizes his own indifference. It is true that earlier he righteously shot a sergeant for desertion (Ch. xxix) shortly before deserting himself. Perhaps that is intentional irony – perhaps not – but it is the closest thing to censure of Henry in the novel. It may seem a slight or even a sophistical distinction to make, but it is an important distinction in the value system of Hemingway's fiction whether the indifference is that of a hero or of a phony or outsider. This fact may account for part of the sense of distortion one gets from Hemingway's handling of the out-group. But the effect of a number of his contrasts is just such a discrimination between the hero and the phony.

To Have and Have Not supplies other examples of people's ironic failure in awareness or sensitivity, the most notorious being Harry Morgan's incoherent attempt to formulate the "social" outlook he has learned by getting shot:

> "A man", Harry Morgan said, looking at them both. "One man alone ain't got. No man alone now." He stopped. "No matter how a man alone ain't got no bloody f—ing chance."
> He shut his eyes. It had taken him a long time to get it out and it had taken him all of his life to learn it.
> He lay there his eyes open again.
> "Come on", said the captain to the mate. "You sure you don't want anything, Harry?"
> Harry Morgan looked at him but he did not answer. He had told them, but they had not heard. (Ch. xxiii)

"He didn't make any sense", the mate says. "He's way out of his head."

Another ironic contrast with a similar effect involves Richard Gordon's and Marie Morgan's misjudgments of each other. In Chapter xix Gordon, a phony of a writer, sees Marie Morgan on her way home, crying, from the sheriff's office where she has learned of Harry's being shot; in "a flash of perception" he gets her dead wrong:

> He was writing a novel about a strike in a textile factory. In today's chapter he was going to use the big woman with the tear-reddened eyes he had just seen on the way home. Her husband when he came home at night hated her, hated the way she had coarsened and grown heavy, was repelled by her bleached hair, her too big breasts, her lack of sympathy with his work as an organizer. He would compare her to the young, firm-breasted, full-lipped little Jewess that had spoken at the meeting that evening. It was good. It was, it could be easily, terrific, and it was true. He had seen, in a flash of perception, the whole inner life of that type of woman.
> Her early indifference to her husband's caresses. Her desire for children and security. Her lack of sympathy with her husband's aims. Her sad attempts to simulate an interest in the sexual act that had become actually repugnant to her. It would be a fine chapter.

The irony is completed in Chapter xxv when Marie Morgan sees Gordon staggering up the road, his face bloody from the beating the bouncer at Freddy's bar gave him for trying to pick a fight with Professor MacWalsey; she also jumps to the wrong conclusion: " 'Some poor rummy', thought Marie. 'Some poor goddamned rummy.' " The over-all effect of the contrast is that of the second category – people's ignorance of one another – but the effect of Gordon's ignorance is closer to the third category: a phony is being shown up.

The nature-human contrast examined in this and the previous chapter perhaps deserves a little further examination, if only to test the validity of Baker's generalizations about Hemingway's use of the device:

... the carefully ordered accounts of natural scenery in his pages reveal, on close examination, a deliberate and intelligent artifice. The description is nearly always directly functional within an action. The beauty – or ugliness – of the land is made to belong to the ugliness – or beauty – of the human events which occur in its midst. Sometimes, as in Frank Norris, natural beauty stands in quiet contrast to whatever it is that men and women are doing in its presence. Hemingway uses this old trick of the naturalistic writers charily and rarely; it is never emphasized in the black-jack manner of, say, Norris in *The Octopus,* or Steinbeck in *The Wayward Bus.* What we tend to get in Hemingway is a subtle interweaving of the natural conditions in the background and the human conditions in the foreground or the middle-distance. (pp. 67-68)

It seems to me that Hemingway's use of the contrast between the natural and the human is neither as peripheral nor as subtle as this account makes it. On the contrary, Hemingway's readiness to expose the sordidness of human affairs by means of the contrast is a fundamental romantic trait of his work.

The nature-human contrast also runs through *To Have and Have Not.* In Chapter xvi we get the contrast as Harry's preparations for murder (putting his submachine gun in order and planning how to get at it easily once the boat is under way) are immediately followed by a paragraph of idyllic nature description:

It was fine clear afternoon, pleasant, not cold, with a light north breeze. It was a nice afternoon all right. The tide was running out and there were two pelicans sitting on the piling at the edge of the channel. A grunt fishing boat, painted dark green, chugged past on the way around to the fish market, the Negro fisherman sitting in the stern holding the tiller. Harry looked out across the water, smooth with the wind blowing with the tide, gray blue in the afternoon sun, out to the sandy island formed when the channel was dredged where the shark camp had been located. There were white gulls flying over the island.

"Be a pretty night", Harry thought. "Be a nice night to cross."

But of course the nice night is turned into a nightmare by the slaughter of Chapter xviii; shortly before the slaughter becomes wholesale Harry points up the contrast again:

It would be a pretty night to cross, he thought, a pretty night. Soon as the last of the afterglow is gone I've got to work her east. If I don't, we'll sight the glare of Havana in another hour. In two, anyway. Soon as he sees the glare it may occur to that son of a bitch to kill me.

After the juxtaposed irony in Chapter xix in which Richard Gordon misjudges Marie Morgan, Chapter xx opens with a description of the appearance of Freddy's boat, the *Queen Conch* (ironically painted "Frolic green"), as it drifts "gay looking in her fresh white and green, against the dark, blue Gulf Stream water". There follows a description of the school of fish around the boat, feeding on the blood which drips over the side. Most of the rest of the chapter is devoted to a description of Harry lying and "taking it", intolerably cold (one of the rare times that cold is definitely bad). The chapter ends with more description of the Gulf Stream, the beauty and purity of nature contrasted with the mire of the human, as it was in the qualitatively similar description in *Green Hills of Africa*:

The launch had been drifting since 10 o'clock of the night before and it was now getting late in the afternoon. There was nothing else in sight across the surface of the Gulf Stream but the gulf weed, a few pink, inflated, membranous bubbles of Portuguese men-of-war cocked jauntily on the surface, and the distant smoke of a loaded tanker bound north from Tampico.

The novel ends with a similar contrast between Marie's bleak thoughts as she sits at the diningroom table ("I guess you find out everything in this goddamned life. I guess you do all right. I guess I'm probably finding out right now. You just go dead inside and everything is easy. You just get dead like most people are most of the time") and the "lovely, cool, sub-tropical winter day" outside, the last paragraphs being a final glimpse of the Gulf Stream:

Through the window you could see the sea looking hard and new and blue in the winter light.

A large white yacht was coming into the harbor and seven miles out on the horizon you could see a tanker, small and neat in profile against the blue sea, hugging the reef as she made to the westward to keep from wasting fuel against the stream.

The text from Ecclesiastes which Hemingway prefaced to *The Sun Also Rises* would be equally apropos here.

6

The ultimate in praise of the indirect or ironic method is doubtless the claim that it is the truest or most real. E. M. Halliday makes this claim for Hemingway at the end of his article "Hemingway's Ambiguity: Symbolism and Irony":

It is the ambiguity of life itself that Hemingway has sought to render, and if irony has served him peculiarly well it is because he sees life as inescapably ironic. But if we must classify him let us do him justice: with all his skilful use of artistic ambiguity, he remains the the great *realist* of twentieth-century American fiction. (p. 22)

But in spite of Hemingway's insistence on telling the truth and presenting what really happened, it seems plain to me that these are not the main purposes or effects of his penchant for indirection. The point of irony can be thoroughly romantic, as it often is with Hemingway. Indirection can be a way of maintaining a greater appearance of dignity than one actually feels, a way of hiding or avoiding unpleasant or "messy" emotions. Objectivity and allusion can serve the evasive purpose of allowing the writer to pretend no personal involvement in feelings that he is obviously not much detached from. Irony, understatement, and indirection can become a mannerism, like any other, even if they pass for greater realism because of historical and literary reasons. *Real*, like *discipline* and *irony* today, is an honorific word. Mark

Spilka calls Jake "at best ... a restrained romantic".[31] I would say that "a restrained romantic" is a good description of Hemingway, in spite of his realistic surface.

The theory of understatement and indirection that Hemingway gives in *Death in the Afternoon* is in part an after-the-fact rationalization of an aesthetic ideal which was widespread in the 1920's (but not confined to the 1920's), which he apparently tried to practice, and which preoccupied him to a considerable extent ever after. Such different writers as Hemingway and Willa Cather, in spite of their belonging to different literary generations and in spite of Hemingway's disdainful remarks about *One of Ours*,[32] share a similar attitude toward artistic method.

Cather's statement of purpose here might have been made by any of a number of writers of the period:

> What I always want to do is to make the "writing" count for less and less and the people for more. In this new novel [*One of Ours*] I'm trying to cut out all analysis, observation, description, even the picture-making quality, in order to make things and people tell their own story simply by juxtaposition, without any persuasion or explanation on my part.
>
> Just as if I put here on the table a green vase, and beside it a yellow orange. Now, those two things affect each other. Side by side, they produce a reaction which neither of them will produce alone. Why should I try to say anything clever, or by any colorful rhetoric detract attention from those two objects, the relation they have to each other and the effect they have upon each other? ... Mere cleverness must go. I'd like the writing to be so lost in the object, that it doesn't exist for the reader – except for the reader who knows how difficult it is to lose writing in the object.[33]

---

[31] "The Death of Love in *The Sun Also Rises*", *Hemingway and His Critics*, ed. Baker, p. 83.

[32] Hemingway wrote to Edmund Wilson, November 25, 1923, "E. E. Cummings' *Enormous Room* was the best book published last year that I read. Somebody told me it was a flop. Then look at *One of Ours*. Prize, big sale, people taking it seriously. You were in the war weren't you? Wasn't that last scene in the lines wonderful? Do you know where it came from? The battle scene in *Birth of a Nation*. I identified episode after episode, Catherized. Poor woman she had to get her war experience somewhere" (*The Shores of Light*, p. 118).

[33] Latrobe Carroll, "Willa Sibert Cather", *The Bookman*, LIII (May 1921), 216.

Contrast and juxtaposition, that is, serve as part of a technique of "objectivity" and implication, just as they do with Hemingway. This technique is, among other things, a studied means of avoiding the high-sounding, pretentious, or too "literary". In "The Novel Démeublé", Cather cites Balzac's work as a bad example of the overfurnished novel: "We have had too much of the interior decorator and the 'romance of business' since his day." [34] (Compare Hemingway's statement in Chapter xvi of *Death in the Afternoon*: "Prose is architecture, not interior decoration, and the Baroque is over.") She concludes, "How wonderful it would be if we could throw all the furniture out of the window . . . and leave the room as bare as the stage of a Greek theatre, or as that house into which the glory of the Pentecost descended. . . ."

A page earlier Cather states a theory of significant omission very much like Hemingway's – claims, in fact, that it is precisely what is not stated but suggested that constitutes the greatest art:

Whatever is felt upon the page without being specifically named there – that, one might say, is created. It is the inexplicable presence of the thing not named, of the overtone divined by the ear but not heard by it, the verbal mood, the emotional aura of the fact or the thing or the deed, that gives high quality to the novel or the drama, as well as to poetry itself.

In "On the Art of Fiction" she restates the theory, calling it simplification (recall the recurring theme of the simple or simplified in Hemingway):

Art, it seems to me, should simplify. That, indeed, is very nearly the whole of the higher artistic process; finding what conventions of form and what detail one can do without and yet preserve the spirit of the whole – so that all that one has suppressed and cut away is there to the reader's consciousness as much as if it were in type on the page.

Utilizing the chillier but more impressive figure cited earlier,

---

[34] *Willa Cather on Writing: Critical Studies on Writing as an Art*, foreword by Stephen Tennant (New York, Alfred A. Knopf, 1949), p. 39. The next two quotations are from pp. 42-43 and 41-42 respectively. The quotation from "On the Art of Fiction" is on p. 102.

Hemingway restates his theory of significant omission in Chapter xvi of *Death in the Afternoon*:

> If a writer of prose knows enough about what he is writing about he may omit things that he knows and the reader, if the writer is writing truly enough, will have a feeling of those things as strongly as though the writer had stated them. The dignity of movement of an ice-berg is due to only one-eighth of it being above water. A writer who omits things because he does not know them only makes hollow places in his writing.

Hemingway recognizes some conditions – writing "truly" enough, the possible boomerang effect of omission – but the "dignity" of the method attracts him. This was a 1932 account of his writing in the early 1920's, but in spite of his lessening of "discipline" in his later work, he repeats the theory in a 1958 interview:

> If it is any use to know it, I always try to write on the principle of the iceberg. There is seven-eighths of it underwater for every part that shows. Anything you know you can eliminate and it only strengthens your iceberg. It is the part that doesn't show. If a writer omits something because he does not know it then there is a hole in the story. ... In writing you are limited by what has already been done satisfactorily. So I have tried to learn to do something else. First I have tried to eliminate everything unnecessary to conveying experience to the reader so that after he or she has read something it will become a part of his or her experience and seem actually to have happened.[35]

In spite of his occasional contrary practice, that is, Hemingway seems still to feel that the understated or implied is truest (with the results to be seen in the next chapter). What the 1958 account also suggests is that Hemingway consciously tried to learn this method in reaction against a more expansive method which he not only distrusted because it was too "literary" but hesitated to attempt because it had "already been done satisfactorily" (meaning that he would have to do it exceedingly well to compare favorably with past writers who used it). Whether or not the method that he consciously adopted was most congenial to him by nature is a moot question. I suspect, and will try to show why later, that a more expansive, hyperbolic style has several attractions for him, too. But it always makes him uneasy.

[35] Plimpton, p. 84.

Both Hemingway and Cather would most likely have agreed with the sentiments of Fitzgerald's letter to Wolfe, July 19, 1937:

I think I could make out a good case for your necessity to cultivate an alter ego, a more conscious artist in you. . . .

Now the more the stronger man's inner tendencies are defined, the more he can be sure they will show, the more necessity to rarefy them, to use them sparingly. The novel of selected incidents has this to be said that the great writer like Flaubert has consciously left out the stuff that Bill or Joe (in his case Zola) will come along and say presently. He will say only the things that he alone sees. So Mme. Bovary becomes eternal while Zola already rocks with age. . . .[36]

Hemingway had already said in *Green Hills of Africa* that besides "talent such as Kipling had" the great writer of prose must have the "discipline of Flaubert" (the qualities of Kipling under the restraint of Flaubert – this suggests nicely an opposition which I think Hemingway found in himself).[37]

In "A Chance Meeting" (with Mme. Grout, Flaubert's niece) Cather contrasts Balzac and Flaubert to the latter's advantage:

The fact remains that Balzac, like Dickens and Scott, has a strong appeal for the great multitudes of humanity who have no feeling for any form of art, and who read him only in poor translations. This is overwhelming evidence of the vital force in him, which no rough handling can diminish. Also it implies the lack in him of certain qualities which matter to only a few people, but matter very much. The time in one's life when one first began to sense the things which Flaubert stood for, to admire (almost against one's will) that peculiar integrity of language and vision, that coldness which, in him, is somehow noble – that is a pleasant chapter of one's life to remember. . . .[38]

A "coldness which . . . is somehow noble" is probably a good description of the appeal that Flaubert had for so many writers in the 1920's and after, though, Cather says, it took some getting used to: "We first read *Bovary* with a certain hostility; the wine is too dry for us" (p. 24).

---

[36] *The Letters of Thomas Wolfe*, ed. Elizabeth Nowell (New York, Charles Scribner's Sons, 1956), p. 641. The passage quoted from Wolfe's reply is on p. 643.

[37] See Edmund Wilson, "Hemingway: Gauge of Morale", in McCaffery, p. 254n, for some provocative conjecture on attitudinal similarities in Kipling and Hemingway.

[38] *Not Under Forty* (New York, Alfred A. Knopf, 1936), p. 25.

Wolfe's reply to Fitzgerald's criticism brings several of the issues here into perspective:

... your argument is based simply upon one *way,* upon one *method* instead of another. ... Now you have your way of doing something and I have mine; there are a lot of ways, but you are honestly mistaken in thinking that there is a "way".

I suppose I would agree with you in what you say about "the novel of selected incidents" so far as it means anything. I say so far as it means anything because every novel, of course, is a novel of selected incidents. There are no novels of unselected incidents. You couldn't write about the inside of a telephone booth without selecting. You could fill a novel of a thousand pages with a description of a single room and yet your incidents would be selected. ... You say that the great writer like Flaubert has consciously left out the stuff that Bill or Joe will come along presently and put in. Well, don't forget, Scott, that a great writer is not only a leaver-outer but also a putter-inner, and that Shakespeare and Cervantes and Dostoievsky were great putter-inners – greater putter-inners, in fact, than taker-outers – and will be remembered for what they put in – remembered, I venture to say, as long as Monsieur Flaubert will be remembered for what he left out.

As Wolfe points out, one method – that of "objectivity", understatement, irony and other forms of indirection – was virtually canonized then (and still receives inordinate critical respect). Furthermore, such "discipline" is not the same thing as selectivity, though the two are often treated as if they were synonyms.

In his essay "Romanticism and Classicism" (written in 1913 but first published in 1924), T. E. Hulme maintains that a new classical revival is due to replace the romantic, which Hulme likens to "spilt religion" or "pouring a pot of treacle over the dinner table".[39] The quality of the classical he calls "dry hardness", while the romantic (which he thoroughly dislikes) is "damp" (p. 9); the classical has the beauty of "small, dry things" (p. 12). The kinship of Hulme's essay with the majority attitude of the times should be obvious. While he does not plump for indirection, but instead talks about "directness and simplicity" and particularly about the "cheerful, dry and sophisticated" verse to

[39] In *Critiques and Essays in Criticism 1920-1948,* ed. Robert Wooster Stallman (New York, The Ronald Press Co., 1949), p. 5.

come (p. 14), it is clear that he shares the ideal which in practice
becomes a method of "objectivity" and implication, by means of
which writers try to insure that emotions will not come spilling
out like treacle.

Certainly the method does not deserve the title of the most real
or true. Too often it is negative – objective because the writer
dreads handling the subjective directly, bare and dry because he
fears sounding pretentious and so becoming ludicrous in the eyes
of his "tough-minded" contemporaries who take such pains not to
wear their hearts on their sleeves. The method of "objectivity"
and indirection can work successfully, but its success is not inevitable. Frequently it is merely cautious, a safe way of writing,
not necessarily a more selective way.

The indirect, ironic method seems to get some of its current
popularity from its protectiveness and from the superior position
it allows one to occupy – above or detached from every position
in which he might be ridiculed or criticized, i.e., every human
position. Accordingly it is thoroughly congenial to the modern
romantic, letting him maintain a greater than human stance under
the guise of hard-boiled objective realism.

The ironic posture can be an intoxicating one to take, not just
for its show of disinterestedness, seeing more than one side to a
question, its display of intelligence and a sense of proportion, but
also for its safety, self-glorification, and "dignity". The complete
ironist is always more than a mere man, picturing human feelings
and actions in whimsical or perhaps in bitter understatements,
which have the effect of keeping him from getting too much involved. In his unheroic presentation of life, that is, the author
manages to come off more heroic, above what he presents.

It is little wonder in an age like ours, overreacting against previous excessive emotionalism and grandiose sentiments, that the
method should seem the ultima Thule of technique to many
critics, writers, and even journalists.[40] However, the difference

[40] See Karl E. Meyer, "Just the Hard Facts: The Divorce of Journalism
and Judgment", *The New Republic*, April 24, 1961, p. 12: " ... different
times bring new styles, and there seems to be a distinct contrast between
the generations of commentators. The old-timers boil with indignation;
the new breed simmers in irony. The modern columnist tends to view his

from earlier romanticism is, I suspect, often more a difference of surface style than it is of spirit. The inhibited feelings beneath the hard-boiled wisecrack, the urbane witticism or irony, the "hard facts" have not gone away: they have gone into hiding, where they continue to exert a twisted influence on today's fashions in "realism".

Hulme makes the point also that the new classicism may be different in form from previous classicism and perhaps not even be recognizable as such because of the preceding period of romanticism (p. 9). I feel that one of the developments which Hulme did not anticipate was the arising of a literature "classical", restrained, and "objective" on its surface but still more than slightly romantic in its underlying and hidden feelings and attitudes. What needs emphasis here is that the "disciplined" or restrained style does not necessarily imply keen selection or subtle feeling. Even with "discipline" the writing can show lapses in selectivity, judgment or feeling. The technique of omission which once seemed so obviously superior, the ultimate style, now seems a manner and sometimes just a mannerism of a period in literature.

---

role as that of a drama critic who must help inept players to understand the script. ... It sometimes seems that the reader has to bring to political commentary the critical apparatus required for studying a stanza of Yeats or Eliot. Somewhere, tucked in all those words, there may be an opinion that can be discovered. The task is rendered more difficult by the fact that what appears to be a judgment often, on closer examination, turns out to be an evasion." Such strategies for avoiding a judgment while seeming to express one are rightly called the "language of caution" and "excessive emphasis on detachment" (p. 15). For cultivating this technique we pride ourselves too often on our superiority to the earlier romantics.

IV

EXPANSIVENESS AND EXAGGERATION

1

Two quotations, one from *The Sun Also Rises* and the other from *For Whom the Bell Tolls*, conveniently introduce many of the issues discussed in this chapter. The first, from Chapter xiv of *The Sun Also Rises*, has Jake thinking that although he likes seeing Mike hurt Robert Cohn, he wishes that Mike wouldn't do it because afterward he feels disgusted with himself for having enjoyed it:

That was morality; things that made you disgusted afterward. No, that must be immorality. That was a large statement. What a lot of bilge I could think up at night. What rot, I could hear Brett say it. What rot! When you were with English you got into the habit of using English expressions in your thinking. The English spoken language – the upper classes, anyway – must have fewer words than the Eskimo. Of course I didn't know anything about the Eskimo. Maybe the Eskimo was a fine language. Say the Cherokee. I didn't know anything about the Cherokee, either. The English talked with inflected phrases. One phrase to mean everything. I liked them, though. I liked the way they talked.

Not only do we see here Jake's (and Hemingway's) liking for understatement, which is one of the appeals of Briticisms for him, but also his concern about not making "large statements". "Large statements" are not true; three times in this brief passage what Hemingway feels is a "large statement" is followed by a deflating comment: "What a lot of bilge I could think up at night" (more distrust of night thoughts); "Of course I didn't know anything about the Eskimo"; "I didn't know anything about the Cherokee, either." What is significant, first of all, is the obvious preference in Hemingway's early work for understatement, which he considers truer. Second, the preference for understatement does not prevent the narrator from making "large statements": perhaps he cannot resist making them, because they are congenial to him. But frequently they are followed immediately by a reaction – almost a reflex – against them, since Hemingway feels that they are untrue: exaggerated, distorted, or pretentious. This mechanism operates in his early work, but it becomes more obvious from about 1932 on.

The second quotation suggests why that is so. In Chapter iii of *For Whom the Bell Tolls* Jordan discusses the problem of blowing up the bridge with Anselmo:

> "For us will be the bridge and the battle, should there be one", Robert Jordan said and saying it in the dark, he felt a little theatrical but it sounded well in Spanish.
> "It should be of the highest interest", Anselmo said and hearing him say it honestly and clearly and with no pose, neither the English pose of understatement nor any Latin bravado, Robert Jordan thought he was very lucky to have this old man. . . .

Now Hemingway deprecates understatement as an "English pose", but as Beach points out, it *is* understatement to say of an enterprise in which they may all be killed, "It should be of the highest interest" (p. 116). That is, although he deprecates understatement, Hemingway still practices it while he also permits himself a more expansive style.

But note that it is necessary to walk a tightrope between opposite poses – understatement and bravado – and that Jordan feels theatrical: i.e., his own words sound maybe a little too pretentious. Another part of the reaction to the potentially high-flown is the assurance that Anselmo spoke "honestly" (feeling that the understated is the truest, Hemingway is often impelled to swear that the "large statement" is really true). Furthermore, it is not a minor detail that "it sounded well in Spanish", for one of the uses of foreignisms in Hemingway is to reintroduce high-sounding words and phrases omitted in English because they are "obscene". That, at any rate, was one reason Frederic Henry gave for preferring the concrete to the "abstract"; another reason, remember, was that the concrete had more *dignity*. The foreignism is often a form of indirection – nearly equivalent to saying *enceinte* instead of *pregnant* – except that for Hemingway the tabu is the high-sounding or "literary".

The abandonment of understatement as an all-purpose method is given theoretical justification in *Death in the Afternoon*, where it does not so much complement as contradict the theory of understatement and significant omission which Hemingway also gives there. But it does not contradict a lot of the practice in the book. Near the end of Chapter i Hemingway makes the following description of Cagancho and his capework, apologizing for but justifying his "flowery" writing:

Cagancho is a gypsy, subject to fits of cowardice, altogether without integrity, who violates all the rules, written and unwritten, for the conduct of a matador but who, when he receives a bull that he has confidence in, and he has confidence in them very rarely, can do things which all bullfighters do in a way they have never been done before and sometimes standing absolutely straight with his feet still, planted as though he were a tree, with the arrogance and grace that gypsies have and of which all other arrogance and grace seems an imitation, moves the cape spread full as the pulling jib of a yacht before the bull's muzzle so slowly that the art of bullfighting, which is only kept from being one of the major arts because it is impermanent, in the arrogant slowness of his veronicas becomes, for the seeming minutes that they endure, permanent. That is the worst sort of flowery writing, but it is necessary to try to give the feeling, and to some one who has never seen it a simple statement of the method does not convey the feeling. Any one who has seen bullfights can skip such flowerishness and read the facts which are much more difficult to isolate and state.

Plainly, according to this explanation, it is not enough to give a simple statement of "the sequence of motion and fact which made the emotion" in order to communicate an emotion. But the theory, like the theory of understatement discussed in the last chapter, is a rationalization of practice – Hemingway having begun to relax his "discipline" an indulge in longer, more "literary" sentences.

However, in his conversations with the "old lady" he continues to show the old distrust of words. In Chapter vii, for instance, he has been holding forth in an expansive manner about the decadence of modern bullfighting; the "old lady" tells him that she finds it hard to understand what he means by *decadence*, whereupon he gives her a lecture about what a poor word it is to use:

I will explain later, madame, but indeed decadence is a difficult word to use since it has become little more than a term of abuse applied by critics to anything they do not yet understand or which seems to differ from their moral concepts.

Old lady: I always understood it to mean that there was something rotten as there is at courts.

Madame, all our words from loose using have lost their edge but your inherent concepts are most sound.

Old lady: If you please, sir, I do not care for all this discussion of words. Are we not here to be instructed about the bulls and those who fight them?

If you so wish, but start your writer to talking of words and he will go on until you are wearied and wish he would show more skill in using them and preach less of their significance.

The last part of this exchange is deflation: Hemingway grows uneasy at the pomposity of his lecture and seeks to puncture it a little by the "old lady's" objection and his own comment about the tendency of writers to preach about words.

But that is not the end of the episode. It is instructive to observe how the author, though he feels he is becoming pompous, cannot resist going on with his lecture, which in turn calls forth more deflation. He goes on to tell the "old lady" an anecdote involving Raymond Radiguet, "a young French writer who knew how to make his career not only with his pen but with his pencil if you follow me, madame":

When the late Radiguet was alive he often wearied of the tenuous, rapturous and querulous society of his literary protector, Jean Cocteau, and spent the nights at an hotel near the Luxembourg Gardens with one of two sisters who were then working as models in the quarter. His protector was greatly upset and denounced this as decadence saying, bitterly, yet proudly of the late Radiguet, "Bebé est vicieuse – il aime les femmes." So you see, madame, we must be careful chucking the term decadence about since it cannot mean the same to all who read it.

Old lady: It repelled me from the first.

The "old lady", that is, punctures his impressive conclusion by reminding him that he was the one who introduced the word in the first place.

In Chapter xi we get more of the distrust of words as the author replies to the "old lady's" objection that she doesn't understand what he means by *love*:

Madame, it is an old word and each one takes it new and wears it out himself. It is a word that fills with meaning as a bladder with air and the meaning goes out of it as quickly. It may be punctured as a bladder is punctured and patched and blown up again and if you have not had it it does not exist for you. All people talk of it, but those who have had it are all marked by it and I would not wish to speak of it further since of all things it is the most ridiculous to talk of and only fools go through it many times. I would sooner have the pox than to fall in love with another woman loving the one I have.

What has this to do with the bulls, sir?

Nothing, Madame, nothing at all, it is only conversation to give you your money's worth.

Note the deflation again at the end of the passage, and also the author's predilection for the expansiveness which calls it forth. Without a tendency toward overstatement, it seems unlikely that Hemingway would be so preoccupied with devices for understating and deflating. By the same token, any increase in expansiveness in a writer having Hemingway's distrust of words is quite sure to be accompanied by an increase in defensive or deflationary reactions.

2

Hemingway's best known early work is usually described as "disciplined" – i.e., severely restrained, extremely "objective" on the surface, reticent about the author's attitude except as it can be inferred from the indirect presentation. One sign of the "discipline", which Fenton traces in Hemingway's revisions of "Chapter" ii of *In Our Time* ("Minarets stuck up in the rain"), is the progressive elimination of adjectives.[1] On the one hand,

[1] Charles A. Fenton, *The Apprenticeship of Ernest Hemingway: The Early Years* (New York, The Viking Press, 1958), pp. 229-236, especially p. 231. This sketch was "Chapter" iii of *in our time*, 1924.

Fenton discusses the removal of adjectives as an attempt to make the sketch more precise and specific (p. 235); on the other, he sees the course of the revision as a move away from the "too explicit" (p. 233). The result he thinks more forceful "by virtue of the new understatement and compression" (p. 233).

Obviously there is a contradiction here, for the relatively unmodified and understated sentence generally lacks the preciseness and specificity of the explicit. It appears rather that as Hemingway learned and practiced a more "disciplined" and understated style he abandoned an earlier more expansive and explicit style, in the process reducing the number of adjectives. (To be accurate, one should really consider all modifiers – adverbs as well as adjectives, perhaps clauses and phrases as well – but the tendency in the change to a more "disciplined" style will be clear from a consideration of adjectives mainly and adverbs occasionally.)

As Fenton points out, Hemingway relies in the final version of the sketch on four basic adjectives – *old, yellow, young*, and *sick* – plus three participles – *loaded, soaked*, and *scared*. The first version, cabled to the Toronto *Daily Star* October 20, 1922, had about three times as many adjectives, including a number of compounds and adjectival sequences: "never-ending, staggering", "ripe, brown", "mud-splashed", "soaked and draggled", "muddy-flanked", "exhausted, staggering". Fenton gives an example of the same practice in a dispatch printed in the *Star* May 1, 1923: "In the cold, grey, street-washing, milk-delivering, shutters-coming-off-the-shops, early morning ... the midnight train from Paris arrived in Strasbourg" (p. 212).

The suppression of adjectives in Hemingway's subsequent early work is only part of the story. In the first place, as Levin points out (pp. 155-156), certain common, unspecific, valuative adjectives – *fine, nice, good, lovely* – are omnipresent in Hemingway. They are allowable in a "disciplined" style, apparently, because they do not have the literary sound that Hemingway eschews (*lovely*, however, seems questionable; perhaps Hemingway feels that he can permit himself an occasional, not too precious literaryism). More to the point here is the observable increase in modifiers, compounds and sequences in some of Hemingway's later work when he begins to relax the "discipline" and experiment again with a more expansive style. The following passage from "Fathers and Sons" (1933) bears repetition:

Could you say she did first what no one has ever done better and mention plump brown legs, flat belly, hard little breasts, well holding arms, quick searching tongue, the flat eyes, the good taste of mouth, then uncomfortably, tightly, sweetly, moistly, lovely, tightly, achingly, fully, finaly, unendingly, never-endingly, never-to-endingly, suddenly ended, the great bird flown like an owl in the twilight. . . .

Several of Hemingway's later descriptions of love or sex have the same torrential quality (in this quality, the strings of modifiers are closely related to another aspect of Hemingway's tendency toward expansiveness and overstatement: his catalogues). In "The Snows of Kilimanjaro" we see some of the increase in modifiers in Harry's reminiscence about an Armenian girl ("she felt as over-ripe as she looked but smooth, rose-petal, syrupy, smooth-bellied, big-breasted and needed no pillow under her buttocks") and in his thoughts about his present companion ("*Town and Country* never showed those good breasts and those useful thighs and those lightly small-of-back-caressing hands").

But the most famous or notorious passages occur in *For Whom the Bell Tolls*:

Where there had been roughness of fabric all was smooth with a smoothness and firm rounded pressing and a long warm coolness, cool outside and warm within, long and light and closely holding, closely held, lonely, hollow-making with contours, happy-making, young and loving and now all warmly smooth with a hollowing, chest-aching, tight-held loneliness that was such that Robert Jordan felt he could not stand it. . . . (Ch. vii)

. . . for her everything was red, orange, gold-red from the sun on the closed eyes, and it all was that color, all of it, the filling, the possessing, the having, all of that color, all in a blindness of that color. For him it was a dark passage which led to nowhere, then to nowhere, then again to nowhere, once again to nowhere, always and forever to nowhere, heavy on the elbows in the earth to nowhere, dark, never any end to nowhere, hung on all time always to unknowing nowhere, this time and again for always to nowhere, now not to be borne once again always and to nowhere, now beyond all bearing up, up, up and into nowhere, suddenly, scaldingly, holdingly all nowhere gone and time absolutely still and they were both there, time having stopped and he felt the earth move out and away from under them. (Ch. xiii)

The repetitions, like the catalogues of modifiers, add to the torrential effect; they may be viewed as means for achieving intensity, but they are also plainly a kind of overstatement or hyperbole, quite different from the impassive understatements of Hemingway's early "disciplined" style.

Not all of the later work shows the increased expansiveness in this form, nor is the increase in modifiers limited to descriptions of sex. The cowardly matador in "The Capital of the World" remembers "how he sighted along the point-dipping blade at the place in the top of the shoulders where it was dusty in the short-haired black hump of muscle above the wide, wood-knocking, splinter-tipped horns. . . ." [2] But Hemingway was obviously experimenting most with series and compounds of modifiers in *For Whom the Bell Tolls*. Here is the first description of Robert Jordan: "The young man, who was tall and thin, with sun-streaked fair hair, and a wind- and sun-burned face, who wore the sun-faded flannel shirt, a pair of peasant's trousers and rope-soled shoes, leaned over, put his arm through one of the leather pack straps and swung the heavy pack up onto his shoulders" (Ch. i).

Particularly noticeable is the great number of compounds and sequences of compounds. A fascist patrol comes looking for one of its members, killed by Jordan: "The leader turned his horse directly toward the opening in the rocks where the gun was placed and Robert Jordan saw his young, sun- and wind-darkened face, his close-set eyes, hawk nose and the over-long wedge-shaped chin" (Ch. xxiii). This is a description of Joaquín, a member of El Sordo's band trapped on the hilltop: ". . . in the last lung-aching, leg-dead, mouth-dry, bullet-spatting, bullet-cracking, bullet-singing run up the final slope of the hill after his horse was killed, the helmet had seemed to weigh a great amount and

---

[2]   There appear to be two misprints in this passage, and I have corrected them in quoting. Both the Modern Library edition and the Scribner's edition of the collected short stories read "he *sighed* along the point-dipping blade" and "*splintered*-tipped horns" (my italics).

to ring his bursting forehead with an iron band" (Ch. xxvii). Pilar wakes Jordan to tell him that Pablo has absconded with his detonating equipment: "Robert Jordan followed her in the dead-ashes, bad-air and sleeping-men smell of the cave" (Ch. xxxiii).

Hemingway extends the practice to the formation of awkward, German-sounding compounds such as this: "He grinned at her, a cracked, stiff, too-tightened-facial-tendoned grin" (Ch. xliii). Here Jordan is thinking about one of the leaders of the loyalists: ". . . the old bald, spectacled, conceited, stupid-as-an-owl, un-intelligent-in-conversation, brave-and-as-dumb-as-a-bull, propaganda-built-up defender of Madrid, Miaja, had been so jealous of the publicity Kleber received that he had forced the Russians to relieve Kleber of his command and send him to Valencia" (Ch. xviii). In Part III of the serialized version of *The Dangerous Summer*, Hemingway returns to the practice but omits the hyphens: "When they came downstairs Antonio had his same dark, reserved, concentrated before the bullfight face with the eyes hooded against all outsiders." [3] The effect of the compounds when pushed to this extreme is the same, I think, as that which Hemingway seeks through deliberate awkwardness: to deflate, to sound pointedly unliterary. But at the same time he gains the foreign, noncolloquial flavor which is also the effect of many of his awkward constructions. In other words, this is a form of expansiveness, a "literary" style with a built-in nonliterary sound, a means by which Hemingway tries to have it both ways at once.

We have already seen that Hemingway was experimenting with such devices in his early dispatches to the Toronto *Daily Star*. Likewise, "chapters" iii and iv of *In Our Time* are experiments with a foreign-sounding style – in this case, British English. The foreign element in Hemingway's style has been frequently remarked but little understood, particularly by those who customarily emphasize his "natural, colloquial, and nonliterary prose style".[4]

The awkward, nonliterary sound of so much of Hemingway's work is not the same thing as colloquialism, though it has long

---

[3]   *Life*, September 19, 1960, p. 81.
[4]   Young, p. 159.

been the custom to describe his style as colloquial.[5] Especially in his earliest work, it is true, Hemingway imitates ordinary speech, but even in "My Old Man" one finds a rather strange mixture of the colloquial and the formal (here, an awkward-sounding conditional-subjunctive): "Seems as though that were the thing that keeps it all going and about the only thing you can figure on is that every day the buses will be going out to whatever track they're running at, going right out through everything to the track." The fact is that though the characters of *The Sun Also Rises* say "those sort", "gents", "swell" or "You got the most class of anybody I ever seen" (Ch. vii), they mix colloquial American English with a language that sounds slightly foreign, well interlarded with Briticisms but also imitative of foreign usage (i.e., an approximation of a foreign language's subjunctive): ". . . I put my worm-can in the shade with the bag, and got a book out of the pack and settled down under the tree to read until Bill should come up for lunch" (Ch. xii).

At any rate, one must term such constructions pointedly non-colloquial in effect, the effect also of Hemingway's obvious foreignisms. From his earliest work, Hemingway experimented with both the colloquial and the foreign, as the vignettes of *In Our Time* show. The awkwardness occasionally complained of in *A Farewell to Arms* is instructive, since the novel contains little actual colloquialism.[6] The awkward sound is partly the result of the repeated use of *and*, which Hemingway says he used consciously "the way Mr. Johann Sebastian Bach used a note in music when he was emitting counterpoint".[7] It is partly due to the word repetition which is both artful and awkward-sounding, sometimes almost dizzying in effect:

[5]   Carlos Baker quickly shows by comparison of the openings of Ch. xix of *Huckleberry Finn* and Ch. xxxi of *A Farewell to Arms* that Twain's practice is far more colloquial than the grammatical usage of Hemingway (p. 181).
[6]   In "Ernest Hemingway and the Psychology of the Lost Generation", in McCaffery, p. 309, Edwin Berry Burgum remarks adversely that the novel "is written in a more awkward style than any other work of Hemingway's".
[7]   Lillian Ross, "How Do You Like It Now, Gentlemen?", *The New Yorker*, May 13, 1950, p. 54.

Troops went by the house and down the road and the dust they raised powdered the leaves of the trees. The trunks of the trees too were dusty and the leaves fell early that year and we saw the troops marching along the road and the dust rising and leaves, stirred by the breeze, falling and the soldiers marching and afterward the road bare and white except for the leaves. (Ch. i)

The awkwardness can be seen in certain "colloquial" constructions too: "It was no great distance to row but when you were out of condition it had been a long way" (Ch. xxxvii), with the (deliberate?) awkwardness of the tense of the last verb; "There was a path went down the mountain but it was steep" (Ch. xxxviii), with its colloquial omission of the relative pronoun. But the awkwardness is frequently the result of hypercorrectness, as with the foreign-sounding conditional-subjunctives: "He could have had anything he wanted if I would have known" (Ch. iv); "I talked with the major and learned that when it should start and our cars should be loaded we would drive them back along the screened road" (Ch. ix).[8] Sometimes Hemingway is so hypercorrect that the result is ungrammatical: "Officers whom I thought could never realize it realize it now" (Ch. xxvi).

Even Levin, who seems momentarily to grasp the connection between Hemingway's distrust of words and his use of the foreign, concludes by finding it "somewhat paradoxical that a writer, having severely cut down his English vocabulary, should augment it by continual importation from other languages, including the Swahili" (p. 151). A page earlier Levin points out a connection which needs further consideration:

The realism of his generation reacted, not only against Wilsonian idealism, but against Wilsonian rhetoric. Hence the famous paragraph from the Caporetto episode describing Frederic Henry's embarrassment before such abstract words as "glory" and "honor", which seem to him obscene beside the concrete names of places and numbers of roads. For a Spaniard, Hemingway notes in *Death in the*

---

[8] Cf. "If we would have hired a good mechanic instead of a half baked kikuyu driver, he would have checked the oil" ("The Snows of Kilimanjaro") or "If he'd have left some money or if there'd been rewards it would have been better but I wouldn't feel no better" (*To Have and Have Not*, Ch. xxvi), in which the hypercorrect combines with the colloquial to produce the awkward unliterary sound.

Afternoon, the abstraction may still have concreteness: honor may be "as real a thing as water, wine, or olive oil". It is not so for us: "All our words from loose using have lost their edge."

What we see in these juxtaposed quotations and in the contradictory theories expressed in *Death in the Afternoon* is Hemingway's preoccupation with understatement (taken to be akin to truth) and an opposed tendency toward expansiveness, even exaggeration, together with one solution to the dilemma: the foreign. However, this solution does not mean an end to the uneasiness that Hemingway experiences when he touches on anything even slightly redolent to him of inflated statement; in Chapter ix of *Death in the Afternoon* he is reduced, as Atkins remarks (p. 83), to laying his hand on his heart and swearing that foreign abstractions are true (and concrete):

In Spain honor is a very real thing. Called pundonor, it means honor, probity, courage, self-respect and pride in one word. Pride is the strongest characteristic of the race and it is a matter of pundonor not to show cowardice. ... This honor thing is not some fantasy that I am trying to inflict on you in the way writers on the peninsula give out their theories on its people. I swear it is true. Honor to a Spaniard, no matter how dishonest, is as real a thing as water, wine, or olive oil.

We shall observe later that the word *true* increases geometrically in Hemingway's later work as he allows himself greater expansiveness but feels uneasy about doing so.

As Delmore Schwartz points out, in spite of Frederic Henry's denunciation of abstract words like glory, honor, courage and hallow, "it is nevertheless precisely glory, honor, and courage which constitute the ideals of conduct in all of Hemingway's writing".[9] Discussing the conversation of Hemingway's characters (and disagreeing with Wyndham Lewis about it having "the rhythms of proletarian speech"), Schwartz continues,

The conversation is, on the contrary, a great heightening of the kinds of speech of our time, an exaggeration in which the whole pattern is embodied. *The foreigner* is necessary for this rhetoric. The foreigner carries over into English the idiom of his native tongue, and in

[9]   P. 120. Cf. Wyndham Lewis, *Men Without Art* (London, Cassell and Co. Ltd., 1934), pp. 35, 40.

that modified English he makes clear the fact that he is living by the values which constitute the code. If, at times, it happens that the honorable one is an American and the foreigner is without honor, this makes no difficulties or falsity, for the honorable Americans are given a style of speech all their own, and the foreigner is made to speak like an American. (pp. 121-122)

What Schwartz says here need not be confined to dialogue. To state it briefly and more generally, one function of the foreign in Hemingway's style is to enable him to reintroduce indirectly material which he finds too high-sounding in English. It is a disguised kind of expansiveness which is impressive, exotic, indirect, and sometimes euphemistic. Taken together with deliberate awkwardness, to which it is related, it gives a tone to Hemingway's style which is not obviously "literary" but which is considerably removed from idiomatic or colloquial American English.

In the dispatch about Strasbourg, Hemingway tried another experiment, the indirect dialogue which imitates foreign speech; Hemingway is talking with a French soldier:

One of them told me there would be a train at 11:15 for Offenburg, a military tram; it was about half an hour to Offenburg, but this droll train would get there about two o'clock. He grinned. Monsieur was from Paris? What did monsieur think about the match Criqui-Zjawnny Kilbane? Ah. He had thought very much the same. He had always had the idea he was no fool, this Kilbane. The military service? Well, it was all the same. It made no difference where one did it. In two months now he would be through. It was a shame he was not free, perhaps we could have a talk together. Monsieur had seen this Kilbane box? The new wine was not bad at the buffet. But after all he was on guard. The buffet is straight down the corridor. If monsieur leaves the baggage here it will be all right.[10]

Hemingway uses the same device twice in the last chapter of *The Sun Also Rises* – first in a conversation at San Sebastian between Jake and the team manager for some bicycle road-racers:

Paris is the town the most *sportif* in the world. Did I know the *Chope de Negre*? Did I not. I would see him there some time. I certainly would. We would drink another *fine* together. We certainly would. They started at six o'clock less a quarter in the morning. Would I be up for the depart? I would certainly try to.

[10]   Quoted by Fenton, p. 213.

The second conversation is between Jake and a fat woman at the Hotel Montana in Madrid:

> Did I want to stay myself in person in the Hotel Montana?
> Of that as yet I was undecided, but it would give me pleasure if my bags were brought up from the ground floor in order that they might not be stolen. Nothing was ever stolen in the Hotel Montana. In other fondas, yes. Not here. No. The personages of this establishment were rigidly selectioned. I was happy to hear it. Nevertheless I would welcome the upbringal of my bags.
> The maid came in and said that the female English wanted to see the male English now, at once.

In *A Farewell to Arms* Hemingway again uses the device in the drunken conversation at the mess (Ch. vii) and in the drunken conversation at the field hospital between Henry, Rinaldi, and the major from the mess (Ch. xii). These experiments, which are in contrast to the understated, "disciplined" style, are another indication of the more expansive side of Hemingway. The foreignism in the preceding examples occurs in extended set pieces, as it does frequently in *For Whom the Bell Tolls*, but very often the foreign flavor comes from an occasional word or construction which does not sound like idiomatic American English. There is, for example, the matter of the ever-present Briticisms, especially *bloody*, which crop up regardless of their appropriateness to a character. To put it another way, they are not present just in the interest of realistic characterization.

It is in character for Brett or Mike or Harris or even Jake to say *bloody*, *frightfully*, *chap* or *I say* (since Jake has been around the others and likes their speech). In the parody *The Torrents of Spring* the Briticisms may be regarded as part of the affectation that Hemingway is burlesquing; just about everyone from Scripps O'Neil to the Indians talks at times like a native Englishman: "He, Scripps, was not the sort of chap that wanted a palace" (Ch. ii); " 'That little chap would have made a pool-player if he hadn't had a bit of hard luck in the war', Red Dog remarked" (Ch. xii). But they become a generalized mannerism of the author, not the characters, so that Frederic Henry is made to say, "We were supposed to wear steel helmets even in Gorizia but they were uncomfortable and too bloody theatrical in a town where the civilian inhabitants had not been evacuated" (Ch. vi).

In his own person Hemingway says in *Green Hills of Africa*, "Our people went to America because that was the place to go then. It had been a good country and we had made a bloody mess of it" (Ch. xiii). The word sounds stranger on the lips of Harry Morgan, an American from Key West: "I have to do it alone, he thought, with that poor bloody Albert" (Ch. xvii); "No matter how a man alone ain't got no bloody f – ing chance" (Ch. xxiii). But it is completely inappropriate to Pilar, supposedly speaking in Spanish, to tell Pablo, "You can stay if you wish and eat of the food and drink of the wine, but not too bloody much, and share in the work if thee wishes" (Ch. iv).

The point is that the foreign in Hemingway's work is primarily a matter of *sound*, not necessarily of any actual foreign idiom. It is true that Hemingway may translate an occasional word or phrase literally, as when the cowardly matador in "The Capital of the World" asks Paco's sister to come to bed with him "for a favor" (*por favor* 'please'), but more often he simply uses something strange to English idiom which sounds foreign. Fenimore remarks, for example, on the inconsistency with which Hemingway employs *thou* and *you* in *For Whom the Bell Tolls*.[11] There is no attempt to be consistent or even accurate – e.g., Pilar's words, "You can stay if you wish ... and share in the work if thee wishes", are not only inconsistent, both *thee* and *wishes* are ungrammatical, not a translation of Spanish or anything else, but a recording of something foreign-sounding.[12]

The same is true of other foreignisms in Hemingway's work – e.g., the recurrent word *much*: "There was much game hanging outside the shops, and the snow powdered in the fur of the foxes and the wind blew their tails" ("In Another Country"); "This matador had an intelligent, very open face and he carried himself with much style" ("The Capital of the World"); "There was much

[11] Edward Fenimore, "English and Spanish in 'For Whom the Bell Tolls' ", in McCaffery, p. 212.
[12] "If thee wishes" is Hemingway foreignism for *si (tu) quieres* 'if thou wishest'. Note that Hemingway has imitated the *-s* ending of the second person singular of Spanish (and French) verbs.

traffic at night and many mules on the roads" (*A Farewell to Arms*, Ch. i); " 'That', said Robert Jordan . . . 'is much horse' " (Ch. i); "He is much fish still" (*The Old Man and the Sea*, p. 84). *Much* is a generalized foreignism – i.e., not idiomatic English usage in this construction – but it cannot be pinned down to any one language or to the nationality of a character. Frederic Henry uses it as readily as Santiago.

When Frederic Henry describes how everyone at the mess ate the spaghetti course, "lifting the spaghetti on the fork until the loose strands hung clear then lowering it into the mouth", the unidiomatic (English) usage of the last definite article cannot be explained as anything but a liking for the foreign sound.[13] Similarly, the use twice of the archaic conditional-subjunctive *were* in the following description of Robert Jordan's thoughts cannot be imitative of Spanish; it is not meant as realistic characterization but as part of the establishment of a mood of the foreign or strange in the novel:

Robert Jordan watching Pablo and as he watched, letting his right hand hang lower and lower, ready if it should be necessary, half hoping it would be (feeling perhaps that were the simplest and easiest yet not wishing to spoil what had gone so well, knowing how quickly all of a family, all of a clan, all of a band, can turn against a stranger in a quarrel, yet thinking what could be done with the hand were the simplest and best and surgically the most sound now that this has happened), saw also the wife of Pablo standing there and watched her blush proudly and soundly and healthily as the allegiances were given. (Ch. iv)

"The wife of Pablo" also sounds slightly foreign.

In this passage we see as well an example of the longer, involved sentence which Hemingway experiments with in his later work – pushed, as the compound modifiers are pushed, to an awkward extreme that undercuts the "literary" quality of the construction. The effect of the long parenthesis here is to make an awkward periodic sentence. As Hemingway's style becomes more

---

13   Cf. the use of the definite article in Frederic Henry's descriptions of himself: "The whites of the eyes were yellow and it was the jaundice" (Ch. xxii): "Hard as the floor of the car to lie not thinking only feeling, having been away too long, the clothes wet and the floor moving" (Ch. xxxii).

expansive, he employs the device frequently, combining the literary and awkward in the desire to get the benefit of amplitude but avoid the danger of sounding inflated. (Cf. the following sentence from Chapter ii of *Across the River and into the Trees*: " 'I don't know what you are talking about', the shooter, who was not a shooter, then, except potentially, and was a Colonel of Infantry in the Army of the United States, reduced from being a general officer, said.")

Several of the critics who have written about Hemingway's use of foreignism in *For Whom the Bell Tolls* have recognized that he did not reproduce exact equivalents of Spanish, but not all recognize that he used the foreign or strange-sounding as a means of getting away from colloquial American English. Accordingly, they sometimes object that the result is not realistic, that Hemingway tries to impress the reader with a linguistic strangeness and loftiness that is actually nonexistent.[14]

Stanley Kauffmann gives one of the most negative appraisals of Hemingway's use of foreignism − not only foreign-sounding phrases but the foreign settings of so many of his stories − in a review of the film version of *The Old Man and the Sea*:

Every strength has an attendant possible weakness. If Hemingway found large themes for his large talent, he succumbed to a certain travel-snobbism. (You there in Omaha, don't you wish you were here with me in this Paris *bistro* or Pamplona *cantina*? Here, I toss you a few foreign phrases and names of wines and streets to dream with.) In addition, his alien view has led him to overvalue certain discoveries. For instance, in Spanish one does indeed say "thou" to friends and one speaks of "the Tigers of Detroit", but Spanish-speaking people don't think that remarkable. You don't often find those forms in good translations of Spanish works; the translator tries to render another language truly (to use one of Hemingway's pet words) in English.

Hemingway, however, taken with the novelty of the forms and the

---

[14] See Arturo Barea, "Not Spain but Hemingway", *Horizon*, III (May 1941), 358-359. Barea objects in particular to Hemingway's giving Spanish peasant speech an abstractness which is the direct opposite of actual usage, which is extremely concrete. This seems further evidence for the view that to Hemingway the foreign represents the abstraction which he finds pompous in English, translated into an acceptable form − become "real" or "true" again.

thrill of being away from home, "thou's" us and insists on a diminish-
ingly effective pseudo-Biblical simplicity. At bottom, there is in this
a wide-eyed juvenile wonder combined with a professional's glee at
finding a pocket of quaint material to mine. Any writer – though
he be as serious and as marvelously gifted as Hemingway – who
spends the bulk of his life away from the place where he grew up
runs the risk of getting his values slightly wrong.[15]

More favorable estimates generally suffer from confining the
discussion of foreignism too narrowly to *For Whom the Bell Tolls*.
Fenimore, for example, sees the foreign-sounding language, with
its archaisms and echoes of Elizabethan English, as a reflection of
the artistic intention in the novel, "the establishment of the epic
spirit" which is appropriate because the novel is "an epic of our
time" (p. 217). The trouble with this is that Fenimore proceeds to
say that it is Hemingway's typical rhythmic patterns rather than
the "Spanish" which give the foreign flavor to the novel (p. 218).
Only an idolator of Hemingway is going to follow these observations to the logical conclusion that his works are all epics. The
increase in the foreign and strange-sounding in *For Whom the
Bell Tolls* should be viewed instead as one aspect of an increased
expansiveness, a more literary and hyperbolic style which
Hemingway experiments with in his later work. The Elizabethan
echoes, found both in constructions and in some of the allusions
mentioned in the previous chapter, are part of a less restrained
manner that is reflected in several other ways.

Doubtless, one effect of the foreign is the exoticism that Kauffmann objects to. It is partly the result of the foreign settings, the
glamour of the strange and unfamiliar, as Frederic Henry recognizes when he considers writing home:

It was a long time since I had written to the States and I knew I
should write but I had let it go so long that it was almost impossible
to write now. There was nothing to write about. I sent a couple of
army Zona di Guerra post-cards, crossing out everything except, I am
well. That should handle them. Those post-cards would be very fine
in America; strange and mysterious. This was a strange and mysterious war zone. . . . (Ch. vii)

[15]   "Hollywood and Hemingway", *The New Republic*, October 6, 1958,
p. 21.

It is like the impressive foreignisms which some critics are prone to, e.g., H. L. Mencken, whom Hemingway satirizes for the habit in *The Torrents of Spring*. Here is Scripps O'Neil talking to the waitress at Brown's Beanery:

"I write stories. I had a story in *The Post* and two in *The Dial*. Mencken's trying to get ahold of me. I'm too wise for that sort of thing. No *politzei* for mine. They give me the *katzenjammers*."

. . . .

"All I want is for them to give me and my bird a square deal. No more *weltpolitik*. Take Doctor Coolidge away." (Ch. v)

As parodists have shown, Hemingway is quite vulnerable to the same kind of burlesquing.[16]

While the foreign can become a pretentious mannerism, it is clear from the following passage that Hemingway is intrigued by its expressiveness. The old distrust of words is somewhat in abeyance as Robert Jordan runs over a series of foreign words, translating a rather high-sounding sentiment into something more acceptable:

... if there is not any such thing as a long time, nor the rest of your lives, nor from now on, but there is only now, why then now is the thing to praise and I am very happy with it. Now, *ahora, maintenant, heute. Now*, it has a funny sound to be a whole world and your life. *Esta noche*, tonight, *ce soir, heute abend*. Life and wife, *Vie* and *Mari*. No it didn't work out. The French turned it into husband. There was now and *frau*; but that did not prove anything either. Take dead, *mort, muerto,* and *todt. Todt* was the deadest of them all. War, *guerre, guerra,* and *krieg. Krieg* was the most like war, or was it? Or was it only that he knew German the least well? Sweetheart, *chérie, prenda,* and *schatz*. He would trade them all for Maria. There was a name. (Ch. xiii)

In *For Whom the Bell Tolls* there is also more of the assurance that a foreign abstraction is real. Maria says of their lovemaking on the night before the bridge is to be blown up, "I am thankful too to have been another time in *la gloria*", and Jordan thinks,

She said La Gloria. It has nothing to do with glory nor La Gloire that the French write and speak about. It is the thing that is in the

---

[16] See, for example, Cornelia Otis Skinner's "For Whom the Gong Sounds", in *Soap Behind the Ears* (New York, Dodd, Mead and Co., 1942), pp. 89-96.

Cante Hondo and in the Saetas. It is in Greco and in San Juan de la Cruz, of course, and in the others. I am no mystic, but to deny it is as ignorant as though you denied the telephone or that the earth revolves around the sun or that there are other planets than this. (Ch. xxxvii)

Schwartz points out an example from "The Gambler, the Nun, and the Radio" of the connection between the foreign and the ideals and values of the code (p. 122). An American detective is questioning the Mexican gambler, who was shot, and asks Mr. Frazer to translate:

"Listen", the detective said. "This isn't Chicago. You're not a gangster. You don't have to act like a moving picture. It's all right to tell who shot you. Anybody would tell who shot them. That's all right to do. Suppose you don't tell who he is and he shoots somebody else. Suppose he shoots a woman or a child. You can't let him get away with that. You tell him", he said to Mr. Frazer.

. . . .

"Listen, amigo", said Mr. Frazer. "The policeman says that we are not in Chicago but in Hailey, Montana. You are not a bandit and this has nothing to do with the cinema."

"I believe him", said Cayetano softly. "Ya lo creo."

"One can, with honor, denounce one's assailant. Every one does it here, he says. He says what happens if after shooting you, this man shoots a woman or a child?"

"One can, with honor, denounce one's assailant." For the Spanish, recall, honor is "as real a thing as water, wine, or olive oil". The foreign abstraction is true. That is, the foreign is an indirect way of reintroducing the "large statement" that Jake distrusted.

Besides being impressive, exotic, or indirect, the foreign may sometimes be euphemistic. For example, Jordan seems to use Spanish euphemistically when thinking about his father, who committed suicide:

I understand it, but I do not approve of it. *Lache* was the word. But you *do* understand it? Sure, I understand it but. Yes, but. You have to be awfully occupied with yourself to do a thing like that.

. . . .

I'll never forget how sick it made me the first time I knew he was a *cobarde*. Go on, say it in English. Coward. It's easier when you have it said and there is never any point in referring to a son of a bitch by some foreign term. He wasn't any son of a bitch, though.

He was just a coward and that was the worst luck any man could have. (Ch. xxx)

Notice, first of all, the vague, indefinite *it* and *that*. Secondly, there comes the recognition of the evasiveness of the foreign and a disavowal of it when used for this purpose.

Hemingway seems to disavow foreignism in general in the first part of the serialized *The Dangerous Summer*, but what he actually repudiates is its misuse to impress and to sound exotic:

I am trying to avoid using a Spanish word whenever I can explain in idiomatic English. This is not always possible but I think it is better than the peppering, larding and truffleing with bullfighting terms and phrases that you get from the newly erudite writers that have disgusted me with trying to read anything about bullfighting in English. By this time, if I were not trying as far as possible to say it in English or whatever it is I write, you could be so snowed under with Manoletinas, Giraldillas, Pedresinas, Trincherillas and other varieties of ballroom bananas that you could not see the paper for the words. Just remember that any pass that ends in *ina* or *illa* is probably a phony and was invented to impress a gullible public. What I could have said in Spanish was that Antonio's father was a great *director de lidia* and that Antonio is very much better so that every pass that is made with the cape from the time the bull comes out and every move of the picadors and the placing of each pic thrust is intelligently directed toward preparing the bull for the last act of the bullfight, his domination by the scarlet cloth of the muleta which prepares him for his death by the sword.[17]

This sounds like a repudiation of much of Hemingway's own past style, especially that of *Death in the Afternoon*. Actually it shows, I think, Hemingway's awareness of the expansive, "literary" function of the foreign – its possible pretentiousness – and the old fear of sounding pompous dictates this attack on foreignisms. Note the deflating self-mockery of "English or whatever it is I write". But note also the long last sentence which gives us the expansive account that Hemingway says he will spare us because it is "phony" and "ballroom bananas". Neatly, if not inconspicuously, he has managed to have it both ways – the expansiveness and the disclaimer of it. While he may reduce the amount of foreignism in his writing, Hemingway never entirely

[17] *Life*, September 5, 1960, p. 86.

abandons this method of making "larger" statements than a strictly colloquial and "disciplined" style would allow.

3

The catalogue is another device which, though often not obviously "literary", may serve the function of expansiveness. It is one of the main forms which Hemingway's tendency toward overstatement takes. (The catalogue, piling up incidental detail, may also give a strong impression of concreteness and immediacy or may serve to establish the expertness and "know-how" of the hero.) While Hemingway was never a radical experimenter such as Joyce and apparently had no desire to help accomplish the "Revolution of the Word", he should have agreed in part with Marinetti's "New Futurist Manifesto". A person with the lyrical faculty ("the exceptional faculty of intoxicating and being intoxicated with life"), says Marinetti, having experienced a "zone of intense life" such as war, will instinctively relate his impressions immediately afterwards in this way:

Disregarding syntax, he will waste no time upon construing sentences. Chucking adjectives and punctuation overboard, he will despise all mannerism or preciosity of style, and will seek to stir you by hurling a confused medley of sensations and impressions at your head.[18]

The catalogue seems unliterary because it is composed so often of "objective" details, but the torrential outpouring is a kind of hyperbole, seeking intensity by exaggeration. Moreover, the "confused medley of sensations and impressions", though it may seem built of incongruous details, frequently intends to be shocking through their juxtaposition. An illuminating example, cited by Levin, is from Hemingway's introduction to *In Sicily*.[19] In a

18   F. T. Marinetti, "The New Futurist Manifesto: Wireless Imagination and Words at Liberty", tr. Arundel del Re, *Poetry and Drama*, I (September 1913), 321-322. Hemingway should have found congenial also Marinetti's urging "a telegraphic lyricism with no sense of the book, and the greatest possible sense of life" (p. 324).

19   Elio Vittorini, *In Sicily*, tr. Wilfrid David (New York, New Directions, 1949), pp. 7-8. Levin discusses the catalogue on pp. 147-148 of *Contexts of Criticism*; I have followed his discussion when it was convenient.

bitter outburst against academicians and critics, whom he connects with aridity, Hemingway says that the good creative writer brings rain (life):

Rain to an academician is probably, after the first fall has cleared the air, H_2O with, of course, traces of other things. To a good writer, needing something to bring the dry country alive so that it will not be a desert where only such cactus as New York literary reviews grow dry and sad, inexistent without the watering of their benefactors, feeding on the dried manure of schism and the dusty taste of disputed dialectics, their only flowering a desiccated criticism as alive as stuffed birds, and their steady mulch the dehydrated cuds of fellow critics; such a writer finds rain to be made of knowledge, experience, wine, bread, oil, salt, vinegar, bed, early mornings, nights, days, the sea, men, women, dogs, beloved motor cars, bicycles, hills and valleys, the appearance and disappearance of trains on straight and curved tracks, love, honor and disobey, music, chamber music and chamber pots, negative and positive Wassermanns, the arrival and non-arrival of expected munitions and/or reinforcements, replacements or your brother. All these are a part of rain to a good writer along with your hated or beloved mother, may she rest in peace or in pieces, porcupine quills, cock grouse drumming on a bass-wood log, the smell of sweet-grass and fresh smoked leather and Sicily.

It is obvious that one thing which calls forth a catalogue from Hemingway is a hated object (or person). Some of the juxtapositions in this series show a bitterness which otherwise seems inexplicable. As Levin points out, the very structure of the second sentence breaks down: the first half is an attempt at an elaborate grammatical construction that gets out of control; after the semicolon the object of the preposition becomes the subject and the new object of the preposition becomes a torrential catalogue. (A similar breakdown in syntax occurs in the long, involved catalogue about the Gulf Stream in Chapter viii of *Green Hills of Africa.*) The suggestion is of feeling so intense that one can hardly find the form to express it in. Words come out in a flood quite unlike Hemingway's "disciplined" style, but the result sounds so awkward that the "literary" quality of the construction is little apparent.

The train of association in the catalogue is sometimes obvious, sometimes roughly deflating. Knowledge is first equated with concrete food and drink connected with the Mediterranean, with bed and its suggestions, with the diurnal cycle, with the heavily jocular Thurber series of men, women, and dogs. More interesting are the deflating combinations:

Then come the great abstractions, love and honor, which are undercut by a cynical negation of the marriage ceremony, "disobey". Since chamber music sounds highbrow, it must be balanced against the downright vulgarity of chamber pots. The pangs of sex are scientifically neutralized by the reference to Wassermann tests, and the agonies of war are deliberately stated in the cool and/or colorless jargon of military dispatches. The final choice, "replacements or your brother", possibly echoes a twist of continental slang (*et ton frère!*); but, more than that, it suddenly replaces a strategic loss with a personal bereavement.

The last sentence continues the bitter and somewhat juvenile shocking juxtapositions (deflation by tough talk), then ends with a whiff of the clean outdoors:

This time love dares to appear in its primary human connection, but only in ambivalence with hatred, and the hazards of sentimentality are hysterically avoided by a trite pun. And though the final images resolve the paragraph by coming back to the Sicilian locale of Vittorini's novel, they savor more of the northern woods of Hemingway's Upper Peninsula.

While catalogues are not confined to Hemingway's later work, those in the later work, like the Gulf Stream passage of *Green Hills of Africa*, are often alike in their rather distorted bitterness and toughness. (Others are concerned frequently with a nostalgic evocation of the past.) This tough tone increases so markedly as Hemingway becomes more expansive in his style that it is almost certainly a defensive deflationary reaction to the uneasiness he feels. It seems to me that it is in large part Hemingway's reactions to his relaxing of understatement which explain what many critics find offensive about his work from *Death in the Afternoon* on.

Notice again the "shocking" juxtapositions and the queer outraged tone of the following catalogue on another hated subject (art or homosexuality?):

Goya did not believe in costume but he did believe in blacks and in grays, in dust and in light, in high places rising from plains, in the country around Madrid, in movement, in his own cojones, in painting, in etching, and in what he had seen, felt, touched, handled, smelled, enjoyed, drunk, mounted, suffered, spewed-up, lain-with, suspected, observed, loved, hated, lusted, feared, detested, admired, loathed, and destroyed. . . . El Greco believed in the city of Toledo, in its location and construction, in some of the people who lived in it, in blues, grays, greens and yellows, in reds, in the holy ghost, in the communion and fellowship of saints, in painting, in life after death and death after life and in fairies. If he was one he should redeem, for the tribe, the prissy exhibitionistic, aunt-like, withered old maid moral arrogance of a Gide; the lazy, conceited debauchery of a Wilde who betrayed a generation; the nasty, sentimental pawing of humanity of a Whitman and all the mincing gentry. Viva El Greco El Rey de los Maricónes. (*Death in the Afternoon,* Ch. xvii)

Compare the tone in Cantwell's description of D'Annunzio in *Across the River and into the Trees:*

writer, poet, national hero, phraser of the dialectic of Fascism, macabre egotist, aviator, commander, or rider, in the first of the fast torpedo attack boats, Lieutenant Colonel of Infantry without knowing how to command a company, nor a platoon properly, the great, lovely writer of *Notturno* whom we respect, and jerk. (Ch. vi)

The disgust expressed in Helen Gordon's denunciation of love and her writer husband in *To Have and Have Not* is further illustration of the tough tone which permeates so much of Hemingway's later work:

"Love was the greatest thing, wasn't it? Love was what we had that no one else had or could ever have. And you were a genius and I was your whole life. I was your partner and your little black flower. Slop. Love is just another dirty lie. Love is ergoapiol pills to make me come around because you were afraid to have a baby. Love is quinine and quinine and quinine until I'm deaf with it. Love is that dirty aborting horror that you took me to. Love is my insides all messed up. It's half catheters and half whirling douches. I know about love. Love always hangs up behind the bathroom door. It smells like lysol. To hell with love. Love is you making me happy and then going off to sleep with your mouth open while I lie awake all night afraid to say my prayers even because I know I have no right to any more. Love is all the dirty little tricks you taught me that you probably got out of some book. All right. I'm through with you and I'm through with love. Your kind of picknose love. You writer." (Ch. xxi)

Notice the similarity in effect between such repetition, massing details for emphasis and intensity, and the catalogue proper: both are a kind of hyperbole.

One of the toughest repetitious catalogues occurs in *For Whom the Bell Tolls* after Pablo has stolen Jordan's detonating equipment; Jordan proceeds to "muck" everybody he can think of in Spain:

Oh, the dirty, vile, treacherous sod. The dirty rotten crut. ... The smart, treacherous ugly bastard. The dirty *cabrón*.

Cut it out and take is easy, he told himself. ... You're just mucked, he told himself. You're mucked for good and higher than a kite. Keep your damned head and get the anger out and stop this cheap lamenting like a damned wailing wall. It's gone. God damn you, it's gone. Oh damn the dirty swine to hell. You can muck your way out of it. You've got to, you know you've got to blow it if you have to stand there and – cut out that stuff, too. Why don't you ask your grandfather?

Oh, muck my grandfather and muck this whole treacherous muck-faced mucking country and every mucking Spaniard in it on either side and to hell forever. Muck them to hell together, Largo, Prieto, Asensio, Miaja, Rojo, all of them. Muck every one of them to death to hell. Muck the whole treachery-ridden country. Muck their egotism and their selfishness and their selfishness and their egotism and their conceit and their treachery. Muck them to hell and always. Muck them before we die for them. Muck them after we die for them. Muck them to death and hell. God muck Pablo. Pablo is all of them. ... Muck all the insane, egotistical, treacherous swine that have always governed Spain and ruled her armies. Muck everybody but the people and then be damned careful what they turn into when they have power.

His rage began to thin as he exaggerated more and more and spread his scorn and contempt so widely and unjustly that he could no longer believe in it himself. If that were true what are you here for? It's not true and you know it. (Ch. xxxv)

Note the reaction at the end of this outburst. Having luxuriated in savage exaggeration, Jordan punctures it by deciding it is not true (after innumerable expansive passages we are told whether they are true or not – as good an indication as any that Hemingway distrusts them in general).

Compare Jordan's tough torrential outburst in Chapter xiv when Pablo taunts him first about the unexpected snow and then about his sleeping outside the cave (where Maria joins him):

"To the snow", Pablo said and touched cups with him. Robert Jordan looked him in the eyes and clinked his cup. You bleary-eyed murderous sod, he thought. I'd like to clink this cup against your teeth. *Take it easy,* he told himself, *take it easy.*

"It is very beautiful the snow", Pablo said. "You won't want to sleep outside with the snow falling."

.   .   .   .

"Yes" (damn your bloody, red pig-eyes and your swine-bristly swines-end of a face). "In the snow." (In the utterly-damned, ruinous, unexpected, slutting, defeat-conniving, bastard-cessery of the snow.)

Not all the catalogues and repetitious detailings are of this nature, of course, nor are they confined to the later work. However, the distorted toughness and bitterness is more peculiar to Hemingway's work from 1932 on, as his style becomes more expansive, and we shall see additional examples of it. In the earlier work, this form of expansiveness is notable in *A Farewell to Arms*, whose style is much less restrained than that of *The Sun Also Rises*, but not marked by the numerous defensive deflationary reactions that spot the still more expansive later work. The tone of the following catalogue, telling how the war was different than during the previous year, is poignant and slightly bitter but lacking the outraged distortion of the preceding examples:

... I was very glad the Austrians seemed to want to come back to the town some time, if the war should end, because they did not bombard it to destroy it but only a little in a military way. People lived on in it and there were hospitals and cafés and artillery up side streets and two bawdy houses, one for troops and one for officers, and with the end of the summer, the cool nights, the fighting in the mountains beyond the town, the shell-marked iron of the railway bridge, the smashed tunnel by the river where the fighting had been, the trees around the square and the long avenue of trees that led to the square; these with there being girls in the town, the King passing in his motor car, sometimes now seeing his face and little long necked body and gray beard like a goat's chin tuft; all these with the sudden interiors of houses that had lost a wall through shelling, with plaster and rubble in their gardens and sometimes in the street, and the whole thing going well on the Carso made the fall very different from the last fall when we had been in the country. (Ch. ii)

In what Fenimore terms the "relentless heaping up of a given observation" and the word repetition, this passage from *A Farewell to Arms* shows one form of expansiveness with which Hemingway gains intensity and the impression of concreteness: [20]

If people bring so much courage to this world the world has to kill them to break them, so of course it kills them. The world breaks every one and afterward many are strong at the broken places. But those that will not break it kills. It kills the very good and the very gentle and the very brave impartially. If you are none of these you can be sure it will kill you too but there will be no special hurry. (Ch. xxxiv)

Observe the similarity in technique in these two examples from *For Whom the Bell Tolls*:

Of course they turned on you. They turned on you often but they always turned on every one. They turned on themselves, too. If you had three together, two would unite against one, and then the two would start to betray each other. Not always, but often enough for you to take enough cases and start to draw it as a conclusion. (Ch. xi)

Dying was nothing and he had no picture of it nor fear of it in his mind. But living was a field of grain blowing in the wind on the side of a hill. Living was a hawk in the sky. Living was an earthen jar of water in the dust of the threshing with the grain flailed out and the chaff blowing. Living was a horse between your legs and a carbine under one leg and a hill and a valley and a stream with trees along it and the far side of the valley and the hills beyond. (Ch. xxvii)

Catalogues and the repetitious massing of details, like the use of incidental detail, serve to achieve emphasis, intensity, and an impression of concreteness. They may be viewed, that is, as an aspect of Hemingway's tendency toward overstatement and also as an aspect of his concentration on the present moment, the now, which is discussed in Chapter v. The sentences which employ repetition for emphasis are often short, and their shortness together with the repetition tends to hide somewhat their "literary" quality, their expansiveness. The sentences in which the catalogues occur are almost inevitably longer, frequently quite involved (if not tortuous), so that they are more obviously related to the expansive side of Hemingway's work in spite of their "objective"

[20] Fenimore, p. 220. He cites the next two examples on p. 219.

details. Both occur early and late, but, as indicated, the later catalogues and repetitious detailings often share a distorted toughness of tone which seems to begin about 1932 and runs through most of Hemingway's subsequent writing.

4

Besides increased toughness, the later work shows an increase in the word *true*, especially in *For Whom the Bell Tolls* and *Across the River and into the Trees*. The emphasis on truth is, of course, the other side of the distrust of words that we have seen in Hemingway and his contemporaries, and it is undoubtedly a result of the disillusionment with World War I. That much is clear in Hemingway's introduction to *Men at War*, from his assertions "A writer's job is to tell the truth" and "The writers who were established before the war had nearly all sold out to write propaganda during it and most of them never recovered their honesty afterwards" to his vow "We who took part in the last war to end wars are not going to be fooled again." [21] Incidentally, he sheds considerable light on his equation of truth with understatement and "objectivity": the writers who wrote about the war after it was over wrote better and truer, he says, because "they had learned to tell the truth without screaming. Screaming, necessary though it may be to attract attention at the time, reads badly in later years" (p. xvi). From reading Tolstoy's distorted theories about Napoleon in *War and Peace*, he says, "I learned ... to distrust my own Thinking with a capital T and to try to write as truly, as straightly, as objectively and as humbly as possible" (p. xviii).

The same fear of lies, connected with the war, appears in Sherwood Anderson's *Dark Laughter*, in which the annual Quat'z Arts Ball the year after the war ended becomes an orgy of life in

[21] Pp. xv, xxxi. On p. xv Hemingway adds some comments about the writers who sold out which show his sternly moral, almost religious fervor about truth and honesty in writing: "All of their reputations steadily slumped because a writer should be of as great probity and honesty as a priest of God. He is either honest or not, as a woman is either chaste or not, and after one piece of dishonest writing he is never the same again."

the raw: "The end of lies, the end of keeping up the pretense, the end of that sort of cheapness – the end of the War":

> Men lying, women lying, children lying, being taught to lie.
> Preachers lying, priests lying, bishops, popes and cardinals lying.
> Kings lying, governments lying, writers lying, artists drawing lying pictures.
> A debauch of lying. Keep it up! The bitter end! Outlast the other liar! Make him eat it! Kill. Kill some more! Keep on killing! Liberty! Love of God! Love of men! Kill! Kill! (Ch. xix)

Years later the heroine, Aline Grey, remembers the account of the orgy that she heard from Rose Frank, a newspaper woman, in Paris:

> After all, most of the women at the ball in Paris were what? Whores? An attempt to throw off pretense, fakiness. So much fake talk during the war. The war for righteousness – to make the world Free. The young men sick, sick, and sick of it. (Ch. xxi)

Understandably enough, this becomes a generalized fear of lies and distrust of thoughts and words: "Under certain circumstances you had thought you knew just about what you would do, but all of your thoughts were, as likely as not, lies. After all, it might be, you never knew anything really until it had touched your own life" (Ch. xvi); "Damn you – no more driveling words here. Words are tender things, leading to poetry – or lies" (Ch. vii). In a letter to George Freitag, August 27, 1938 (thirteen years later), on the problems of the young writer, Anderson sounds very much like Hemingway as he talks about his "best and truest work" and warns against the dangers of "faking, trying to give people what they think they want. . . ." [22]

Hemingway must have encountered similar advice as a young

---

[22] *Letters of Sherwood Anderson*, ed. Howard Mumford Jones, with Walter B. Rideout (Boston, Little, Brown and Co., 1953), pp. 406, 407. Cf. Hemingway's advice to the young aspirant writer in "Monologue to the Maestro": "Good writing is true writing. If a man is making a story up it will be true in proportion to the amount of knowledge of life that he has and how conscientious he is; so that when he makes something up it is as it would truly be. If he doesn't know how many people work in their minds and actions his luck may save him for a while, or he may write fantasy. But if he continues to write about what he does not know about he will find himself faking. After he fakes a few times he cannot write honestly any more" (p. 21).

writer. Here, for example, is Ezra Pound in "The Serious Artist" (1913):

Bad art is inaccurate art. It is art that makes false reports.

. . . .

If an artist falsifies his report as to the nature of man, as to his own nature, as to the nature of his ideal of the perfect, as to the nature of his ideal of this, that or the other, of god, if god exist, of the life force, of the nature of good and evil, if good and evil exist, of the force with which he believes or disbelieves this, that or the other, of the degree in which he suffers or is made glad; if the artist falsifies his reports on these matters or on any other matter in order that he may conform to the taste of his time, to the proprieties of a sovereign, to the conveniences of a preconceived code of ethics, then that artist lies. If he lies out of deliberate will to lie, if he lies out of careless-ness, out of laziness, out of cowardice, out of any sort of negligence whatsoever, he nevertheless lies and he should be punished or despised in proportion to the seriousness of his offence.

. . . .

Purely and simply . . . good art can NOT be immoral. By good art I mean art that bears true witness, I mean the art that is most precise.[23]

To consider practice as well as theory, this passage from Gertrude Stein's *Melanctha* shows similarities to Hemingway not only in the sophisticated repetitions and "simplicity" but in the recurrence of the word *true* (and related words such as *certainly, honest, real* and *sure*):

Melanctha never talked much, now, when they were together. Some-times Jeff Campbell teased her about her not talking to him. "I cer-tainly did think Melanctha you was a great talker from the way Jane Harden and everybody said things to me, and from the way I heard you talk so much when I first met you. Tell me true Melanctha, why don't you talk more now to me, perhaps it is I talk so much I don't give you any chance to me, or perhaps it is you hear me talk so much you don't think so much now of a whole lot of talking. Tell me honest Melanctha, why don't you talk more to me." "You know very well Jeff Campbell", said Melanctha "You certainly do know very well Jeff, you don't think really much, of my talking. You think a whole lot more about everything than I do Jeff, and you don't care much about what I got to say about it. You know that's true what I

[23] *Literary Essays of Ezra Pound*, ed. T. S. Eliot (Norfolk, Conn., New Directions, 1954), pp. 43-44.

am saying Jeff, if you want to be real honest, the way you always
are when I like you so much." Jeff laughed and looked fondly at her.
"I don't say ever I know, you ain't right, when you say things like
that to me, Melanctha. You see you always like to be talking just
what you think everybody wants to be hearing from you, and when
you are like that, Melanctha, honest, I certainly don't care very
much to hear you, but sometimes you say something that is what
you are really thinking, and then I like a whole lot to hear you
talking." [24]

At times the conversation sounds almost like that in *Across the
River and into the Trees*:

"Oh! Oh!" cried Jeff Campbell, laughing, "I ain't going to be so bad
for always, sure I ain't, Melanctha, my own darling. And sure you
do forgive me really, and sure you love me true and really, sure,
Melanctha?" (p. 161)

With Hemingway, the insistence on truth-telling and exposing
the fake first becomes the loud protestation it does in *Death in the
Afternoon*, a book which also shows a growing expansiveness and
even exaggeration. On the one hand, "there remains a determination to tell the truth, to discern faking wherever it may be, that
becomes almost pathological. Perhaps more of Hemingway's
explanation of bullfighting is devoted to how to tell the fake stuff
than to how to recognize the real." [25] On the other hand, "Almost
everything he does is exaggerated. The fine spoofing which is so
natural a part of *The Sun Also Rises* and *A Farewell to Arms*
now becomes the garrulous joking with the Old Lady interlocutor
in *Death in the Afternoon*" (p. 280).

Frohock does not cite examples of what he means, but the
introduction to "A Natural History of the Dead" which the author
gives the "old lady" is probably a fair sample: "It's written in
popular style and is designed to be the Whittier's *Snow Bound* of
our time and at the end it's simply full of conversation" (Ch. xii).
Here Hemingway seems to be reacting self-consciously to criticism
of his work, and elsewhere we get more of this disturbing reaction
(somewhat reminiscent of the author's addresses to the reader in
the early *The Torrents of Spring*):

---

[24] *Three Lives* (Norfolk, Conn., New Directions, 1933), pp. 134-135.
[25] W. M. Frohock, "Violence and Discipline", in McCaffery, p. 281.

But, you say, there is very little conversation in this book. Why isn't there more dialogue? What we want in a book by this citizen is people talking; that is all he knows how to do and now he doesn't do it. The fellow is no philosopher, no savant, an incompetent zoologist, he drinks too much and cannot punctuate readily and now he has stopped writing dialogue. Some one ought to put a stop to him. He is bull crazy. Citizen, perhaps you are right. Let us have a little dialogue. (Ch. xi)

Whereupon the author instructs the "old lady" about the love life of the bulls, which she finds sad, and follows it up with a lecture on the dangers of using words like *love*.

There is more of this painful joking in Chapter xiv on the subject of Faulkner's work and his prolificacy:

... as age comes on I feel I must devote myself more and more to the practice of letters. My operatives tell me that through the fine work of Mr. William Faulkner publishers now will publish anything rather than to try to get you to delete the better portions of your works, and I look forward to writing of those days of my youth which were spent in the finest whorehouses in the land amid the most brilliant society there found. I had been saving this background to write of in my old age when with the aid of distance I could examine it most clearly.

Old lady: Has this Mr. Faulkner written well of these places?

Splendidly, Madame. Mr. Faulkner writes admirably of them. He writes the best of them of any writer I have read for many years.

Old lady: I must buy his works.

Madame, you can't go wrong on Faulkner. He's prolific too. By the time you get them ordered there'll be new ones out.

Old lady: If they are as you say there cannot be too many.

Madame, you voice my own opinion.

One wonders whether it is partly the subject matter of these interludes which accounts for their painful tone or whether it is the way in which Hemingway tries to puncture or cover up the dubious feelings that he now expresses more openly.

At any rate, we have here the attempt to deflate by humor, a device which Hemingway uses with hilarious success in Chapter xii of *Green Hills of Africa* when he gets the "braggies" in a long conversation with the "Roman" (an old African) who cannot understand a word he says except for "Simba, Simba, Faro, Nyati, Tendalla, Tendalla" ("lion, lion, rhino, buffalo, kudu,

kudu"). The device is less successful in Chapter xi of *The Torrents of Spring*, where Hemingway in the guise of Yogi Johnson delivers a lecture on war to two Indians, in the course of which he criticizes Sherwood Anderson for Fred Grey's thoughts about war in *Dark Laughter* (Ch. xxi), explains how war is like football (unpleasant), gives a little inside information about how Allied soldiers shot prisoners, delivers a theory of four phases in the psychology of the soldier, and reveals that Willa Cather knew nothing about war and took the war scenes for *One of Ours* from *Birth of a Nation*.

After this ponderous lecture comes some rather heavy-handed humorous deflation: one of the Indians has fallen asleep; Yogi asks the other how he liked the speech. "White chief have heap much sound ideas", the Indian answers. "White chief educated like hell." Yogi, touched, feels that he has found true communion "among the simple aborigines, the only real Americans". Then we get the complete bursting of the balloon. The Indian asks, "Was white chief in the war?"

"I landed in France in May, 1917", Yogi began.

"I thought maybe white chief was in the war from the way he talked", the Indian said. "Him", he raised the head of his sleeping companion up so the last rays of the sunset shone on the sleeping Indian's face, "he got V.C. Me I got D.S.O. and M.C. with bar. I was major in the Fourth C.M.R.'s."

"I'm glad to meet you", Yogi said. He felt strangely humiliated. Here we see an early indication of the tendency toward pontificating and the attempt at deflation by humor which dogs Hemingway throughout *Death in the Afternoon*.

At the same time tough talk and the word *true* (and similar words) show a pronounced increase. The first is illustrated by an exchange at the end of Chapter ix when the "old lady" asks the author whether he is not prejudiced:

Author: Madame, rarely will you meet a more prejudiced man nor one who tells himself he keeps his mind more open. But cannot that be because one part of our mind, that which we act with, becomes prejudiced through experience and still we keep another part completely open to observe and judge with?

Old lady: Sir, I do not know.

Author: Madame, neither do I and it may well be that we are talking horseshit.

Old lady: That is an odd term and one I did not encounter in my youth.

Author: Madame, we apply the term now to describe unsoundness in an abstract conversation or, indeed, any overmetaphysical tendency in speech.

Old lady: I must learn to use these terms correctly.

Elsewhere, when he enlarges on "this honor thing" in Chapter ix, he tries to reassure the reader and himself that it is not a lie by saying, "I swear it is true." In Chapter i there is not only the emphasis on "knowing truly what you really felt" but the assurance that spectators at the bullfight, once they have learned to appreciate values instead of romantic and picturesque things, seek "honesty and true, not tricked, emotion and always classicism and the purity of execution of all the suertes" (this is by way of explanation why the true *aficionado* prefers horses without protective padding). At the end of Chapter xx Hemingway returns again to the subject of truth in writing – "Let those who want to save the world if you can get to see it clear and as a whole. Then any part you make will represent the whole if it's made truly" – after having devoted the rest of the chapter to a catalogue meaningful primarily to himself of all the other things that he might have said about Spain but didn't. (This kind of catalogue, like Harry's reminiscences about the Place Contrescarpe in "The Snows of Kilimanjaro", seems to me illegitimate writing, a private indulgence in nostalgia.)

Green Hills of Africa, advertised in the preface as an attempt "to write an absolutely true book to see whether the shape of a country and the pattern of a month's action can, if truly presented, compete with a work of the imagination", continues the "same desire to get at true feeling, and true things, and how for example to kill in the honest and true way" (Frohock, p. 281). But the declaration that the writer of prose with a fourth or fifth dimension must have "an absolute conscience as unchanging as the standard meter in Paris, to prevent faking" comes near the end of a pretentious lecture in Chapter i, in the course of which Hemingway delivers himself of the exaggeration, "All modern American literature comes from one book by Mark Twain called *Huckle-*

berry Finn", explains how critics and money destroy good writers, and finally grows uneasy at his pompousness when his straight man Kandisky asks him what else harms writers:

I was tired of the conversation which was becoming an interview. So I would make it an interview and finish it. The necessity to put a thousand intangibles into a sentence, now, before lunch, was too bloody.

"Politics, women, drink, money, ambition. And the lack of politics, women, drink, money and ambition", I said profoundly.

After Kandisky leaves, Hemingway's wife remarks that he did not have much chance to talk after "B'wana M'Kumba" (the natives' name for Hemingway – obviously the original of the name Macomber) got started: " 'I did have verbal dysentery', I said."

In Chapter viii Hemingway describes the horror he felt when in a hospital with his arm broken (apparently the experience on which he based "The Gambler, the Nun, and the Radio"), a little out of his head, thinking that he was being punished for all hunters. The description serves as a transition to the long passage about the Gulf Stream, an elaborate bit of conscience-salving with some key *trulys* and a *cleanly* in it:

Then, getting well, decided if it was a punishment I had paid it and at least I knew what I was doing. I did nothing that had not been done to me. I had been shot and I had been crippled and gotten away. I expected, always, to be killed by one thing or another and I, truly, did not mind that any more. Since I still loved to hunt I resolved that I would only shoot as long as I could kill cleanly and as soon as I lost that ability I would stop.

If you serve time for society, democracy and the other things quite young, and declining any further enlistment make yourself responsible only to yourself, you exchange the pleasant, comforting stench of comrades for something you can never feel in any other way than by yourself. That something I cannot yet define completely but the feeling comes when you write well and truly of something and know impersonally you have written in that way and those who are paid to read it and report on it do not like the subject so they say it is all a fake, yet you know its value absolutely; or when you do something which people do not consider a serious occupation and yet you know, truly, that it is as important and has always been as important as all the things that are in fashion. . . .

Hemingway seems here to be defending his interest in bullfighting and hunting against his critics. However, the critics appear to have the best of it in regard to *Green Hills of Africa* – for example, Edmund Wilson, who finds the "absolutely true book" a failure, "what must be one of the only books ever written which make Africa and its animals seem dull"; "He delivers a self-confident lecture on the high possibilities of prose writing; and then produces such a sentence as the following: 'Going down-hill steeply made these Spanish shooting boots too short in the toe and there was an old argument, about this length of boot and whether the bootmaker, whose part I had taken, unwittingly first, only as interpreter, and finally embraced his theory patriotically as a whole and, I believed, by logic, had overcome it by adding onto the heel' " (Ch. v).[26] The long, tangled, awkward sentence is just one sign of the increased expansiveness which occurs in the book along with the emphasis on truth.

But the real proliferation of *trues* begins with *For Whom the Bell Tolls*. Coming at the time that it did and reflecting, at least in its surface message, the turn away from isolation to internationalism, the novel was undoubtedly overvalued and is still difficult to evaluate free of stock responses. In 1941 Beach called it "the most accomplished in technique, and the strongest in effect" of anything Hemingway had yet written (p. 69), and in 1944 Cowley termed it "the best of Hemingway's novels", though he printed only Chapter xxvii (El Sordo on the hilltop) while printing the whole of *In Our Time* and *The Sun Also Rises*.[27] Part of Beach's judgment seems due to Hemingway's having come around to affirming positive ideals (abstractions) more explicitly, which he previously distrusted as "proud words" (a phrase that Beach borrows from Sandburg). The fact is, however, that Hemingway still distrusts all high-sounding sentiments, so that Robert Jordan is continually reassuring himself that they are true.

Sometimes, as in the following example which Beach cites

---

[26] "Hemingway: Gauge of Morale", p. 246.
[27] The Viking Portable *Hemingway*, ed. Malcolm Cowley (New York, The Viking Press, 1944), p. 340.

(p. 90), Jordan gives himself a talking to about their reality – a device which contributes very much to the talkiness of the novel and at the same time makes one doubt his belief in these once "obscene" abstractions which need so much justification. In Chapter xviii, in one of the long passages of introspection that frequent the novel, Jordan feels he is taking part in a crusade, with this reaction:

That was the only word for it although it was a word that had been so worn and abused that it no longer gave its true meaning. You felt, in spite of all bureaucracy and inefficiency and party strife something that was like the feeling you expected to have and did not have when you made your first communion. It was a feeling of consecration to a duty toward all of the oppressed of the world which would be as difficult and embarrassing to speak about as religious experience and yet it was authentic as the feeling you had when you heard Bach, or stood in Chartres Cathedral or the Cathedral at León and saw the light coming through the great windows; or when you saw Mantegna and Greco and Brueghel in the Prado. It gave you a part in something that you could believe in wholly and completely and in which you felt an absolute brotherhood with the others who were engaged in it. It was something that you had never known before but that you had experienced now and you gave such importance to it and the reasons for it that your own death seemed of complete unimportance; only a thing to be avoided because it would interfere with the performance of your duty.

But as Beach also points out, Jordan like Hemingway finds it embarrassing to talk about such high-sounding ideals because "Jordan shares Hemingway's fear of romantic falsification". The old distrust of "large statements" is still there, with the result that Jordan, like Hemingway in *Death in the Afternoon*, has to swear that they are really true:

In all the work that they, the *partizans* did, they brought added danger and bad luck to the people that sheltered them and worked with them. For what? So that, eventually, there should be no more danger and so that the country should be a good place to live in. That was true no matter how trite it sounded. (Ch. xiii)

After worrying over one trite phrase, Jordan goes on to make another "large statement" which he immediately doubts:

Enemies of the people. That was a phrase he might omit. That was a catch phrase he would skip. That was one thing that sleeping with

Maria had done. He had gotten to be as bigoted and hidebound about his politics as a hard-shelled Baptist and phrases like enemies of the people came into his mind without his much criticizing them in any way. Any sort of *clichés* both revolutionary and patriotic. His mind employed them without criticism. Of course they were true but it was too easy to be nimble about using them. But since last night and this afternoon his mind was much clearer and cleaner on that business. Bigotry is an odd thing. To be bigoted you have to be absolutely sure that you are right and nothing makes that surety and righteousness like continence. Continence is the foe of heresy.

How would that premise stand up if he examined it? (Ch. xiii)

The patriotic pep talks that Jordan keeps giving himself are repeatedly followed by some reassurance about their truth:

This was the greatest gift that he had, the talent that fitted him for war; that ability not to ignore but to despise whatever bad ending there could be. This quality was destroyed by too much responsibility for others or the necessity of undertaking something ill planned or badly conceived. For in such things the bad ending, failure, could not be ignored. It was not simply a possibility of harm to one's self, which *could* be ignored. He knew he himself was nothing, and he knew death was nothing. He knew that truly, as truly as he knew anything. (Ch. xxxix)

Jordan protests too much and Hemingway feels it, for he has Jordan telling himself again and again not to lie to himself. Here, for example, Jordan explains to Agustín the one great difference between himself and Kashkin (whom he shot):

"I am alive and he is dead", Robert Jordan said. Then: what's the matter with you? he thought. Is that the way to talk? . . . Is that all it means to you, now? It never meant much, he told himself truly. You tried to make it mean something, but it never did. There is no need to lie in the time that is left. (Ch. xxiv)

Two pages earlier, after having told himself that killing is an extra sacrament for the Spanish, an act of faith of their earlier religion, Jordan recoils upon himself once more:

Stop making dubious literature about the Berbers and the old Iberians and admit that you have liked to kill as all who are soldiers by choice have enjoyed it at some time whether they lie about it or not. Anselmo does not like to because he is a hunter, not a soldier. Don't idealize him, either. Hunters kill animals and soldiers kill men. Don't lie to yourself, he thought. Nor make up literature about it. (Ch. xxiii)

One could hardly find a more explicit statement of Hemingway's distrust of words than in this association between literature and lying. It is no wonder that the "large statements" in the novel make both author and character so uneasy. Occasionally Santiago in *The Old Man and the Sea* sounds like Jordan in his introspections, especially in his concern about not lying to himself (a reminder that the latter book is not a complete reversal of form from the earlier more expansive works): "Fishing kills me exactly as it keeps me alive. The boy keeps me alive, he thought. I must not deceive myself too much" (p. 117).

Besides the longer assurances of the truth of high sentiments and the admonitions against lying, there are countless *trues* and *trulys* sprinkled throughout *For Whom the Bell Tolls*, generally occurring in passages where the feelings or ideas might be considered pretentious. For example, Pilar asks Jordan if he has faith in the Republic:

> "Yes", he said, hoping it was true.
> "I am happy", the woman said. "And you have no fear?"
> "Not to die", he said truly.
> "But other fears?"
> "Only of not doing my duty as I should."
> "Not of capture, as the other had?"
> "No", he said truly. (Ch. ix)

The result is, of course, that the words themselves become a pretentious mannerism, virtually a self-parody. Maria asks Jordan,

> "But tell me truly. Did the earth never move for thee before?"
> "Never", he said truly.
> "Now I am happy", she said. "Now I am truly happy." (Ch. xiii)

Jordan wakes in the night and holds Maria tight: "He held her feeling she was all of life there was and it was true" (Ch. xx). Pilar even smiles *truly*: "She smiled at him again, smiling fairly and truly with the harsh lips and the wide mouth, and said, 'I care for thee very much, *Inglés*'" (Ch. xxxviii). At the end Jordan tells himself *truly* that he is not afraid to die: "There are many worse things than this. Every one has to do this, one day or another. You are not afraid of it once you know you have to do it, are you? No, he said, truly" (Ch. xliii).

I think that Young is quite right in saying that Jordan's expressions of faith and belief do not ring true and that Hemingway
is involved here in the difficulty of "knowing what you really felt,
rather than what you were supposed to feel, and had been taught
to feel" (p. 78). At the same time Hemingway is involved in the
difficulty of expressing openly all sorts of ideals and abstractions
which Frederic Henry thought "obscene", and he never convinces
himself that big words, if not words in general, are not false.
Moreover, he distrusts the open expression of feeling so thoroughly, fearing sentimentality, that he must resort to various means to
camouflage, deflate, or hide it – or, conversely, he must swear to
its truth.

A reminiscence of Jordan's about his childhood, when he first
went away to school, is instructive on this point. He was afraid to
go but so much more embarrassed by his father's open display of
emotion that his distaste overcame his fear:

... his father had kissed him good-by and said, "May the Lord
watch between thee and me while we are absent the one from the
other." His father had been a very religious man and he had said it
simply and sincerely. But his moustache had been moist and his eyes
were damp with emotion and Robert Jordan had been so embarrassed
by all of it, the damp religious sound of the prayer, and by his
father kissing him good-by, that he had felt suddenly so much older
than his father and sorry for him that he could hardly bear it.

On the train the brakeman asked him if he didn't mind going away
to school: " 'No', he had said and it was true. It would not have
been true before but it was true that minute" (Ch. xli). The
embarrassment at open feeling, even as remembered from the
past, is so strong that the reaction of distaste sets in at once,
together with the repetition three times that his unconcern was
true. The word seems to come to Hemingway almost automatically
as feelings or ideals become too explicit, possibly sentimental, or
too pretentious-sounding.

In *Across the River and into the Trees*, Hemingway's most
distorted work since *To Have and Have Not*, the mannerism becomes completely ludicrous, and the deflating tough talk just
painful. Cantwell tells a boatman that he might be able to get him
an old jeep engine for his boat: "Don't talk about such things", the

boatman says. "Things like that don't happen. I don't want to
think about it." "You can think about it", Cantwell answers. "I'm
talking true" (Ch. vi). Renata is not only his "last and true and
only" love, but she has *honest* eyelashes:

> ... look at Renata's eyes, he thought. They are probably the most
> beautiful of all the beautiful things she has, with the longest honest
> lashes I have ever seen and she never uses them for anything except
> to look at you honestly and straight. What a damn wonderful girl
> and what am I doing here anyway? It is wicked. She is your last and
> true and only love, he thought, and that's not evil. It is only unfor-
> tunate. No, he thought, it is damned fortunate and you are very
> fortunate. (Ch. ix)

The example shows also one of the simplest forms of deflation by
tough talk – the combination of the high-flown and the low, the
tendency toward the big word undercut by a curse. Compare
Cantwell's description of fishing boats: "It's not that they are
picturesque. The hell with picturesque. They are just damned
beautiful" (Ch. v).[28] *Picturesque* is too literary, a term of dis-
praise which Hemingway had already used in Chapter i of *Death
in the Afternoon* in reference to the spectators at bullfights who
are not *aficionados*, do not appreciate values, and accordingly
prefer "useless and romantic things". Cantwell's description of the
mistress of a Milanese war profiteer is similar: "She is a beautiful,
hard piece of work. She is damned beautiful, actually" (Ch. vi).

There are presages of the method in earlier work – for example,
in Jake's description of Brett: "Brett was damned good-looking.
She wore a slipover jersey sweater and a tweed skirt, and her hair
was brushed back like a boy's. She started all that. She was built
with curves like the hull of a racing yacht, and you missed none
of it with that wool jersey" (Ch. iii). Atkins remarks, "The picture
of a writer and the emotion of a Rotarian" (p. 189), seeming to
agree in part with Gertrude Stein.[29]

It is obvious also that *straight*, like *honest* and *true* (and *cold*),
is an honorific word: "They kissed for a long time, standing

---

[28] See Levin, pp. 155-156, and Atkins, pp. 189-190.

[29] *The Autobiography of Alice B. Toklas* (New York, The Literary
Guild, 1933), p. 270: "Finally I heard her [Gertrude Stein] say, Hemingway, after all you are ninety percent Rotarian. Can't you, he said, make
it eighty percent. No, said she regretfully, I can't."

straight, and kissing true, in the cold of the open windows that were onto the Grand Canal" (Ch. xi). These and other honorific words which Hemingway leans on so heavily in the novel are pushed to a ludicrous extreme: "Then she chewed well and solidly on her steak and said, 'Do you think it is true that men make their own faces after fifty?' " (Ch. xii); " 'Take a glass of this', the Colonel said, reaching accurately and well for the champagne bucket" (Ch. xiii).

Their being pushed to such an extreme is a sign both of Hemingway's increased overstatement and exaggeration and of his uneasiness at it ("I swear it is true"). The result is a self-parody more devastating than any burlesque of Anderson or others in *The Torrents of Spring*:

The Colonel whispered; holding her tight, and with his heart broken, honestly and fairly, in his whisper that was as barely audible as a silent dog whistle heard close to the ear, "I love you, devil. And you're my Daughter, too. And I don't care about our losses because the moon is our mother and our father. And now let's go down to dinner."

He whispered this last so low that it was inaudible to anyone who did not love you. (Ch. xi)

Along with more *trues* too numerous to cite, there is a lot of concern about not lying:

This was a comparatively safe place, I'm really not lying, not me nor anybody else. You can't fool those that were in Hurtgen, and if you lied they would know it the minute you opened your mouth, Colonel or no Colonel. (Ch. xxxv)

The belligerent tone toward the war stories of writers who don't know what they are talking about is reminiscent of *The Torrents of Spring*, while the association between writing and lying is like that in *For Whom the Bell Tolls*: "Everything about war bores those who have not made it. Except the tales of liars" (Ch. xii; cf. "Soldier's Home"). This is just one of Cantwell's comments after Renata tells him that he ought to write:

"You ought to write", the girl said. "I mean it truly. So someone would know about such things."

"No", the Colonel disagreed. "I have not the talent for it and I know too much. Almost any liar writes more convincingly than a man who was there."

The discussion naturally carries over to the "pitted man with the caricature face", a phony of a writer whom they cannot leave alone in their conversations: "If he is a mediocre writer he will live forever", says Cantwell. "But you're not a writer. How do you know this?" "No", Cantwell says. "By the grace of God. But I've read several books. ... I can tell one writer from another and I tell you that a mediocre writer has a long span of life." The same distrust of writing and writers occurs in Robert Jordan's self-mockery when he feels that he is getting too pompous (reflecting to some extent Hemingway's feeling that he is over-stating?):

The bombers were high now in fast, ugly arrow-heads beating the sky apart with the noise of their motors. They *are* shaped like sharks, Robert Jordan thought, the wide-finned, sharp-nosed sharks of the Gulf Stream. But these, wide-finned in silver, roaring, the light mist of their propellers in the sun, these do not move like sharks. They move like no thing there has ever been. They move like mechanized doom.

You ought to write, he told himself. (Ch. ix)

As one might expect, the heroes are truth-tellers; at least they do not lie very much. Renata begins,

"The *Gran Maestro* doesn't lie. Isn't it wonderful to have people who do not lie?"

"Very wonderful and quite rare", the Colonel said. "I was thinking just now of a man named Georgie Patton who possibly never told the truth in his life."

"Do you ever lie?"

"I've lied four times. But each time I was very tired. That's not an excuse", he added.

"I lied a lot when I was a little girl. But mostly it was making up stories. Or I hope so. But I have never lied to my own advantage."

"I have", said the Colonel. "Four times."

"Would you have been a general if you had not lied?"

"If I had lied as others lied, I would have been a three-star general." (Ch. xii)

This reminds me of Bluntschli's answer to Raina in Act III of Shaw's *Arms and the Man* when she claims that she has told only two lies in her life. He says that he considers himself fairly honest, but that number wouldn't get him through the average morning. The posturing is much more ridiculous in *Across the River and into the Trees* because of the pompousness of Cantwell and the total lack of humor with which Hemingway makes this claim for him. Put another way, it is one more indication of Hemingway's loss of perspective in the novel.

5

The toughness and tough talk which increases so jarringly in Hemingway's work in the 1930's has already received some illustration.[30] It appears in the original version of "A Natural History of the Dead" when the story is told to the "old lady" in *Death in the Afternoon*:

The only natural death I've ever seen, outside of loss of blood, which isn't bad, was death from Spanish influenza. In this you drown in mucus, choking, and how you know the patient's dead is; at the end he shits the bed full. (Ch. xii)

When the story was reprinted in the collected short stories Hemingway altered this to read,

how you know the patient's dead is: at the end he turns to be a little child again, though with his manly force, and fills the sheets as full as any diaper with one vast, final, yellow cataract that flows and dribbles on after he's gone.

It appears indirectly in *Green Hills of Africa* as Hemingway's bitter jealousy when Karl shoots a bigger rhino, though it is Pop (the professional hunter) who says, "I never felt more a four-letter man" (Ch. iv) – a self-conscious euphemism which recurs in "The Short Happy Life of Francis Macomber":

"You have such a pretty way of putting things, Francis", Margot Macomber said. Wilson looked at them both. If a four-letter man marries a five-letter woman, he was thinking, what number of letters would their children be?

[30] The toughness is an extension of an early trait. Sean O'Faolain in *The Vanishing Hero: Studies in Novelists of the Twenties* (London, Eyre and Spottiswoode, 1956) sees it as a fear of sentimentality or tenderness, a "roughness which rings false", as in the early poem "Oklahoma" (pp. 148-149): "Pull an arrow out:/If you break it/The wound closes./Salt is good too/And wood ashes./Pounding it throbs in the night – /(or is it the gonorrhea)." "Oklahoma" was first printed in *Three Stories and Ten Poems* (Paris, Contact Publishing Co., 1923), p. 50.

(I suspect that it is some more disguised overstatement which also produces these thoughts of Wilson's: "This Macomber was an odd one though. Damned if he wasn't. Now the wife. Well, the wife. Yes, the wife. Hm, the wife. Well he'd dropped all that.")

It appears more directly in *Green Hills of Africa* when Hemingway gives himself a tongue lashing for gut-shooting a sable bull:

But that damned sable bull. I should have killed him; but it was a running shot. ... Yes, you bastard, but what about the cow you missed twice, prone, standing, broadside? ... Every damned thing is your own fault if you're any good. I thought I could shoot a shotgun better than I could and I had lost plenty of money backing my opinion but I knew, coldly and outside myself, that I could shoot a rifle on game as well as any son of a bitch that ever lived. Like hell I could. ... Hell, everybody is off sometime. You've got no bloody business to be off. Who the hell are you? My conscience? Listen, I'm all right with my conscience. I know just what kind of a son of a bitch I am and I know what I can do well. (Ch. xiii)

Several of Robert Jordan's tough dialogues with himself sound remarkably similar. After he has killed a fascist cavalryman, he and "himself" have an argument in which "himself" tells him that he has no right to kill unless to prevent something worse happening to others:

So get it straight and do not lie to yourself.

But I won't keep a count of people I have killed as though it were a trophy record or a disgusting business like notches in a gun, he told himself. I have a right to not keep count and I have a right to forget them.

No, himself said. You have no right to forget anything. You have no right to shut your eyes to any of it nor any right to forget any of it nor to soften it nor to change it.

Shut up, he told himself. You're getting awfully pompous.

Nor ever to deceive yourself about it, himself went on. (Ch. xxvi)

From this Jordan goes on to recite his credo – "You believe in Liberty, Equality and Fraternity. You believe in Life, Liberty and the Pursuit of Happiness" – then to reassure himself that what he feels for Maria is *true* and that he is lucky even if he dies tomorrow. The feelings which are brought out in the open here and argued make Hemingway uneasy, as does the garrulous argument, partly because he thinks them dangerous and partly because they sound pretentious to him; the result, I think, is various defensive reactions: deflation by toughness, having Jordan call himself pompous, assure himself it is true.

In terms of the novel, Jordan recognizes the tough talk, like talking too much, to be a reaction to danger; rage, like many other reactions, is escapist. (Cantwell later recognizes that there is something wrong with his tough talk and is continually telling himself not to be so rough.) In terms of Hemingway and his work, I think it is talking too much which he feels to be the danger, with a following reaction of tough talk which he also feels to be a false note.

Let us observe first of all the association between danger and talking too much. After a close brush with a fascist cavalry patrol searching for the cavalryman that Jordan shot, Jordan "felt the need to talk that, with him, was the sign that there had just been much danger. He could always tell how bad it had been by the strength of the desire to talk that came after"; "It must have been bad enough when the leader of the first patrol of cavalry had pointed toward the entry because they were all talking very much. Too much, Robert Jordan thought" (Ch. xxiii).

This is like the reaction of Nick in "A Way You'll Never Be" when he feels "it coming on again" (a crazy spell, the result of his fear); he tries to "hold it in" but can't, babbling a lecture about locusts and grasshoppers and telling Captain Paravicini why he is qualified to command: "You can read and write, can't you?" After a heart attack, Colonel Cantwell delivers an amusing lecture to the concierge about "energy crackers", which have "something in it that keeps you from getting erections. It's like the atomic bomb, only played backwards": "He was talking too much to regain confidence quickly" (Ch. xxiii). That Hemingway feels the talking itself to be a danger appears clearly in *Green Hills of Africa* when Kandisky starts him lecturing on American literature: "You must take more beer to loosen your tongue", Kandisky says, and Hemingway replies, "It's loose. ... It's always too bloody loose" (Ch. i).

Jordan sounds more than a little like Nick babbling about the locusts when he is placing the charges under the bridge:

"The other side now, *viejo*", he shouted up to Anselmo and climbed across through the trestling, like a bloody Tarzan in a rolled steel forest, he thought. ... Come on. Don't get excited. Do it. Clean and fast as the last one. Don't fumble with it. Take your time. Don't try to do it faster than you can. ... You're shaking, like a Goddamn woman. What the hell is the matter with you? You're trying to do it too fast. I'll bet that Goddamn woman up above isn't shaking. ... She'll shake if she gets in enough. Like everybody bloody else.

. . . .

You have a nice thinking head old Jordan. Roll Jordan, Roll! They used to yell that at football when you lugged the ball. Do you know the damned Jordan is really not much bigger than that creek down there below. At the source, you mean. So is anything else at the source. This is a place here under this bridge. A home away from home. Come on Jordan, pull yourself together. This is serious Jordan. ... I'm all right now however she goes. As Maine goes so goes the nation. As Jordan goes so go the bloody Israelites. The bridge, I mean. As Jordan goes, so goes the bloody bridge, other way around, really. (Ch. xliii)

(Cf. Nick's trying to slow down his sensations in "Big Two-Hearted River", II, as the excitement of fighting a trout makes him feel sick.)

While waiting for the bombing to begin which will signal that the bridge is to be blown up, Jordan gives himself another patriotic pep talk, with the admonition not to lie to himself at the beginning, not to get excited in the middle, and not to be so pompous at the end:

This is just a holding attack. You must not get illusions about it now. Suppose we got a break-through today? This is our first big attack. Keep your sense of proportion. But what if we should have it? Don't get excited, he told himself. Remember what went up the road. You've done what you could about that. ... You just watch now and do what you should.

Today is only one day in all the days that will ever be. But what will happen in all the other days that ever come can depend on what you do today. It's been that way all this year. It's been that way so many times. All of this war is that way. You are getting very pompous in the early morning, he told himself. (Ch. xliii)

When Jordan worries about his orders, we get some lofty sentiments, followed by toughness and directed thinking about something else:

... there are no people that things must not happen to. Neither you nor this old man is anything. You are instruments to do your duty. There are necessary orders that are no fault of yours and there is a bridge and that bridge can be the point on which the future of the human race can turn. As it can turn on everything that happens in this war. You have only one thing to do and you must do it. Only one thing, hell, he thought. If it were one thing it was easy. Stop worrying, you windy bastard, he said to himself. Think about something else.

So he thought about the girl Maria. ... (Ch. iii)

Besides his talkiness which annoys him, Jordan has an elaborate list of don'ts which are a reaction to fear and expansiveness. Again, in terms of the novel, Jordan has to fight against various attractive escapes, which he does by prescribing for himself as though he were his own doctor; but in terms of Hemingway's relation to his work, these are various pretentious poses to avoid, in the name of the plain hard truth:

Don't worry, he told himself. ... Either you will have to blow that bridge in the morning or you will not have to. But do not start deceiving yourself into thinking you won't have to blow it. ... It is not you who decides what shall be done. You follow orders. Follow them and do not try to think beyond them.

The orders on this are very clear. Too very clear. But you must not worry nor must you be frightened. For if you allow yourself the luxury of normal fear that fear will infect those who must work with you.

. . . .

Don't kid yourself, he said. You do it all perfectly O.K. Cold. Without kidding yourself. You aren't going to see Durán any more and it is of no importance. Don't be that way either, he told himself. Don't go in for any of those luxuries.

Nor for heroic resignation either. We do not want any citizens full of heroic resignation in these hills. (Ch. xxx)

It is obvious that Jordan (and Hemingway) feels that he must walk a tightrope between poses, like "the English pose of understatement" and "Latin bravado". Neither silence (or its verbal equivalent, understatement) nor talking (or its verbal equivalent, expansiveness) is safe.

This is the picture of a man who sees potential danger in every feeling – even feelings that are not overt (except on the pages of the novel). Accordingly, he sees anger and tough talk also as escapist – i.e., as feelings that may give him away:

He grinned at Maria again but the grin was still no deeper than the skin that felt tight over his cheekbones and his mouth.

She thinks you're wonderful, he thought. I think you stink. And the *gloria* and all that nonsense that you had. You had wonderful ideas, didn't you? You had this world all taped, didn't you? The hell with all of that.

Take it easy, he told himself. Don't get into a rage. That's just a way out too. There are always ways out. You've got to bite on the nail now. There isn't any need to deny everything there's been just because you are going to lose it. Don't be like some damned snake with a broken back biting at itself; and your back isn't broken either, you hound. Wait until you're hurt before you start to cry. Wait until the fight before you get angry. (Ch. xxxviii)

Everything is a "way out" – a falsification. The figure of the snake biting at itself is reminiscent of the hyena in *Green Hills of Africa*, snapping at its own entrails when it is shot, a dirty joke to the gun bearer M'Cola (Ch. ii). It is the image of misdirected anger which is both obscene and ludicrous – a recognition on Hemingway's part that there is something wrong with the outbursts of rage and tough talk in his later work.

Colonel Cantwell also expresses this sense of having hit a false note when he repeatedly tells himself not to be rough (at the same time he cannot resist the tough talk, and Hemingway presents him as something out of the ordinary because of his "wild-boar truculence"). Here Cantwell breaks the "spell" in joking with the *Gran Maestro* and thinks,

why am I always a bastard and why can I not suspend this trade of arms, and be a kind and good man as I would have wished to be.

I try always to be just, but I am brusque and I am brutal, and it is not that I have erected the defense against brown-nosing my superiors and brown-nosing the world. I should be a better man with less wild boar blood in the small time which remains. We will try it out tonight, he thought. With whom, he thought, and where, and God help me not to be bad. (Ch. vii)

However, this "wild boar blood" is clearly a sign of the hero:

The Colonel took the drink Arnaldo, the glass-eyed waiter, made him. He did not want it, and he knew that it was bad for him.

But he took it with his old wild-boar truculence, as he had taken everything all of his life, and he moved, still cat-like when he moved, although it was an old cat now, over to the open window. ... (Ch. viii)

We even get passages in which Cantwell instructs Renata in the pose of toughness, as when he has successfully knocked two sailors unconscious, in spite of his bad heart: "Let's walk so we make even the backs of our legs look dangerous" (Ch. xl). Earlier he teaches her a little tough talk to use on the writer with the pitted face, which she practices on the *Gran Maestro*: " 'Listen, Mac. You hired out to be tough, didn't you?' the girl hard-worded him" (Ch. xxvi). Observe the grotesque simile when Renata has told him that he is going to have to tell her more about his war experiences:

"*Have to?*" the Colonel said and the cruelty and resolution showed in his strange eyes as clearly as when the hooded muzzle of the gun of a tank swings toward you.
"Did you say *have* to, Daughter?" (Ch. xii)

What is wrong with such passages is not primarily a matter of the author intruding, as Halliday suggests.[31] Rather, it is the all-pervasive nature of the tough reaction, which, like other reactions to expansiveness, seems to get entirely out of hand in *Across the River and into the Trees*. Its deflationary intent is quite plain in passages like these:

She kissed him kind, and hard, and desperately, and the Colonel could not think about any fights or any picturesque or strange incidents. He only thought of her ... and how close life comes to death when there is ecstasy. And what the hell is ecstasy and what's ecstasy's rank and serial number? ... Yes, ecstasy is what you might have had and instead you draw sleep's other brother.
Death is a lot of shit, he thought. (Ch. xxviii)

"Don't you feel better to be loved?"
"Yes", the Colonel said. "I feel as though I were out on some bare-assed hill where it was too rocky to dig, and the rocks all solid, but with nothing jutting, and no bulges, and all of a sudden instead of being there naked, I was armoured. Armoured and the eighty-eights not there."

"You should tell that to our writer friend with the craters of the moon face so he could write it tonight."

"I ought to tell it to Dante if he was around," the Colonel, suddenly gone as rough as the sea when a line squall comes up, said. (Ch. xii)

(Note the awkward periodic construction of the last sentence.)

Together with a number of would-be humorous deflating wisecracks, this directionless toughness creates much of the embarrassingly distorted tone of the novel:

You have to be a tough boy in this town to be loved, the Colonel thought. ... And what is a tough boy, he asked himself. You use it so loosely you should be able to define it. I suppose it is a man who will make his play and then backs it up. Or just a man who backs his play. And I'm not thinking of the theatre, he thought. (Ch. vi)

What a fine, compact and, yet, ready to be air-borne building, he thought. I never realized a small church could look like a P47. ... Damn, I wish I might walk around this town all my life. All my life, he thought. What a gag that is. A gag to gag on. A throttle to throttle you with. Come on, boy, he said to himself. No horse named Morbid ever won a race. (Ch. ix)

Hemingway continues to use the device in Part I of *The Dangerous Summer*, with no more success: "... Miguel looks and behaves the best in adversity of any man I've ever seen and I have seen many men in adversity. It is a tough town to play." [32]

Occasionally Cantwell sounds like Jordan mulling over words and their foreign equivalents to see which is the most expressive; but, characteristically, Cantwell winds up the expansive with a silly deflating wisecrack:

... do not even think rough, he told himself. You have to be good now in every way until you say good-bye. What a word, he thought, good-bye.

It sounds like a Valentine slogan.

Good-bye and *bonne chance* and *hasta la vista*. We always just said *merde* and let it go at that. Farewell, he thought, that is a nice word. It sings well, he thought. Farewell, a long farewell and take it with you where you go. With handles, he thought. (Ch. xxxviii)

At other times the characters themselves become self-conscious about their dialogue in a way reminiscent of some of the conversations in *For Whom the Bell Tolls*:

"I have known you a long time, Colonel. Or maybe it just seems a long time", the surgeon told him.

"It's been a long time", the Colonel said.

"We sound like song writers", the surgeon said. "But don't you ever run into anything, or let any sparks strike you, when you're really souped up on nitroglycerin. They ought to make you drag a chain like a high-octane truck." (Ch. ii)

Having seen the connection between toughness and overstatement (expansiveness) in other work should make the toughness more understandable in *To Have and Have Not*. What might otherwise seem a rather pointless rage and bitterness is very likely part of the toughness that Hemingway employs to deflate exaggeration. The exaggeration is not just a matter of style but of "satiric" scenes where Hemingway is exposing phonies. For example, the whole incident between Frederick Harrison, his secretary, and Captain Willie is unbelievable. Harrison tries to take it upon himself to arrest Harry Morgan for bootlegging, informing Captain Willie, "For your information, I'm one of the three most important men in the United States today." Captain Willie maneuvers close to Harry's boat to warn him, but the others think that he is helping them:

"You're really capturing him single-handed", said the secretary admiringly.

"And unarmed, too", said Frederick Harrison.

"With no G men nonsense", said the secretary.

"Edgar Hoover exaggerates his publicity", said Frederick Harrison. "I feel we've given him about enough rope." (Ch. vii)

Instead of helping them, Captain Willie shouts to Harry, "I got a guy here on board some kind of a stool from Washington", and, "I'm taking this big alphabet man fishing until dark." The chapter ends with him doing just that, taunting Harrison about his importance. Atkins is right in saying, "When hatred or dislike get the better of him Hemingway's accuracy suffers" (p. 83). And nothing brings out this hatred, or one might call it this exposé motive, in Hemingway so readily and with such likelihood of distortion as a phony does. The exposé motive is surely related to

Hemingway's passion for truth-telling, but nearly always it is truth-telling, exposing the lie or the fake, in its distorted form so familiar in Hemingway's later work.

It is partly in reaction to such overdone scenes, I think, that Hemingway overdoes the toughness of so much dialogue. Here are a pair of exchanges between Harry and Bee-lips, the lawyer:

"I'll get a boat. I'll carry them to hell."

"That isn't a bad idea."

"Don't mouth that now. Keep your mouth off my business."

"Listen, you big murdering slob", said Bee-lips, "I try to help you out and get you in on something – "

"And all you do is poison me. Shut up. You're poison to anybody that ever touched you."

"Cut it out, you bully."

"Take it easy", Harry said. (Ch. xiii)

"You are a goddamn rat."

"Well, I never killed anybody", Bee-lips told him.

"Nor you never will. Come on, let's get out of here. Just being with you makes me feel crummy."

"Maybe you are crummy."

"Can you get them from talking?"

"If you don't paper your mouth."

"Paper yours then." (Ch. xv)

The sophomoric tough talk is not limited to dialogue, but occurs in Harry's talking to himself as well. In the following passage he is preparing to shoot the Cubans on Freddy's boat:

Quit stalling, he said to himself. Come on, quit stalling. Where're your balls now? Under my chin, I guess, he thought.

. . . .

Twenty-one to a clip is four bursts of five at the most, he thought. I got to be light-fingered. All right. Come on. Quit stalling, you gutless wonder. Christ, what I'd give for another one. Well, there isn't any other one now. (Ch. xviii)

This passage is reminiscent of Robert Jordan tongue-lashing himself or of Hemingway doing the same thing in *Green Hills of Africa*.

It is tougher than most of Santiago's interior monologues in *The Old Man and the Sea*, though they sometimes have a note of asperity:

It is silly not to hope, he thought. Besides I believe it is a sin. Do not think about sin, he thought. There are enough problems now without sin. Also I have no understanding of it.

I have no understanding of it and I am not sure that I believe in it. Perhaps it was a sin to kill the fish. I suppose it was even though I did it to keep me alive and feed many people. But then everything is a sin. Do not think about sin. It is much too late for that and there are people who are paid to do it. Let them think about it. (pp. 115-116)

(Is it accidental that in so many of these passages the thinker is wrestling with the question of killing? I suspect a guilty conscience.)

The Old Man and the Sea, as Levin remarks in the preface to his reprinted article on Hemingway's style, is Hemingway "neither at his best nor at his worst but at his most typical", but the hero, "described by the author as 'simple', turns out to be a garrulous character who talks to himself in the Hispanese of *For Whom the Bell Tolls*, translated or explained by Hemingway in a manner which is pedagogical, if not pedantic" (p. 140). Enough of Levin's comment is true for us to see how *The Old Man and the Sea* is connected with the expansiveness of Hemingway's later work. In this novel, however, he seems to have come to grips more successfully with that tendency of his style, so that many of the reactions which marred the other late work are absent or less apparent.

6

A frequent appraisal of Hemingway's later work is that its failures are the result of a lack of "discipline" – "discipline" not merely in the sense of perspective or selectivity, but "the strictly modulated feelings, the flat tones which were to impress themselves on a section of American prose", "a sort of rigidity, an iron restraint".[33] For example, compare Edmund Wilson's judgments of *in our time* and *Death in the Afternoon*. In a review titled "Mr. Hemingway's Dry-Points" Wilson praises *in our time* (the early short sketches) for its "cool objective manner", its "dry sharpness" and

[33] Geismar, p. 144.

"artistic dignity". The conclusion to his criticism of *Death in the Afternoon* is, "In short, we are compelled to recognize that, as soon as Hemingway drops the burning-glass of the disciplined and objective art with which he has learned to concentrate in a story the light of the emotions that flood in on him, he straightway becomes befuddled, slops over." [34] It sounds as though Hemingway is a good writer as long as he keeps his feelings thoroughly hidden beneath an "objective", indirect, and inhibited style but becomes a bad writer when he allows those feelings to come out in the open where they may be seen.

Too much criticism of Hemingway implies the same thing, although the idea is rarely stated so explicitly. The point of view is part of a widespread, still current predilection for understatement, irony, and other forms of indirection which is apparent in a review of the film *Exodus*, in which the director is praised like this:

... he has forced his camera to understate. Detention camp, general's garden, stark streets, all bustle into just enough – not too much – life. The very first shot of a line of refugees being loaded on to Army lorries at dockside sets the tone of the film. There are no weeping faces, no winsome tots tugging at their mothers' skirts. There is just a long file of tired, dirty people, carrying everything they own, accustomed to being policed and prodded, simply intent on the business of once more being loaded on to something and shipped off somewhere. That is all; and in it the whole story, from Diaspora to Dachau, is implicit.[35]

It seems to me that this century has not yet recovered from its over-reaction against the excess emotionalism of much of the art of the last century, to the extent that we suffer from the opposite malady – emotional inhibition. As a result movies are praised for

[34] "Mr. Hemingway's Dry-Points", a review in the *Dial*, October 1924, is reprinted in Wilson's *The Shores of Light*; the phrases quoted are on pp. 120-121. The criticism of *Death in the Afternoon* is from "Hemingway: Gauge of Morale", p. 243. Cf. the similar opinions of Frohock, pp. 263-264, and Hoffman, *The Modern Novel in America*, pp. 99 ff. Hoffman sees even *A Farewell to Arms* as a sign of Hemingway's "slowly but perceptibly losing hold of the discipline learned in the early years in Paris".
[35] Stanley Kauffmann, "Double Feature", *The New Republic*, December 19, 1960, p. 22.

having "just enough – not too much – life", and Hemingway is praised when he expresses indirectly feelings for which he is damned when he states them more overtly. The fact is that people still do weep, and the idea that art is best or most realistic when it pictures numb despair is partly an inheritance from the early Hemingway (e.g., "Chapter" ii of *In Our Time*, "Minarets stuck up in the rain", sounds very much like what Kauffmann admires in the film).

It is true that something seems to go wrong when Hemingway becomes more expansive. But the distortion and loss of perspective appears to result in large measure from his sharing the same distrust of emotion, which shows up variously as distrust of words, distrust of talking or thinking, emphasis on simplicity or truth, and so on. Many of the failures of his later work are due to greater expansiveness and explicitness only in the sense that they make him so profoundly uneasy that he exaggerates a number of mannerisms and deflationary reactions to try to get back the "truth" which he associates with restraint.

Why he is better able one time than another to handle expansiveness successfully is a matter of conjecture, but obviously the success of his work is not just a matter of the presence or absence of adjectives, to take one example. Any device, from the use of foreignism to the increased conscious use of symbolism in his later work, can be well or poorly done – and it is here that the writer's selectivity and judgment must be measured, not by whether he understates less than he used to. Yet the critical view that the restrained and indirect method is somehow innately superior or more truthful appears to me to account for some of the current high opinion of *The Sun Also Rises*, though the more expansive *A Farewell to Arms* is (I think) by far the better novel.

Related to the question of the stylistic method of "discipline" is another problem which may be termed that of Jamesian realism. The "objective" method, that is, seems most real to many readers and critics because they view fiction according to the conventions which James elaborated (in theory, at least) – for example, consistency of point of view and absence of authorial comment. However, it is a grave mistake to try to judge Hemingway's work by these conventions, for he simply does not aim at that sort of realism. It is one thing to say, with Young, that among the reasons for the failure of *Across the River and into the Trees* is the lack of distance between Hemingway and his hero (p. 90), so that Cantwell sounds almost as though he thinks he is being interviewed (like Hemingway himself in *Green Hills of Africa*). But it is something quite different to say, with Levin, "An increasing tendency for the author to intrude, commenting in his own person, is one of the weaknesses of *Across the River*" (p. 162).

On this point I find myself in complete disagreement with E. M. Halliday in his article "Hemingway's Narrative Perspective". Briefly, Halliday posits that Hemingway is a realist of the Jamesian variety, then criticizes him whenever he fails to maintain the realistic conventions. Thus he treats the first-person point of view in *The Sun Also Rises* and *A Farewell to Arms* as an expression of the theme of emotional isolation but finds the latter less realistic because there are more subjective passages where he looks for "objective epitome" (pp. 209-210). Similarly, he thinks most of the trouble with *To Have and Have Not* is its lack of consistent narrative perspective and the intrusive omniscient author who knows and tells all about the disagreeable characters at the yacht basin at Key West (pp. 211, 213-214). Of *For Whom the Bell Tolls* he contends that the third-person point of view is "very well suited to the investigation of human interdependence" (p. 215), without mentioning Hemingway's many short stories in the third person which have the opposite or a different theme. With *Across the River and into the Trees* he again concentrates on "the same intrusive commentator, gone sentimental, who plagued the reader of *To Have and Have Not*" (p. 217).

There are two main objections to this line of criticism. First of all, the so-called intrusive comments may be intrusive from the view of Jamesian realism, but there is nothing to indicate that Hemingway feels bound to any such view. Some of the most renowned and most frequently quoted passages even in Hemingway's early work are bits of philosophizing or "moralizing" to establish a theme and have little to do with any theory of absolute verisimilitude or consistency of point of view. They include Jake's alcoholic philosophizing in Chapter xiv of *The Sun Also Rises* ("I did not care what it was all about. All I wanted to know was how to live in it. Maybe if you found out how to live in it you learned from that what it was all about") and in *A Farewell to Arms* such passages as Frederic Henry on the obscenity of abstract words (Ch. xxvii), the difference between the night and the day and how the world breaks and kills everyone (Ch. xxxiv), and how they "threw you in and told you the rules and the first time they caught you off base they killed you" (Ch. xli).

This leads to my second objection: that Hemingway is more interested in establishment of mood or theme than he is in strict verisimilitude in the Jamesian sense. His style, for example, rarely characterizes a given person. There is little difference in style whether Pilar or Jordan is supposed to be thinking or talking, and Andrés sounds almost exactly like Jordan talking to himself:

You have no family but a brother who goes to battle tomorrow and you own nothing but the wind and the sun and an empty belly. The wind is small, he thought, and there is no sun. You have four grenades in your pocket but they are only good to throw away. You have a carbine on your back but it is only good to give away bullets. You have a message to give away. And you're full of crap that you can give to the earth, he grinned in the dark. You can anoint it also with urine. Everything you have is to give. Thou art a phenomenon of philosophy and an unfortunate man, he told himself and grinned again. (Ch. xxxiv)

The style is appropriate, if anything, to the mood or tone that Hemingway wants to create. For example, observe the difference in style between the first sentence and the last two in this description of Marie Morgan looking at her husband:

She watched him go out of the house, tall, wide-shouldered, flat-backed, his hips narrow, moving, still, she thought, like some kind of animal, easy and swift and not old yet, he moves so light and smooth-like, she thought, and when he got in the car she saw him blonde, with the sunburned hair, his face with the broad mongol cheek bones, and the narrow eyes, the nose broken at the bridge, the wide mouth and the round jaw, and getting in the car he grinned at her and she began to cry. "His goddamn face", she thought. "Everytime I see his goddamn face it makes me want to cry." (Ch. xiv)

The style of the first sentence is certainly not a realistic approximation of Marie's thinking, in spite of the words "she thought". This is Hemingway's more expansive lyrical style, used for hyperbolic effect, just as Marie's *goddamns* are tough talk used for deflation and to suggest "reality".

In the same way Santiago's "thoughts" about birds on the sea are not realistic characterization of the old man; the style conveys the author's attitude, sets a tone or mood:

He was sorry for the birds, especially the small delicate dark terns that were always flying and looking and almost never finding, and he thought, The birds have a harder life than we do except for the robber birds and the heavy strong ones. Why did they make birds so delicate and fine as those sea swallows when the ocean can be so cruel? She is kind and very beautiful. But she can be so cruel and it comes so suddenly and such birds that fly, dipping and hunting, with their small sad voices are made too delicately for the sea. (p. 32)

This is no more realistic than some of Frederic Henry's "literary" thoughts about Catherine.

It is simply a mistake to view Hemingway as a Jamesian realist, a mistake which leads to inaccurate descriptions of his work. It leads Beach, for instance, to say that as a realist seeking unvarnished truth Hemingway on the whole "doesn't aim at satire; that in itself is too showy a line" (p. 99). Yet Hemingway cannot portray a fake, phony, or tourist without attempting satire, and his feelings are apparently so violent on the subject of such people and of exposing them that the result is often serious distortion.

The attempt to fit Hemingway into so stringent a mold, like the praise of his "discipline" and objectivity, seems part of the general reaction against excesses of nineteenth-century literature, a reaction that includes James's theories of verisimilitude and consistency of narrative perspective. We are so steeped in the conventions and assumptions of realism that we find it difficult even when someone points it out to recognize how thoroughly they determine our ideas of what is good art and what is artistically "true". Hemingway, like many modern writers, emphasizes the truth or reality of his writing (though more than most). Still, protestations and indirection do not make either his method or his content the most real.

V

PHONIES AND HEROES

1

A great deal has been written about Hemingway's heroes and their "code" but not very much about their opposite number, Hemingway's phonies. Yet (the heroes are often defined by contrast with the phonies, just as truth is very often defined for Hemingway by exposing the fake or the lie.) It is not enough to describe the rejects from Hemingway's value system, morality, or "code" as *outsiders* (the heroes also are generally outsiders, but good ones): they are *fakes* for him, to be exposed with the same single-minded purpose we see in his stern moralistic determination to tell the truth and give the lie) While this may sound like a noble undertaking, Hemingway's overemphasis frequently results in his phonies being given short shrift. Caricature, distortion, exaggeration, "satire", "irony" are common practice in his exposure of fakes.

The phony most conceded to be a phony in Hemingway's stories is doubtless Robert Cohn, "perhaps the most fashionable whipping boy of modern American literature" because of "the mistake of adopting uncritically the prejudices of the book's characters" (i.e., the heroes' prejudices).[1] It is understandable but regrettable that a critical article should have to be devoted to Cohn's defense. The fact is, however, that an examination of what is supposedly wrong with Cohn, the most skillfully handled of Hemingway's phonies, can show us a lot about what is wrong with other fakes – and vice versa. As James T. Farrell observes

[1] Arthur L. Scott, "In Defense of Robert Cohn", *College English*, XVIII (March 1957), 309.

(p. 225), Cohn's difference from the other characters is one of the central concerns of *The Sun Also Rises*.

Here I must add that this is Hemingway's value system, not mine: the article defending Cohn repeatedly accuses critics of condemning him when they seem to be trying to explain the code and how he fails to live up to it.[2] However, the critics themselves may be partly to blame, for in Hemingway's best noncommittal manner they often describe without explicitly evaluating, so that it is possible to take them as championing the code – as Baker sometimes does champion it. Therefore at the outset I want to make clear that I think the code decidedly questionable.

Just what is wrong with Robert Cohn? Among other things, he is a Jew, a fact that the other characters do not let us forget in remarks like Jake's about Cohn's "hard, Jewish, stubborn streak" (Ch. ii) or Brett's about how difficult it has been to have "that damned Jew" around (Ch. xvi). Since the whole question of anti-Semitism is such a vexed one today, it is virtually impossible to treat this matter as the minor point it is – i.e., by mentioning it in an offhand way or relegating it to a footnote. I want to discuss the point first so that we can get on to Cohn's more serious faults, those that he shares with other phonies.

Cohn's Jewishness bears about the same relation to his other failings as the pitted face of the tourist-writer so ridiculed in *Across the River and into the Trees* does to his being a phony. Each seems to be just one more, slightly irrelevant item in a thoroughgoing dislike; neither item is particularly "reasonable" except perhaps in emotional terms, as when one finds more and more reasons to confirm a dislike that he already holds. Yet each appears early in the presentation of the phonies, before their other failings are known, so that its logic again is more emotional

---

[2] One example is Scott's accusing Atkins of condemning Cohn for kissing and telling (p. 311) and for refusing to admit defeat in his courtship of Brett (p. 312), actions which Scott proceeds to defend. But the passage that Scott objects to is one where Atkins is explaining the code: "The code is best illustrated in *Fiesta*, particularly in the passages where Cohn persistently breaks it by refusing to admit defeat, by discussing his own emotions, and by being altogether too loquacious about certain 'banned' subjects" (p. 192). (*Fiesta* is the title of the British edition of *The Sun Also Rises*.)

than chronological (e.g., Cantwell dislikes the pitted face long before he learns that the man is a tourist-writer).

To be sure, a Jew can be a villain or a phony like anyone else; the difficulty is that the Jew *is* the traditional scapegoat of Christians, and I think it a mistake to fall into such convolutions of irony that one gets lost in anti-anti-prejudice.[3] The simple fact appears to be that Hemingway shared what was a fashionable attitude of the 1920's when he made an issue of Cohn's Jewishness – in spite of his protests to the contrary.[4] Cohn's Jewishness seems to represent for Hemingway a kind of symbol of the supercilious New York critics and rich literary dilettantes whom he has always hated. It is also connected with Cohn's sensitivity, his readiness to take offense and to fight, and with his air of superiority: the first thing Jake tells us about Cohn is how he learned to box, though

[3] Malcolm Cowley in *Exile's Return*, pp. 20-21, explains how "we" (himself and Kenneth Burke?) evolved a theory of convolutions while at Peabody High School in Pittsburgh. The "first convolution" was to say the opposite of what one's audience expected; the "second convolution" was to say what one's audience might conventionally expect one to say, when they were expecting the opposite; etc. The pitfalls of such extremes of "irony" are evident when it is used to try to dissociate a writer from his time in order to make him more "proper" and acceptable for contemporary times (the attempt to "sterilize" Shakespeare's attitude in his presentation of Shylock is a classic example of misused ironic detachment, the kind of thing that should be avoided with Hemingway). I doubt that Hemingway is that detached.

[4] Scott quotes Hemingway as saying, when he learned that the anti-Semitic comments were deleted from a paperback reprint of *The Sun Also Rises* without his or Scribner's knowledge, "If you think the book is anti-Semitic you must be out of your mind or at least not in full possession of your critical faculties" (p. 310). If Hemingway is quoted accurately (I have been unable to trace the original of this statement), he is not entirely ingenuous. A letter to Sherwood Anderson, May 21, 1926, in which Hemingway tries to explain his motives in writing *The Torrents of Spring*, suggests that he did hold an attitude common then but become socially inadmissible since. The letter is in the Anderson manuscript collection of The Newberry Library, Chicago. Now cf. Ch. xix in which Mike explains that Brett has no money because she pays 350 pounds in interest to Jews every year: "They're not really Jews. We just call them Jews. They're Scotsmen, I believe"; or cf. Ch. iii in which Jake makes fun of Cohn for the way he stares at Brett: "He looked a great deal as his compatriot must have looked when he saw the promised land. Cohn, of course, was much younger. But he had that look of eager, deserving expectation."

he disliked boxing, in order to "counteract the feeling of in-
feriority and shyness he had felt on being treated as a Jew at
Princeton"; Bill phrases both his and Jake's dislike when he says
that Cohn is too "superior and Jewish" (Ch. x). Jewishness does
not appear as a count against subsequent phonies, but being rich
or being the wrong sort of writer often does.

Like his original, Harold Loeb, Cohn is a former rich boy who
backed a little magazine until his money ran out. When the novel
opens, he is a tourist-writer, "fairly happy, except that, like many
people living in Europe, he would rather have been in America,
and he had discovered writing" (Ch. i). In all this, Cohn closely
resembles the phony tourist-writer of "Mr. and Mrs. Eliot". (I
doubt that the name is sheer accident, since in 1924, in a tribute
to the recently deceased Conrad, Hemingway announced hyper-
bolically that if he could bring Conrad back to life by grinding
T. S. Eliot into a fine dry powder and sprinkling the powder over
Conrad's grave, he would set off the next morning for London
with a sausage grinder.[5] "Mr. and Mrs. Elliot" was first published
in the *Little Review*, Autumn and Winter 1924-25.)

Here are some of the counts against the Elliots: "He was a
poet with an income of nearly ten thousand dollars a year. He
wrote very long poems very rapidly" (Hemingway wrote slowly
and carefully). "He was twenty-five years old and had never gone
to bed with a woman until he married Mrs. Elliot. He wanted to
keep himself pure" (he is sexually deficient and a prude). He
learned how to kiss "from hearing a fellow tell a story once".
They are sexual failures not only on their wedding night, but
they keep trying to have a baby "as often as Mrs. Elliot could
stand it". Finally Mrs. Elliot's girl friend joins them, takes over
the typing and sleeps with Mrs. Elliot, while Elliot occupies his
nights by writing long poems. They and their friends congregate
at the Café du Dome, "avoiding the Rotonde across the street
because it is always so full of foreigners", and they do not appreciate Touraine, which they merely find to be "a very flat hot
country very much like Kansas". When Mr. Elliot has enough
poems for a book, he pays a publisher to publish them.

[5] *the transatlantic review*, II (September 1924), 341-342.

The last paragraph of the story is a fair sample of its "irony", the kind of distorted tone that comes over Hemingway so often when he deals with phonies:

Elliot had taken to drinking white wine and lived apart in his own room. He wrote a great deal of poetry during the night and in the morning looked very exhausted. Mrs. Elliot and the girl friend now slept together in the big mediaeval bed. They had many a good cry together. In the evening they all sat at dinner together in the garden under a plane tree and the hot evening wind blew and Elliot drank white wine and Mrs. Elliot and the girl friend made conversation and they were all quite happy.

According to Fenton (p. 261), Hemingway thought of "Mr. and Mrs. Elliot" as a funny story. Perhaps it is funny if one adopts the point of view of the Hemingway hero; otherwise it is unpleasant, like other stories devoted to the absurdity of outsiders and fakes. What humor there is, is too much tinged with the superiority of the hero, looking out or down on those unfortunates not "in the know". "Whenever Hemingway tries to write about the Elliots of this world, or the rich people in *To Have and Have Not*, he does not give them half a chance." [6]

Being (relatively) rich is one of Robert Cohn's minor sins, a sin mainly because it is associated with his failure to appreciate values. It is not a sin with the rich Count Mippipopolous, whom Brett calls "one of us", because he has "lived very much" and therefore now "can enjoy everything so well". Jake agrees "absolutely" with the Count's conclusion: "That is the secret. You must get to know the values" (Ch. vii). Cohn has not only lost or squandered most of his inheritance, in the process learning how much he enjoyed being sole editor of the little magazine supported by his money, but his mother has rescued him, settling an allowance on him of about three hundred dollars a month (Ch. i). (Somehow it is different with Mike, who is also on an allowance from home.) By contrast, Jake, who knows values, realizes, "You paid some way for everything that was any good. . . . Either you paid by learning about them, or by experience, or by taking chances, or by money" (Ch. xiv).

[6] George Hemphill, "Hemingway and James", in McCaffery, p. 338.

In the 1930's Hemingway tends to take the fact of being rich as prima-facie evidence of loss of values. Thus Harry, the sold-out writer of "The Snows of Kilimanjaro", has been corrupted by the "bloody money" of his "rich bitch" companion – though he is an equivocal figure, not a clear-cut phony, since he accuses himself of having destroyed his talent with luxury. Yet that does not prevent him from indulging in bitter tirades on the wrong done him: "Your damned money was my armour. My Swift and my Armour." Besides, he thinks of himself as not really being one of the very rich but a spy in their country, and Hemingway has him recall an anecdote about "poor Julian" (Fitzgerald) and his romantic awe of the rich – "how he had started a story once that began, 'The very rich are different from you and me.' And how someone had said to Julian, Yes, they have more money." [7]

The most serious distortion occurs in *To Have and Have Not* in the sketches of the "haves" on the yachts at Key West (Ch. xxiv). Except for the "Intrepid Voyagers", Esthonians sailing around in a 34-foot yacht and selling their "sagas" to Esthonian newspapers, the "haves" are a sexually deficient or abnormal lot. The sixty-year-old grain broker, who "had been admirably endowed for a speculative career because he had possessed extraordinary sexual vitality which gave him the confidence to gamble well", with his "now useless and disproportionately large equipment that had once been his pride", is unable to sleep from remorse at having tried to outsmart the Internal Revenue Bureau and must drink some "chemical courage" though the doctor warns it will kill him.

[7] By 1950 Hemingway has apparently become enough of a "have" himself, or identified himself sufficiently with the "haves", that he now finds the new rich to be the phonies (they are late comers, like the tourists he dislikes). Renata explains, "Did you think I was a snob because I come from an old family? We're the ones who are not snobs. The snobs are what you call jerks, and the people with all the new money. Did you ever see so much new money?" (Ch. xxxvii). In "The Helpless Hero of Ernest Hemingway", *Science and Society*, XVII (Winter 1953), 19, Lois L. Barnes comments with asperity on the aristocratic strain in Hemingway: "Not having born to the purple, making his way up, he has been envious of the American aristocracy and has made heavy fun of tourists and of young men out of the clubs of Princeton and Yale. But he has modeled his heroes after their aloof, arrogant, dead-pan manner, and has taught them to perfect it."

On the next yacht "a pleasant, dull and upright family are asleep", rich from selling an unnamed product which costs three cents a quart to make and sells for a dollar a bottle in the large pint size "and the product's really good"; the fiancé of the daughter, Frances, is a Skull and Bones man, voted most likely to succeed: "The type of man who is tapped for Bones is rarely also tapped for bed; but with a lovely girl like Frances intention counts as much as performance." On another yacht is Henry Carpenter, postponing "his inevitable suicide by a matter of weeks if not of months", by indulging the "rather special pleasures" of his homosexual rich host, Wallace Johnston. Finally, there is Dorothy Hollis, mistress of "a professional son-in-law of the very rich", putting herself to sleep with luminol and masturbation.

By contrast, we get the outlaw hero Harry Morgan, who is poor but sexually proficient – unlike another foil, Richard Gordon, not only an unsuccessful lover with the rich Helène Bradley, who collects writers, but also a sexual failure with his wife, who leaves him for the drunken but manly Professor Mac-Walsey (Ch. xxi). Similarly, Margot Macomber's ill-concealed affair with Wilson marks the nadir of Macomber's life before his conversion to courage and reassertion of male dominance: "The great American boy-men", Wilson thinks. "Damned strange fellow. Probably meant the end of cuckoldry too. . . . Damned good thing. . . . Fear gone like an operation. Something else grew in its place. Main thing a man had. Made him into a man. Women knew it too."

Note that Robert Cohn has been left by a rich wife and dominated by another woman, Frances Clyne – "moulded by the two women who had trained him", Jake says (Ch. vi). "I do not know how people could say such terrible things to Robert Cohn", Jake remarks ironically shortly afterward when Frances is giving Cohn a very bad time. Cohn is one of those people you can say terrible things to, as Mike shows later when he tells Cohn that he ought to like the life of a steer (Ch. xiii). Not the least of Cohn's sexual deficiencies, of course, is the fact that Brett wants nothing more to do with him after their trial interlude at San Sebastian.

Another failing that Cohn shares with numerous other phonies is being a tourist. On the surface, this may seem rather odd, since most of Hemingway's heroes are perennial tourists and Hemingway himself was a sojourner in foreign countries much of his life. But a class of tourists (actually, most of them aside from the hero and his group), very often Americans, are distinguished as tourist-phonies. The distinction lies in the phonies' not having the right sense of values: not being in the know or not recognizing the importance of what they observe, not liking the foreign country or its inhabitants or simply thinking it and its people all very "quaint" – in general, not liking what the heroes like.

Consider, for example, how much of the point of "A Canary for One" is exposé of the lady on the *rapide* to Paris who looks "very wholesome and middle-aged and American", who couldn't have her daughter marrying a foreigner because a friend once told her, "No foreigner can make an American girl a good husband." "American men make the best husbands", the American lady tells the American narrator (who starts "to say suspenders and changed it to braces in the mouth, to keep my English character") and his wife; the story ends with the narrator's "ironic" statement, "We were returning to Paris to set up separate residences." Neither Hemingway nor his heroes have any use for such tourists. When they are phony tourist-writers, they are the worst fakes that Hemingway can conceive.

Cohn is a phony tourist-writer. Even before Cohn's affair with Brett, which Jake admits makes him "blind, unforgivingly jealous" (Ch. x), Jake has a few caustic things to say about Cohn's "stubbornness" – i.e., Cohn doesn't like Paris and he wants to go to South America: "I was sorry for him, but . . . right away you ran up against the two stubbornnesses: South America could fix it and he did not like Paris. He got the first idea out of a book, and I suppose the second came out of a book too" (Ch. ii). It is one of the worst things that Hemingway can say of a writer, to say that he talks like a book or gets his ideas out of books. Jake explains in the same chapter that Cohn got his passion for going to South America from reading *The Purple Land* by W. H. Hudson: "Cohn, I believe, took every word of 'The Purple Land' as literally as though it had been an R. G. Dun report." Later Jake comments "ironically", "I wondered where Cohn got that incapacity to enjoy Paris. Possibly from Mencken. Mencken hates Paris, I believe. So many young men get their likes and dislikes from Mencken" (Ch. vi). In Hemingway's value system it is bad enough to get one's ideas out of books without getting them from Mencken. Cohn is obviously a phony.

But Cohn is not only not *simpático* for failing to appreciate Paris, he fails to appreciate other values of the heroes and the clime. For example, when Jake informs him, "Nobody ever lives their life all the way up except bull-fighters", Cohn retorts, "I'm not interested in bull-fighters. That's an abnormal life." "Did you ever think of going to British East Africa to shoot?" Jake asks. "No", Cohn says, "I wouldn't like that." Jake remarks waspishly, "That's because you never read a book about it. Go on and read a book all full of love affairs with the beautiful shiny black princesses" (Ch. ii). If all this sounds slightly like a vaudeville routine, I think the resemblance is more than accidental: exposing the phony somehow usually brings out the unreal note in Hemingway.

The others are quite offended, of course, at Cohn's saying "I'm only afraid I may be bored" when Jake and Bill try to explain how to watch a bullfight selectively so that you won't mind the horses too much – especially Bill, who takes it as a sign of Cohn's "Jewish superiority" (Ch. xv). After the first bullfights Bill asks him repeatedly whether he was bored, joined by Mike, who razzes him about how green he looked, until Cohn has to beg for mercy. But Cohn's failure to appreciate the bullfights, his sympathy for the horses and the steers (the wrong animals to feel sympathy for), is just more of his failure to appreciate values – as, for example, on the drive by open car from Bayonne to Pamplona, when Jake sees some impressive scenery: "I was up in front with the driver and I turned around. Robert Cohn was asleep, but Bill looked and nodded his head" (Ch. x). Clearly there was little likelihood of it being Bill asleep and Cohn nodding his head in understanding.

A number of scenes in *The Sun Also Rises* are exposures of

other tourists, too. For instance, even the *poule* that Jake picks up can see through Frances Clyne, "speaking French very rapidly and not seeming so proud and astonished as Mrs. Braddocks at its coming out really French" (Ch. iii). In this case, Frances tries to patronize the Frenchwoman for not liking Paris. "Who's she?" Georgette asks Jake. "Do I have to talk to her?"

It is also American tourists who irritate Jake when he and Bill go to Madame Lecomte's restaurant on the Ile Saint Louis. The restaurant is so crowded with American tourists that Jake and Bill have to stand and wait for a table: "Some one had put it in the American Women's Club list as a quaint restaurant on the Paris quais as yet untouched by Americans, so we had to wait forty-five minutes for a table" (Ch. viii). After the delayed meal they get the bill, "chalked up the same as ever on a slate, that was doubtless one of the 'quaint' features", and Madame Lecomte (who of course knows them both by sight) says, "You never come here any more, Monsieur Barnes." "Too many compatriots", is Jake's explanation. There is in all this a con-siderable amount of snobbery toward the newcomer from the old hand who arrived a few years earlier, and considerable ill will toward the hoi polloi for causing the heroes such inconvenience.

On the train to Bayonne Jake and Bill encounter all sorts of inconvenience because of seven cars of "pilgrims" from Dayton, Ohio, on their way to Biarritz and Lourdes, who have reserved the first four services of lunch, so that the heroes have to get along on sandwiches and wine until 4:15 before they can be served. Both become righteously indignant, Bill buttonholding a priest to demand, "When do us Protestants get a change to eat, father?" and Jake angry that he can't get a meal even though he is a Catholic (Ch. ix). Meanwhile they are forced to listen to an American couple (who push their way into the first service) tell them how good fishing is back in Montana and how hard traveling is on their son Hubert.

During the fiesta at Pamplona, Jake does his duty by bull-fighting by advising the hotel owner Montoya, a fellow *aficionado*, not to deliver an invitation to Romero from the American am-bassador and his party. They both agree that the American tourists would ruin Romero: "They're a fine lot", Jake says. "There's one American woman down here now that collects bull-fighters" (Ch. xvi). (Compare the passage in Chapter viii of *Across the River and into the Trees* in which Cantwell decides not to go to Harry's bar until the "riff-raff from the American Consulate" leave.)

The heroes are disturbed also by the English tourists from Biarritz who have come up for the fiesta. "Let's go and look at the English", Mike says. "They're awful", Bill says. "Where did they all come from?" "They come from Biarritz", Mike says. "They come to see the last day of the quaint little Spanish fiesta." "I'll festa them", Bill says. "What the hell are they doing at this fiesta?" (Ch. xvi).[8] Jake, who establishes with a glance and a nod between him and Montoya that Romero is "a real one" (Ch. xv; note the indefiniteness), has to listen to the critical judgment of the "Biarritz bull-fight experts" on Romero's performance:

The Biarritz crowd did not like it. They thought Romero was afraid, and that was why he gave that little sidestep each time as he transferred the bull's charge from his own body to the flannel. They preferred Belmonte's imitation of himself or Marcial's imitation of Belmonte. There were three of them in the row behind us.

"What's he afraid of the bull for? The bull's so dumb he only goes after the cloth."

"He's just a young bull-fighter. He hasn't learned it yet." (Ch. xviii)

Phonies never recognize the real thing when they see it. That is the same point made at the end of *The Old Man and the Sea*, when the tourists not only cannot tell a marlin's skeleton from a shark's but cannot understand the foreign language (so that to them the natives remain merely quaint). A woman tourist points down to the skeleton of the fish and asks a waiter at the Terrace what it is:

---

8 In "Pamplona Letter", *the transatlantic review*, II (September 1924), 301, Hemingway protests that he can't write about the Pamplona fiesta: "Either it would bore a lot of people or else next year Cooks would be running tours down there. The less publicity it has the better. Practically all the people that deserved to be at Pamplona were there this year. . . . The more people that think it is a terrible, brutal degrading relic of etc. the better."

"Tiburon", the waiter said, "Eshark." He was meaning to explain
what had happened.
"I didn't know sharks had such handsome, beautifully formed
tails."
"I didn't either", her male companion said.

Immediately we go back to the old man, asleep on his face in his
shack, by the contrast to feel the keener, supposedly, the poignancy and heroism of the old man's suffering and the disgusting
ignorance of those unaware of it (and, by implication, incapable
of being aware of it or too self-centered to bother finding out).[9]
Of the things wrong with *To Have and Have Not* and *Across
the River and into the Trees*, one of the most disturbing is the
identification and treatment of phonies. Besides the instances
already cited, some rather excruciating passages are concerned
with the exposure of tourist-writers. It is hardly accidental that
Helen Gordon, in her outburst against her husband and love,
should accuse him of having got his "dirty little tricks" out of
some book and end with the most abusive term she or Hemingway can think of – "You writer." [10] She adds that if he had been
a good writer she might have stood everything else, but he was
only a lickspittle and timeserver – a phony (Ch. xxi). Moreover,

[9]   Saul Bellow, in "Hemingway and the Image of Man", *Partisan Review*,
XX (May-June 1953), 341, comments on the exemplary and exclusive
character of Hemingway's heroes: "Manhood, as Hemingway views it,
must necessarily be the manhood of the few. In *The Old Man and the Sea*
a young boy chooses the fisherman as his symbolic father. The actual
father is not good enough. He is out. The tourist at the end of the story
is out, too. He is not one of those who know. (It's strange how Hemingway detests tourists. – Other tourists. Every traveler, I suppose, has felt
the enmity of the American who 'hit the place first' and considers himself practically a native.)"
[10]   Malcolm Cowley remarks, "It is the final insult. But since Hemingway
is a writer himself, this aversion is also a self-aversion" ("Hemingway:
Work in Progress", p. 305). I agree. With Hemingway's distrust of words,
he must at least half-feel that writers, himself included, are fakes. Bill
Gorton, a tourist-writer who is not presented as a fake, drunkenly asks
Jake to tell Romero something quite similar: "Tell him I think writing is
lousy. ... Go on, tell him. Tell him I'm ashamed of being a writer"
(Ch. xvi). In the tribute to Conrad in *the transatlantic review*, Hemingway
says that he once saved up four of Conrad's books to read "until I needed
them badly, when the disgust with writing, writers and everything written
of and to write would be too much" (p. 342).

in Chapter xv, a combination of distorted exposé and distorted tough talk, Gordon spouts high-flown jargon which sounds like it came out of a sociology book crossed with a dilettantish liberal literary journal. Of Helène Bradley he says, "She interests me both as a woman and as a social phenomenon." When his wife asks if going to bed with a social phenomenon is part of the homework of a writer, he retorts, "A writer has to know about everything. ... He can't restrict his experience to conform to Bourgeois standards."

Laughton, the other tourist-writer at the bar, doesn't work, just drinks, and is kidded unmercifully by Professor MacWalsey:

"My name's Laughton", the tall one said. "I'm a writer."

"I'm glad to meet you", Professor MacWalsey said. "Do you write often?"

Freddy's thoughts about the Laughtons clinch their status as phonies, if it was ever in doubt, when Mrs. Laughton calls Harry "beautiful" and her "dream man" (Harry calls her a whore):

All this time the writer sat there with a sort of stupid look on his face except when he'd look at his wife admiringly. Any one would have to be a writer or a F.E.R.A. man to have a wife look like that, Freddy thought. God, isn't she awful?

Even Baker concedes that Richard Gordon is a "strategic error" of *To Have and Have Not*, a foil whose purpose is that of "enlarging Harry Morgan's character" (p. 212) – a caricature somewhat akin to Macomber before his conversion (p. 213). But though Gordon and Macomber are both playboys, tourists, and sexual failures, Gordon has the additional failing of being a phony writer, like the phonies Harry sees in "The Snows of Kilimanjaro" on his return to Paris from the Greco-Turkish war where he has seen such horror that "he could not talk about it or stand to have it mentioned":

... there in the café as he passed was that American poet with a pile of saucers in front of him and a stupid look on his potato face talking about the Dada movement with a Roumanian who said his name was Tristan Tzara, who always wore a monocle and had a headache. ...

The clear implication is that there is something quite phony about

their bandying around empty words, literary talk, when the hero
has just returned, scarred, from the wars.

The situation is similar in *Across the River and into the Trees*
regarding the blemished writer whom the hero and his circle
cannot stop ridiculing. This party sport begins with identification
of the man as a phony, when Cantwell wonders aloud to Renata
who that "son of a bitch" in Harry's bar is:

> They looked at the man at the third table. He had a strange face
> like an over-enlarged, disappointed weasel or ferret. It looked as
> pock-marked and as blemished as the mountains of the moon seen
> through a cheap telescope and, the Colonel thought, it looked like
> Goebbels' face, if Herr Goebbels had ever been in a plane that
> burned, and not been able to bail out before the fire reached him.
>
> Above this face, which was ceaselessly peering, as though the an-
> swer might be found by enough well directed glances and by queries,
> there was black hair that seemed to have no connection with the
> human race. The man looked as though he had been scalped and
> then the hair replaced. Very interesting, the Colonel thought. Can he
> be a compatriot? Yes, he must.
>
> A little spit ran out of the corner of his mouth as he spoke,
> peeringly, with the elderly, wholesome looking woman who was
> with him. She looks like anybody's mother in an illustration in "The
> Ladies' Home Journal", the Colonel thought. (Ch. ix)

Not only the description but the association with "anybody's
mother in an illustration in 'The Ladies' Home Journal' " is
ominous. Equally ominous is the sinister fascination that the man
holds for Cantwell. "He looks like a caricature of an American
who has been run one half way through a meat chopper and then
been boiled, slightly, in oil", Cantwell thinks. (Certainly he *is* a
caricature of some American writer whom Hemingway would
not mind grinding up or watching being ground up in that
sausage grinder of his.) Turning to the waiter Ettore, Cantwell
asks, "Who is that spiritual character?" Ettore doesn't know, but
he gathers "his intelligence rapidly and as a Venetian should" and
delivers it to the Colonel:

> "My colleague who works at his hotel, says that he drinks three or
> four highballs, and then writes vastly and fluently far into the night."
> "I dare say that makes marvelous reading."
> "I dare say", Ettore said. "But it was hardly the method of Dante."

"Dante was another *vieux con*", the Colonel said. "I mean as a man. Not as a writer."

Our suspicions are confirmed, but there is more to come yet. Now the *Gran Maestro* reports on the man: "He condescends to me. He speaks bad Italian assiduously. He goes everywhere in Baedeker, and he has no taste in either food or wine." "Does he speak of us?" Cantwell wants to know:

"He asked me who you were. He was familiar with the Contessa's name and had book-visited several palaces that had belonged to the family. He was impressed by your name, Madam, which I gave to impress him."
"Do you think he will put us in a book?"
"I'm sure of it. He puts everything in a book." (Ch. xii)

Obviously, this phony has just about every characteristic imaginable of the very worst class of phony tourist-writers.

Subsequently, the heroes' circle has a lot of fun verbally grinding the fake up: "But what is my pitted compatriot thinking three tables down?" Cantwell interrupts his disquisition on war to ask. "About his next book, or about what it says in Baedeker", Renata answers. "Should we tell the pitted man that we are going?" Cantwell says. "I think he has the same pits on his heart and in his soul and maybe in his curiosity." "*Gran Maestro*", the Colonel asks a little later, "did my illustrious compatriot look up the *Barone* in Baedeker?" "Truly, my Colonel. I have not seen him pull his Baedeker during the meal." "Give him full marks", the Colonel says. Near the end of the same chapter, when Renata gives Cantwell a large portrait of herself, she asks, "Should we have them take it and the chairs down and make a special showing of it for your compatriot? The *Gran Maestro* could tell him the address of the painter and he could visit the picturesque studio." In Chapter xxxviii when Cantwell and the *Gran Maestro* enroll Renata in the Order and Cantwell is about to reveal to her the secrets of the Order, he must first determine that there are no phonies within earshot:

"I reveal", the Colonel said. "There are no pitted folk about?"
"No. He is out with his Lady. Miss Baedeker."

Besides getting his ideas out of books, and the wrong books to boot, Cohn has other failings as a writer that we have seen in some of the phony tourist-writers. For example, he tries to act impressive, cultured, "literary" when he, Jake and Bill look at the cathedral in Bayonne: "Cohn made some remark about it being a very good example of something or other, I forget what. It seemed like a nice cathedral, nice and dim, like Spanish churches" (Ch. x). He has too many phony writer friends like the Braddockses and their friends (Jake and Georgette decide that there are too many writers and artists on the left bank): Mrs. Braddocks introduces Jake to another "rising new novelist" also named Robert (Prentiss), who offends Jake by questioning his liking for Paris and then by telling him that he gets angry "charmingly". "Don't be cross with Robert", Mrs. Braddocks says to Jake. "He's still only a child, you know." "I wasn't cross", Jake tells her. "I just thought perhaps I was going to throw up" (Ch. iii).

Then Frances Clyne has some bitter things to throw in Cohn's face, especially about how he looks at everything in life as potential material for a book (he is having trouble writing his second novel):

"Listen, Robert, dear. ... Don't have scenes with your young ladies. Try not to. Because you can't have scenes without crying, and then you pity yourself so much that you can't remember what the other person's said. You'll never be able to remember any conversations that way. Just try and be calm. I know it's awfully hard. But remember, it's for literature. We all ought to make sacrifices for literature." (Ch. vi)

Worst of all, Cohn has come back from America rather conceited about his first novel, which his publishers praised highly (Ch. ii), though Jake informs us it was a poor novel: "He wrote a novel, and it was not really such a bad novel as the critics later called it, although it was a very poor novel" (Ch. i).

Lack of competence, skill, or expertness in his field is one of the clearest signs of the phony. In an incredible scene in *A Farewell to Arms*, Hemingway establishes this point about the doctors who first examine Frederic Henry's knee:

... three doctors came into the room. I have noticed that doctors who fail in the practice of medicine have a tendency to seek one another's company and aid in consultation. A doctor who cannot take out your appendix properly will recommend to you a doctor who will be unable to remove your tonsils with success. These were three such doctors. (Ch. xv)

Indifferently, they force him to bend his knee although it hurts, and they keep calling each other "doctor". Then one of them, a first captain, asks for the x-rays again:

The third doctor handed him one of the plates. "No. The left leg, please."
"That is the left leg, doctor."
"You are right. I was looking from a different angle."

Next the three incompetents (the house doctor included) decide that they must wait six months before operating. Henry asks the house doctor to have another doctor look at his leg, since a doctor who is a first captain can't be much good: "If he was any good he would be made a major. I know what a first captain is, doctor" (heroes have this kind of know-how).

Immediately afterward, for contrast, we get a doctor who is a hero. Dr. Valentini is a major; he is loud, jocular, and self-confident; he knows how much it hurts to bend the knee and how indifferent doctors are about their patients' pain; he has a keen eye for a pretty girl (Catherine); he accepts a drink at once when Henry offers it to him (the house doctor never drinks). Finally, when Henry asks him when the knee can be operated on, he says, "To-morrow morning. Not before." As he goes out the door, Henry notes again that he is a major. Comment would be superfluous.

Cohn is undoubtedly the most complex of Hemingway's phonies and the one given the most extensive treatment, so that he does not seem to be condemned offhand like the other phonies. Bill and Jake agree, for instance, that Cohn is nice "but just so awful" (Ch. x). After Mike insults Cohn by calling him a steer, Bill has mixed feelings: "I don't like Cohn, God knows, and I think it was a silly trick for him to go down to San Sebastian, but nobody has any business to talk like Mike" (Ch. xiii). When Brett tells Jake how badly Cohn has behaved ("He can't believe it didn't mean anything"), Jake at least partly defends Cohn:

"Everybody behaves badly", I said. "Give them the proper chance."
"You wouldn't behave badly." Brett looked at me.
"I'd be as big an ass as Cohn", I said. (Ch. xvi)

It is part defense, but only part, for the implication is that Jake would never behave so badly and that to say one would be "as big an ass as Cohn" is bottoms in superlatives.

When it is granted that there is an occasional suggestion about Cohn's side of things, it is still largely giving the devil his due, while most of the evidence – some of it pretty flimsy – is devoted to exposing him. It is not enough to say that Cohn is an outsider because he does not share the heroes' assumptions about the value of action, skill, knowledge, courage, honesty, or stoicism (enduring without complaint), nor because he is a hopeless romantic who gets his ideas from books like *The Purple Land* and who refuses to face the reality of what Brett is, as Jake does.[11]

The fact that Cohn seems to be enjoying the "childish, drunken heroics of it" and is "ready to do battle for his lady love" when Mike tries to make him go away (Ch. xvi) is only one more count in the case against him, like all the other failings already given. If he stubbornly refuses to admit that Brett does not love him, sure that "true love would conquer all", in Jake's ironic phrase (Ch. xvii), if he doesn't know when he isn't wanted and picks a fight when Jake pimps for Brett by calling Jake a pimp, these failings are set beside the more tenuous charges that he never gets drunk like the rest and passes out when he does drink (Ch. xiv, xv). His beating up Jake, Mike, and Romero and being defeated finally by Romero's dauntless spirit, his crying and wanting to shake hands and be friends again (Ch. xvii) are somehow made equivalent to his looking sad and suffering during the fiesta when everyone else is trying to drink himself into a good time (Ch. xvi). His following Brett around, showing his feelings and talking about them (a blatant violation of the code of understatement and "disciplined" emotion) are nearly on a par with his sending a three-word telegram, "Vengo Jueves Cohn" ("I come Thursday"), when he could have sent ten words for the same price (more about

---

[11]   James B. Colvert, "Ernest Hemingway's Morality in Action", *American Literature*, XXVII (November 1955), 380-382.

values): "It gives you all the dope that's of interest to Cohn",
Bill remarks (Ch. xiii).

The mixture of the tenuous and the trifling with the telling
weakens the whole case, suggesting that Cohn was first judged a
phony, after which reasons – any reasons – were sought out to
bolster the judgment. Somehow things are wrong for him which
are all right for others: he mustn't dislike Paris or bullfighting,
though Georgette may dislike Paris, and it is apparently all right
for the Spanish waiter at the café not to like bullfighting (Ch. xvii).
It is all right for the heroes to patronize Madame Lecomte's
restaurant or Harry's bar but somehow all wrong for phonies to be
there.[12]

Accordingly, in the last analysis the definition or specifications
of the phony remain somewhat elusive. Thus in *Across the River
and into the Trees* the bartender at the Gritti Palace hotel is
"still outside of the Order for some small, not defined, un-stated
reason" (Ch. vii). The reason may be that he does not share
Cantwell's and the *Gran Maestro*'s war experience, their wounds,
or their attitudes; it may be that he cannot speak Spanish. The
Order's full name is *"El Ordine Militar, Nobile y Espirituoso de
los Caballeros de Brusadelli*. The Colonel and the head waiter both
spoke Spanish, and since that is the best language for founding
orders, they had used it in the naming of this one" (named,
ironically, in honor of a Milanese profiteer who had accused his
young wife, "publicly and legally through due process of law, of
having deprived him of his judgment through her extraordinary
sexual demands"). The association is clear once more between
the foreign and the code; this is foreignism made yet more esoteric
and exclusive, so that the "secrets" of the initiates are safely in-
accessible to outsiders.

The nearest thing to definition of a phony comes when Cantwell calls the pock-marked writer a jerk and Renata asks him to
define *jerk:* "It is a little rough to state. But I think it means a

[12] In "A Visit with Hemingway: A Situation Report", *Look*, September 4,
1956, p. 24, Hemingway is still distressed by "the jerks and twerps, the
creeps and the squares and the drips" who not only exist but flourish and
overrun all his favorite places, "while people that you care for die
publicly or anonymously each month".

man who has never worked at his trade (*oficio*) truly, and is presumptuous in some annoying way" (Ch. ix). Renata sounds like the "old lady" of *Death in the Afternoon* as she responds, "I must learn to use the term properly" (heroines are often students of the heroes). Again skill and honesty are criteria for belonging to the inner circle, but ultimately the decision is the heroes': is the person in question "presumptuous in some annoying way"? That is a criterion which can cover a multitude of dislikes, from a person's inconveniencing the heroes to his disliking what the heroes like, or vice versa. With such a broad definition, Hemingway or his heroes can classify as phony just about anyone who annoys them. That too is part of the value system or code.

2

Delmore Schwartz quotes Ezra Pound as saying, "Mr. Hemingway is preëminently the wise guy", then hastens to add that this is the "popular and superficial aspect of his writing", mentioned for the sake of moving immediately beyond it (p. 114). But can the "wise-guy" aspect of Hemingway's work be so lightly dismissed by calling it "popular and superficial", on the assumption that whatever is popular must be superficial? One suspects that Hemingway's popular appeal makes critics uneasy, so that they feel obligated to look beyond and try to ignore both his slickness and his knowledgeability about things of sometimes doubtful importance, seeking deeper, hidden, and more dignified reasons for giving him their attention. It is true, of course, that cleverness and inside information are not the sum total of Hemingway, but they are certainly important parts, resulting in the wise-guy air when pushed to their extreme. The expertness and know-how of heroes and author alike are not simply superficial aspects of Hemingway: they are very important in the value system, in giving a character claim to hero status, and in supplying him a measure of security in a hostile world.

Like other claims to heroism, expertness occasionally backfires, becoming self-parody, but the urgency of establishing the expertness of the hero is only substantiated the more by the lapses it sometimes produces in sense of proportion. One such lapse comes in "Big Two-Hearted River" after the reader has learned from the detailed description of Nick's activities how to make camp expertly, how to pitch a tent so that the canvas is "drum tight", how and when to catch grasshoppers for bait (before the dew evaporates), and how to make coffee and flapjacks in camp. When we get to the details of Nick's preparing his fishing tackle, we learn that the technique includes not getting the fishhook stuck in the finger: "He fastened a hook on the end of the leader. It was a small hook; very thin and springy. . . . He tested the knot and the spring of the rod by pulling the line taut. It was a good feeling. He was careful not to let the hook bite into his finger" (Part II).

In *For Whom the Bell Tolls* Jordan first wins the confidence of the Spanish guerrillas by showing that he is an expert about their horses (Ch. i); it is his examination before acceptance into the circle, very much like the "oral spiritual examination" that Jake undergoes (by men quite embarrassed by their strong feelings) before being accepted by Spaniards as an *aficionado* (Ch. xiii). Something like Nick, Jordan is also an expert at making a bed out of boughs (Ch. xx), but he is in addition an expert at gun emplacement and concealment (Ch. xxii) and of course an expert at blowing up bridges. It is while he is placing the charges under the bridge, telling himself to go slow so that he will make no mistake, that the know-how again becomes funny. The correct technique includes not lashing down the levers of the grenades being used as detonators: "He checked that the grenades, lashed on their sides, had room for the levers to spring when the pins were pulled (the wire that lashed them ran through under the levers)" (Ch. xliii).

From Jordan we also learn that being an insider, in the know, has its drawbacks as well as its advantages, but that being in the know compensates for most unpleasantness – even for being a party to lies:

In a revolution you could not admit to outsiders who helped you nor that any one knew more than he was supposed to know. He had learned that. If a thing was right fundamentally the lying was not supposed to matter. There was a lot of lying though. He did not care for the lying at first. He hated it. Then later he had come to like it. It was part of being an insider but it was a very corrupting business. (Ch. xviii)

Part of being an insider includes as well knowing "how it really was", being shockproof about it once you do know, and exposing the truth for the less fortunate who are not in the know.

Cantwell's claim to hero status is based, among other things, on his being an expert on duck shooting (Ch. i), on painting and architecture (Ch. iii), on Venice (Ch. iv), on marine engines (Ch. vi), on all "or nearly all" the tricks for self-inflicted wounds and feigning illness to dodge front-line duty (Ch. vii), on food and wine and the generals of World War II (Ch. xii), and on trees (Ch. xxvi). But he is also an expert spitter: "It was a long spit and he just made it. 'I couldn't spit that night nor afterwards for a long time', he said. 'But I spit good now for a man who doesn't chew' " (Ch. iii). He is an expert on raw clams, on cutting them out of the shell, and on their edibility, who asks the clam seller in the market where his clams came from: "They came from a good place, without sewerage and the Colonel asked to have six opened. He drank the juice and cut the clam out, cutting close against the shell with the curved knife the man handed him. The man had handed him the knife because he knew from experience the Colonel cut closer to the shell than he had been taught to cut" (Ch. xxii).

He also knows how to die with style, the last thing he does being to shut the rear door of the automobile "carefully and well" (Ch. xlv). (In dying "correctly" he is lucky: cf. Jordan telling himself at the end, "Dying is only bad when it takes a long time and hurts so much that it humiliates you. That is where you have all the luck, see?" A code that prescribes even that one must die in a dignified manner, without showing "humiliating" feelings, seems to me the last word in "discipline" which is not improved much by calling it "existentialist".[13])

To establish the hero's (and author's) expertness is one reason

[13] See John Killinger, *Hemingway and the Dead Gods: A Study in Existentialism* (Lexington?, University of Kentucky Press, 1960), pp. 70, 75-79. In his conclusion Killinger says that his book is "in a sense" a defense of Hemingway's work against those who find it philosophically limited or unsatisfactory (p. 100).

for a good deal of seemingly extraneous and incidental detail. Besides Jake's more obvious expertness in such things as how to preserve trout in hot weather (Ch. xii), in how to watch a bullfight and in the true, unfaked technique of bullfighting, "so slow and so controlled" (Ch. xv, xviii), and in diving "cleanly and deeply" and swimming "slowly and steadily" (Ch. xix), he has a lot of less obvious know-how. For example, the detailed description of Jake's and Bill's walk from Madame Lecomte's restaurant to the Café Select (Ch. viii), whose purpose Baker finds hard to discover (p. 52), establishes Jake and Hemingway as authorities on Paris, no mere tourists newly arrived. Jake's description of the sights around San Sebastian which he could see from the raft while swimming serves a similar purpose.

Likewise, some of Jake's information about prices, while a part of his interest in values and getting one's money's worth, also shows how in the know he is about, say, the going rates for room and board at the inn at Burguete (Ch. xi). His comments about the difference between Spain and France, how France "is the simplest country to live in. . . . If you want people to like you you have only to spend a little money" (Ch. xix), give more of his knowledgeability which new tourists lack. His attempt to go native by purchasing wineskins to drink from – and informing us how much they cost and how much it cost to have them filled with wine – is the same motive become slightly ludicrous (Ch. xv).

In *A Farewell to Arms*, besides getting information about how to pour wine with the same hand holding the glass and how the Italians ate the spaghetti course at mess (Ch. ii) and about the sensible procedure for drinking in hotels ("I would get a bottle of whiskey and have them bring ice and soda"; Ch. xl), we get this kind of incidental description which not only informs us about the exotic foreign country but also makes the hero an expert on it:

The army had not stood at the Tagliamento. They were falling back to the Piave. I remembered the Piave. The railroad crossed it near San Dona going up to the front. It was deep and slow there and quite narrow. Down below there were mosquito marshes and canals.

There were some lovely villas. Once, before the war, going up to Cortina D'Ampezzo I had gone along it for several hours in the hills. Up there it looked like a trout stream, flowing swiftly with shallow stretches and pools under the shadow of the rocks. The road turned off from it at Cadore. (Ch. xxxv)

The fact that the hero is so often an outsider in a foreign country encourages the reader's identification with him, since the reader is usually a stranger also to the country in which the hero finds himself and is inclined to accept information from the hero who knows more about it: "This attitude is not limited to acceptance of fact, but after conditioning the reader to accept him as guide to the facts of the situation, the author is in a more authoritative position in any statement he makes or impression he conveys." [14]

An added advantage of being a stranger in a foreign country is that one can be merely an observer or spectator if he doesn't like what is happening around him. "In another country" the hero is not really involved unless he chooses to be. It is much easier and less reprehensible, for instance, for Frederic Henry to desert from a foreign army than from an American army. Or as Enrique Emmunds, the narrator-writer, tells the old waiter at Chicote's Bar in Madrid during the Spanish civil war, "I am a foreigner and it is your war and your problem." [15] If Robert Jordan subsequently chooses to make it his war, he is yet always fundamentally detached from it in a way that the Spanish never are. His duties are self-imposed, an ennobling choice of values which are true because of their foreign setting. The tourist hero is thus in an enviable position: on the one hand, he cannot be blamed much for rejecting foreign values which he dislikes; on the other hand, he is ennobled when he imposes foreign values on himself because he believes in them.

Far from being superficial traits, foreignism and expertness perform an important persuasive function in Hemingway's work, inclining the reader to identify himself with the heroes and their system of values. The password of the secret order of the heroes

---

[14] John Graham, "Ernest Hemingway: The Meaning of Style", *Modern Fiction Studies*, VI (Winter 1960-61), 306n.
[15] "The Denunciation", *Esquire*, November 1938, p. 113.

is frequently appreciation of correct technique, in nonfiction as well as in fiction: *Death in the Afternoon* is an extensive inquiry into correct technique in bullfighting, and *Green Hills of Africa* is much concerned with the correct technique of hunting and shooting, in each case with Hemingway himself the undisguised expert.[16]

Santiago is not an American in a foreign land, but he is an expert in an exotic situation and country with which the reader is not likely to be so familiar. *The Old Man and the Sea* (like the first part of *To Have and Have Not*) is devoted in large part to the technique of deep-sea fishing, in which Santiago is an expert. For example, he is superior to the other fishermen because he keeps his lines straighter than anyone else:

He looked down into the water and watched the lines that went straight down into the dark of the water. He kept them straighter than anyone did, so that at each level in the darkness of the stream there would be a bait waiting exactly where he wished it to be for any fish that swam there. Others let them drift with the current and sometimes they were at sixty fathoms when the fishermen thought they were at a hundred.

But, he thought, I keep them with precision. Only I have no luck any more. ... It is better to be lucky. But I would rather be exact. Then when luck comes you are ready. (pp. 35-36)

Other bits of seemingly extraneous information also testify to the expertness of the old man and the author (cf. Chapters iii and xvi of *To Have and Have Not* in which we learn that Harry knows how to keep guns from rusting on a boat and how to make a sling for a submachine gun so that it can be managed with one hand). Santiago knows, for instance, the signs of a hurricane at sea, so that unlike the timorous fishermen who stay near shore he is not afraid to go far out:

He thought of how some men feared being out of sight of land in a small boat and knew they were right in the months of sudden bad weather. But now they were in hurricane months and, when there are

---

[16] See Joseph Beaver, " 'Technique' in Hemingway", *College English*, XIV (March 1953), 327. However, Beaver's conclusion is tenuous in the extreme: "When this technique is properly handled, the result is characters who are genuine heroes, and novels which are genuinely great" (p. 328).

no hurricanes, the weather of hurricane months is the best of all
the year.

   If there is a hurricane you always see the signs of it in the sky for
days ahead, if you are at sea. They do not see it ashore because they
do not know what to look for, he thought. (pp. 67-68)

   It is apparent from the last two examples that know-how and
observance of details are not only a way of establishing the expertness of the hero but are also protective, a form of security, safety,
or good luck. They may not actually cause good luck, but they
help one be ready when luck comes and they help keep the hero
from being more badly wounded. Like know-how, discrimination
of details "*implies* order – an order deliberately and self-
consciously supplied by the individual himself to his own experience. It is a bulwark against *nada*."[17] Likewise, expertness in
work or sport and observance of the "rules" provide an order and
a concentration on the here and now which, if they cannot assure
safety and luck, can guarantee against needless risks or at least
can help one temporarily forget the unendurable threat that he
cannot control. The observance of details, then, whether as "rules"
or ritual of performance, as apparently incidental description, or
as "concrete" dwelling on the immediate moment, is often both a
kind of control and a kind of drug.

   The security provided by the know-how and code of the bull-
fighter is one of the fascinations for Hemingway of that formal,
stylized occupation with violence and death. The very word
suertes (akin to English 'surety' or 'security'), which Hemingway
defines in the glossary of *Death in the Afternoon* as "all predetermined manoeuvres in a bullfight; any move in a bullfight
which has rules for the manner of its execution", "in the singular
also means luck". Just as lack of know-how about details brought
about the death of the would-be bullfighter Paco in "The Capital
of the World", so the poor matador is the one who does not
control his danger through scrupulous observation of the *suertes*:
... the matador, if he knows his profession, can increase the amount
of the danger of death that he runs exactly as much as he wishes.

[17] E. M. Halliday, "Hemingway's Hero", *The University of Chicago
Magazine*, XLV (May 1953), 13.

He should, however, increase this danger, *within the rules provided for his protection.* In other words it is to his credit if he does something that he knows how to do in a highly dangerous but still geometrically possible manner. It is to his discredit if he runs danger through ignorance, through disregard of the fundamental rules, through physical or mental slowness, or through blind folly. (Ch. ii)

Lack of attention to the details of technique is what Hemingway castigates himself for in *Green Hills of Africa* when he gut-shoots the sable bull: "It came from over-confidence in being able to do a thing and then omitting one of the steps in how it is done"; "Every damned thing is your own fault if you're any good" (Ch. xiii). It is the thing that Cantwell frets about when he fails to notice the Milan profiteers leave the bar: "I'm getting awfully slow, he thought. Somebody will take me any day now" (Ch. vi). Proper attention to detail is seen in the *Gran Maestro*'s seating Cantwell in the corner of the bar "where the Colonel had both his flanks covered": ". . . he would no more have seated his Colonel in the middle of a room than he would have taken up a stupid defensive position" (Ch. xii).

Attention to concrete detail, like word repetition and the "relentless heaping up of a given observation", gives "a concentration upon the solitary fact which alone can be mastered and held to and made a kind of anchor" against the destructive power of the world.[18] That is, it may be more of a drug, a control over fear, than a control over danger. For example, Nick in "Now I Lay Me" occupies his mind at night by imaginatively fishing trout streams in great detail to keep himself awake, because he fears that "if I ever shut my eyes in the dark and let myself go, my soul would go out of my body". In "A Way You'll Never Be" Nick "noticed everything in such detail to keep it all straight so he would know just where he was" (see the catalogue of debris on

[18] Fenimore, p. 220. See Hoffman, *The Twenties*, pp. 190-191, and *The Modern Novel*, p. 80, for discussion of Gertrude Stein's advocacy of "beginning again and again" (repetition) as a way of achieving the "continuous present" or "prolonged present" – a technique and an emphasis that Hemingway must have learned from her or had confirmed by her practice. Stein's "explanation" of her method can be found in "Composition as Explanation", *Selected Writings of Gertrude Stein*, ed. Carl Van Vechten (New York, Random House, 1946), pp. 453-461.

the battlefield at the beginning of the story; Nick has "crazy spells" – the result of fear stemming from memories of battle). Mr. Frazer in "The Gambler, the Nun and the Radio" concentrates on the radio all night, when his nerves go bad, so that he can stop thinking. Nick's detailed routine in "Big Two-Hearted River" obviously serves a similar purpose.

In *For Whom the Bell Tolls* the detailed imagining that Jordan does about the trip he will take to Madrid with Maria after the bridge has been blown up is a deliberate temporary escape from thoughts of impending death (Ch. xviii, xxxi), just like Cantwell's and Renata's imagining the motor trip they will take across America (Ch. xxxvii). It is for the purpose of controlling his fears and uncertainty about blowing up the bridge that Jordan tells himself to think about "something concrete and practical" like his grandfather's war souvenirs. Momentarily he doubts that even that will work when his brain "gets to racing like a flywheel with the weight gone" and decides, "You better not think at all. ... Soon you will be with Maria and you won't have to think" (she too is a drug). However, he manages to capture a good feeling "with the confidence that had come from thinking back to concrete things" which, like the knowledge that he will surely have to blow up the bridge, is the comfort of certainty: "It's much better to be sure, he thought. It's always much better to be sure" (Ch. xxx).

Here we see the reason for the concentration on the now, on the present moment or detail, to the exclusion of everything else. Cowardice, as Hemingway explains in his introduction to *Men at War*, is "almost always simply a lack of ability to suspend the functioning of the imagination. Learning to suspend your imagination and live completely in the very second of the present minute with no before and no after is the greatest gift a soldier can acquire" (p. xxvii). When he cannot turn off his thinking, he can try to control it, as Jordan does so often – most noticeably when, lying with a broken leg and waiting for the fascist cavalry, he forces himself repetitiously to imagine the details of the others' escape:

Think about them being away, he said. Think about them going through the timber. Think about them crossing a creek. Think about them riding through the heather. Think about them going up the slope. Think about them O.K. tonight. Think about them travelling, all night. Think about them hiding up tomorrow. Think about them. God damn it, think about them. *That's just as far as I can think about them,* he said.

Think about Montana. *I can't.* Think about Madrid. *I can't.* Think about a cool drink of water. *All right.* That's what it will be like. Like a cool drink of water. *You're a liar.*

Emphasis on the now is nowhere more overt than in *For Whom the Bell Tolls* – e.g., in Jordan's mulling over whether *now, ahora, maintenant,* or *heute* is the most expressive; he immediately sets them against *dead* and *war* and their foreign equivalents, making *sweetheart, chérie, prenda, schatz,* and *Maria* virtual synonyms for the precious now. Hemingway shows more acumen perhaps than Browning or Hopkins when he equates the timeless moment with the moment of orgasm (but less acumen, maybe, in his representation of it). Here is part of the description of Maria's and Jordan's lovemaking the night before the bridge is blown up, with *now* as the pedal point (note the suppressed image of the bird in flight):

Then they were together so that as the hand on the watch moved, unseen now, they knew that nothing could ever happen to the one that did not happen to the other, that no other thing could happen more than this; that this was all and always; this was what had been and now and whatever was to come. ... They were having now and before and always and now and now and now. Oh, now, now, now, the only now, and above all now, and there is no other now but thou now and now is thy prophet. Now and forever now. Come now, now, for there is no now but now. Yes, now. Now, please now, only now, not anything else only this now ... and not why, not ever why, only this now; and on and always please then always now, always now, for now always one now; one only one, there is no other one but one now, one, going now, rising now, sailing now, leaving now, wheeling now, soaring now, away now, all the way now, all of all the way now. ... (Ch. xxxvii)

If you love Maria so much, Jordan tells himself, "you had better love her very hard and make up in intensity what the relation will lack in duration and in continuity. ... You have it *now* and that is all your whole life is; now. There is nothing else than now

There is neither yesterday, certainly, nor is there any tomorrow.
... There is only now, and if now is only two days, then two days
is your life and everything in it will be in proportion" (Ch. xiii).
One thing that will give it proportion and also make the moment
more timeless is close attention to each small detail; it is like the
hero's trying to slow things up, not wanting to rush his sensations.
Waiting for the bombing which will signal that the bridge must be
blown up, Jordan thinks, "If we are going to blow it I would like
to breathe very slowly and slow up the time again and feel it"
(Ch. xliii). The desperate intensity of the love affair and the
attempt to slow time up by observance of details is the same as in
Across the River and into the Trees or in *A Farewell to Arms*
where Henry recites to Catherine, "But always at my back I hear
Time's wingèd chariot hurrying near" (Ch. xxiii), and later comments, "We knew that the baby was very close now and it gave
us both a feeling as though something were hurrying us and we
could not lose any time together" (Ch. xl).

The sense of impending death which gives such intensity to
every detail of the present moment is the condition of crisis and
war, of life viewed as something as dangerous and precarious as
war (or bullfighting), of life as seen by one in extremity. Faulkner
repeats the point in *Soldiers' Pay*: "In wartime one lives in to-day.
Yesterday is gone and tomorrow may never come" (Ch. v, 1). Not
only does one seek to make up for duration in intensity, but he
may seek out danger and the threat of death precisely in order to
give intensity to the present moment. As Cowley explains it, the
experience of World War I gave many of his generation a taste for
strong pleasures:

The war created in young men a thirst for abstract danger, not suffered for a cause but courted for itself. ... Danger was a relief from
boredom, a stimulus to the emotions, a color mixed with all others
to make them brighter. There were moments in France when the
senses were immeasurably sharpened by the thought of dying next
day, or possibly next week. The trees were green, not like ordinary
trees, but like trees in the still moment before a hurricane; the sky
was a special and ineffable blue; the grass smelled of life itself; the
image of death at twenty, the image of love, mingled together into

a keen, precarious delight. And this perhaps was the greatest of the lessons that the war taught to young writers.[19]

The explanation doubtless applies to Hemingway: "If death no longer generally exists, he must seek it out; battles being over, the bull ring must do, or the jungles of Africa, the matador or the kudu" (Geismar, p. 162).

Several things follow from seeing life as danger, the world as a war world. As just suggested, one is an association between beauty and danger or death. Jake points out that the other bullfighters faked their danger, so that afterward "all that was faked turned bad and gave an unpleasant feeling. Romero's bull-fighting gave real emotion, because he kept the absolute purity of line in his movements and always quietly and calmly let the horns pass him close each time. . . . Brett saw how something that was beautiful done close to the bull was ridiculous if it were done a little way off" (Ch. xv).

The intensity of feeling is so great during a good *faena* (the matador's work with the *muleta*, the cape), Hemingway says in *Death in the Afternoon*, that it is "as profound as any religious ecstasy", adding, "The greatest pass with the muleta, the most dangerous to make and the most beautiful to see is the natural" (Ch. xviii). Emotion reaches the climax of ecstasy, of course, at the "moment of truth": ". . . the beauty of the moment of killing is that flash when man and bull form one figure as the sword goes all the way in, the man leaning after it, death uniting the two figures in the emotional, aesthetic and artistic climax of the fight" (Ch. xix).[20] Compare "the old hollow, singing feeling" that Harry Morgan gets after shooting the Cuban gunmen (Ch. xviii), the same "strange, hollow singing in his heart" that he gets on coming into port after a rough crossing (Ch. viii). Much of the beauty and intensity of the moment comes from the danger, the

---

[19] *Exile's Return*, pp. 41-42. Spilka thinks that "chiefly the risk of death lends moral seriousness to a private code which lacks it. The risk is arbitrary; when a man elects to meet it, his beliefs take on subjective weight and he is able to give meaning to his private life" (p. 87n).
[20] Melvin Backman points out the similarity between the ecstasy of the moment of killing and the moment of orgasm (p. 5). Each is a "moment of truth", a timeless moment.

threat of death once more averted (even vicariously or symbolically).

Among the familiar ideas in *The Old Man and the Sea*, as Young observes, is that of "death, expertly delivered and received, as the source of much of life's intensity" (p. 96). Also familiar are other corollaries of viewing life as dangerous, precarious, and fearful as wartime – e.g., the high premium set on courage, on endurance or "taking it", on toughness. The old man repeatedly tries "not to think but only to endure" (p. 50), showing the fish "what a man can do and what a man endures" (p. 73). "Keep your head clear and know how to suffer like a man. Or a fish, he thought" (p. 102). "A man can be destroyed but not defeated" (p. 114). This is the theme not only of "The Undefeated" but of "Today Is Friday", the crucified Christ being the type of the hero who is not lucky but who knows how to take it: "He was pretty good in there today", the first soldier repeats six times (he has seen "plenty of them"). It is high praise coming from a soldier. Jesus is a real man because he suffers with style or "discipline"; like a good soldier, he knows how to die. The code "summarizes the virtues of the soldier":

It is tested by conduct in the face of death; it is the ethic of wartime. And it operates, in a way, off duty, for when the soldier is not at war he is in escape of it – on leave or, at the very least, in the reserve. And escaping this world is but to imitate it: one kills, instead of other soldiers, ducks, marlin, kudu, lions, bulls and horses. This escape functions to keep alive the conditions escaped, until the real thing comes along again. ... The activities of escape go according to the rules of sport, which make up the code of the armistice, the temporary, peacetime modification of the rules of war. (Young, p. 215)

Jordan holding onto himself at the end so that he won't lose consciousness, so that he can kill a few more fascists before they kill him, Harry Morgan who "lay quietly and took it" after being shot (Ch. xviii) are further illustrations of the virtues of the code, just as Ad Francis ("The Battler") and the punch-drunk veteran of *To Have and Have Not* (Ch. xxii) in their masochistic pride at being able to take it are perversions of the code.

If there was ever any doubt about Harry Morgan's being a

hero, it is dispelled by courtesy of Captain Willie: "... so Harry crossed last night. That boy's got *cojones*" (Ch. vii). Talking about the *capea* (amateur bullfight), Hemingway explains in *Death in the Afternoon* how the sport requires more of the courage that he equates with manliness in the word *cojones*:

> I am afraid however due to the danger of death it involves it would never have much success among the amateur sportsmen of America and England who play games. We, in games, are not fascinated by death, its nearness and its avoidance. We are fascinated by victory and we replace the avoidance of death by the avoidance of defeat. It is a very nice symbolism but it takes more cojones to be a sportsman when death is a closer party to the game. (Ch. ii)

I would say that Hemingway is more in accord with the popular culture of his country (at least now) than he seems to think he is: he shares its notions, in large part, of what traits are masculine.[21]

That life is a dangerous game for Hemingway, like bullfighting or war, is quite clear in the well-known statement from *A Farewell to Arms* (even though the figure sounds like one from baseball): "You did not know what it was about. You never had time to learn. They threw you in and told you the rules and the first time they caught you off base they killed you" (Ch. xli). Living in a war world, the hero will bear honorable wounds, which he exhibits (as though against his will) as his title to hero status; the wounds show that he has been in the thick of life at its most dangerous and intense, hence vital, and he has the marks to prove it: "The world breaks every one and afterward many are strong at the broken places" (Ch. xxxiv). Those whom the world seems

---

[21] See Tom Burnam, "Primitivism and Masculinity in the Work of Ernest Hemingway", *Modern Fiction Studies*, I (August 1955), 21. Commenting on Hemingway's insistence that fear is not to be condoned, Atkins makes an interesting point about Hemingway's value system: "Among the christian virtues is courage but fear is not rated as a sin. Indeed, the christian is expected to show fear in certain situations, else he will be accused of pride. But Hemingway, Macomber and especially Mrs. Macomber are driven by a hard logic to regard fear as a sin that must be punished mercilessly" (p. 129). Between such stern morality and the fear of being unmanly, Hemingway can only see fear as the most shameful of all failings – at any rate, when it is translated into action or given too open expression.

most anxious to kill or break are the best people – the brave, the good, the gentle – and those who are strong at the broken places are the heroes.[22]

The author explains this fact to the "old lady" in *Death in the Afternoon* when she laments the prevalence of venereal disease among bullfighters: "Ah, madame, you will find no man who is a man who will not bear some marks of past misfortune. Either he has been hit here, or broken this or contracted that, but a man throws off many things" (Ch. x). In *Green Hills of Africa* Hemingway regrets not having formal tribal marks like the natives; still, he has some manly scars of his own: "The tribal marks and the tattooed places seemed natural and handsome adornments and I regretted not having any of my own. My own scars were all informal, some irregular and sprawling, others simply puffy welts" (Ch. iii).

Several things are clear. The wound is symbolic as much as realistic: it is a sign of the hero. The wound is not so much "unreasonable" as it is meaningful (see Chapter ii). The wound is not primarily "an outward and visible sign of an inward and spiritual dis-grace" (Young, p. 13), though it may symbolize spiritual decay or wounding as in "The Snows of Kilimanjaro" or *The Sun Also Rises*. It is primarily the hero's title to manhood, his claim to distinction. It shows that he has been crucified or castrated by the world (sometimes one metaphor is more appropriate, sometimes the other; sometimes both are applicable), that he is a kind of martyr who has "been there". But above all it shows that he *is* the hero.

All of the important heroes and many of their friends have been wounded one way or another. Here I must object to Young's distinction between the "code hero" and the "real hero", useful though it sometimes is (pp. 36-38). According to Young, the real hero is "the generic Nick Adams" with Hemingway's own background, while the code hero is the outlaws and professional sportsmen who show the real hero a possible code to live by. Thus Harry Morgan, for example, is a code hero, not a real hero. This distinction, I feel, is too arbitrary. The so-called code heroes

---

[22]   See Barnes, p. 13.

too often have the same honorable scars as the real hero. They represent, I would say, an alter ego of the hero – another aspect of the hero's personality, a way he wishes frequently that he could be.

Starting with Nick in "Chapter" vi of *In Our Time*, who is wounded in the spine and has made a "separate peace", the heroes bear a physical mark of the punishment they have absorbed from life. (Young seems correct in saying that the wound is the culminating objectification of all the spiritual wounds that Nick has been getting as a growing boy.) Most of Jake's circle (if not the whole "lost generation") have psychic wounds of some sort, while Jake himself has a rather mysterious sexual wound. Many critics have referred to Jake as castrated or emasculated, but Hemingway denied vehemently in his interview with Plimpton that such was the case:

Actually he had been wounded in quite a different way and his testicles were intact and not damaged. Thus he was capable of all normal feelings as a *man* but incapable of consummating them. The important distinction is that his wound was physical and not psychological and that he was not emasculated. (p. 77)

It seems to me that Hemingway protests too much here, as he does when he disparages Young's "trauma theory of literature" (p. 69) – that in each case there must be at least a kernel of truth to cause these reactions. In any event, Jake has been "saved by his physical disability" – not merely saved from possible destruction by Brett but saved from having to prove himself.[23]

Count Mippipopolous also bears "marks of past misfortune". After informing Jake and Brett that he has been in seven wars and four revolutions, he partially undresses to show them the scars of his arrow wounds under the ribs. This time Brett explains

[23] Edmund Wilson, "Hemingway: Gauge of Morale", p. 254, says that Jake was saved from Brett. Hesitating to portray a love affair which he had not experienced, perhaps rejecting the possibility of attempting to do so from the beginning, Hemingway had to devise some means by which Jake could be Brett's true love and yet could not have intercourse with her. What is interesting is that he should have hit on a sexual wound as the explanation. For some of the facts of the situation in real life, see Harold Loeb, *The Way It Was* (New York, Criterion Books, Inc., 1959), pp. 249-257, 274-299.

the significance of the wound, turning to Jake: "I told you he was one of us. Didn't I? ... I love you, count. You're a darling" (Ch. vii).

In *A Farewell to Arms* Catherine has been psychically wounded by the earlier death in the war of a man she loved (also part of Brett's background). Frederic Henry, like the "I" of "In Another Country", is wounded in the knee, and at the end of the novel he is marked by the death of Catherine. When Hemingway is telling the "old lady" about love in *Death in the Afternoon*, he informs her that "those who have had it are all marked by it. . . ." She asks, "What way are people marked who have had this thing or is that only a way of speaking?" "All those who have really experienced it are marked, after it is gone, by a quality of deadness", Hemingway replies, adding hastily, "I say this as a naturalist, not to be romantic" (Ch. xi).

The last description is remarkably similar to the description Hemingway gives in Chapter vi of the mark to be seen on the matador:

> The matador, from living every day with death, becomes very detached, the measure of his detachment of course is the measure of his imagination and always on the day of the fight and finally during the whole end of the season, there is a detached something in their minds that you can almost see. What is there is death and you cannot deal in it each day and know each day there is a chance of receiving it without having it make a very plain mark. It makes this mark on every one.

Like lovers marked by the death of their loved one, these are people who have drunk life to the lees, "Made weak by time and fate, but strong in will To strive, to seek, to find, and not to yield" (Tennyson, "Ulysses"). Or as Jake expresses it, "Nobody ever lives their life all the way up except bull-fighters" (Ch. ii). The mark signifies one who has lived his life "all the way up", in the process receiving the inevitable, honorable wound.

Harry Morgan first loses an arm, then his life in the battle of existence. Robert Jordan suffers a broken leg which will cost him his life, but he had also been wounded earlier: as a child (rather like Nick) when he witnessed the lynching of a Negro in Ohio (Ch. x) and later when his father committed suicide (Ch. xxx).

Cantwell is covered with the marks of wounds and so are the real men that he loves:

He only loved people, he thought, who had fought or been mutilated.

Other people were fine and you liked them and were good friends; but you only felt true tenderness and love for those who had been there and had received the castigation that everyone receives who goes there long enough.

So I'm a sucker for crips, he thought. ... And any son of a bitch who has been hit solidly, as every man will be if he stays, then I love him. (Ch. viii)

Moreover, in a passage that looks backward to *Death in the Afternoon* and forward to *The Old Man and the Sea*, Cantwell reflects on the ignorance of two young Italians (former fascists) whom he frightens off by smiling at them "his old and worn death smile":

... couldn't those badly educated youths realize what sort of animal they were dealing with? Don't they know how you get to walk that way? Nor any of the signs that combat people show as surely as a fisherman's hands tell you if he is a fisherman from the creases from the cord cuts. (Ch. xxi)

It is a part of the code to speak of the wound in a tough or deprecating manner, not just as one who would hide his feelings about the harrowing experience but as one who would not boast about his exploits. Notice, for example, the "disciplined" offhand tone in which Cantwell recalls his first big wound (the wound, it is clear, which had profound effects on Hemingway):

... he had become quite confident of his personal immortality since he knew he should have been killed in the heavy artillery bombardment that always preceded the attacks. Finally he did get hit properly and for good. No one of his other wounds had ever done to him what the first big one did. I suppose it is just the loss of the immortality, he thought. Well, in a way, that is quite a lot to lose. (Ch. v)

(The deprecation is reminiscent of Mike's in Chapter xiii of *The Sun Also Rises* when Brett tells the others that he was a very distinguished soldier in the war. He has little to say beyond "How I wish those dear days were back" and "I suppose I've the usual medals. But I never sent in for them.")

Santiago's hands have "deep-creased scars from handling heavy fish on the cords", scars "as old as erosions in a fishless desert" (p. 10). At the end of the short novel his hands are so cut that when the boy sees them he starts to cry (pp. 134-135). This is how we know how badly they are cut and how much Santiago has suffered: in spite of the story's being largely his monologue, he is pretty reticent about his pain, continually understating it.

The fact that so many of the heroes are wounded, together with the fact that three of them have wounds in the hands which are explicitly compared to Christ's stigmata, has tempted some critics to find a Christian meaning in Hemingway, making the heroes types of Christ or Christian martyrs. Even Robert Jordan, who is not one of those wounded in the hands, becomes "a quasi-Marxist sacrificing himself in Christian terms", meeting a series of temptations "on his self-imposed path to martyrdom. . . ."[24] I think that the meaning of the wounds and of the Christian references is something different − but first let us see who has the wounds in the hands.

Santiago's wounds are compared to Christ's when he sees the first of the two sharks come to attack the marlin: " 'Ay', he said aloud. There is no translation for this word and perhaps it is just a noise such as a man might make, involuntarily, feeling the nail go through his hands and into the wood" (p. 118). Returning to the village after his three-day ordeal at sea, he climbs the hill to his shack with the mast over his shoulder and falls asleep face down "with his arms out straight and the palms of his hands up" (p. 134). The cruciform sleeping position is deliberate symbolism, the climb up the hill doubtless an allusion to the ascent of Calvary; the old man's name literally translated means Saint James.[25]

In *Across the River and into the Trees* Renata wants to feel Cantwell's badly wounded hand because she has been dreaming for a week that it is "the hand of Our Lord" (Ch. ix). The earliest explicit Christian comparison that I know of comes in *A Farewell to Arms* when Frederic shows Catherine his hands,

[24] William T. Moynihan, "The Martyrdom of Robert Jordan", *College English*, XXI (December 1959), 128.
[25] See Baker, pp. 319-329, 293n, and Backman, p. 10.

blistered raw from rowing all night, with the comment, "There's no hole in my side" (Ch. xxxvii).

The question is, as Lois Barnes points out (p. 7), in what sense does the hero suffer for mankind – how is he a Christian martyr? O'Faolain seems closer to the meaning when he suggests that the traditional hero has given way to a new type, the tortured martyr, with writers making themselves scapegoats (p. 30) – or Rosenfeld when he suggests that Hemingway gave the "lost generation" an image of itself that it was glad to accept as ennobling and self-justifying in his portrayal of his characters as wounded (pp. 148-149). Briefly, I think that the comparisons to Christ are intended glorification of the heroes, who are only "technically" Christian but very much messianic in their outlook and their fantasies. The wounds and Christian comparisons imply that the hero has been so tortured and martyred by the world that he deserves the honorific comparison, especially when he shows how he can take it and be "pretty good in there" (see Young, p. 101).

It is significant, I think, that as Frederic Henry sits outside Catherine's room in the hospital, remembering the time in camp when he threw a log full of ants on the fire, he muses, "I remember thinking at the time that it was the end of the world and a splendid chance to be a messiah" (Ch. xli). How little Christian such terminology is becomes quite clear in *Death in the Afternoon*. On the first page Hemingway says that from a Christian point of view the whole bullfight is indefensible, and in Chapter xix he explains that one of the pleasures of killing is that of taking to yourself one of the Godlike attributes, giving out death: "These things are done in pride and pride, of course, is a Christian sin, and a pagan virtue. But it is pride which makes the bullfight and true enjoyment of killing which makes the great matador." [26] How-

---

[26] In "Pamplona Letter" Hemingway makes a similar explanation about the fiesta of San Firmin, during which the bullfights are held: "San Firmin is the local deity in the system of local idolatry which the Spaniards substitute for catholicism" (p. 301). Cf. Jordan's thoughts about how killing is the "extra sacrament" for the Spanish, a part of their earlier pagan religion which they have never abandoned but only suppressed to bring out again in wars and inquisitions: "They are the people of the Auto de Fé; the act of faith" (Ch. xxiii).

ever, explaining this does not prevent Hemingway from saying in Chapter ix that what bullfighting needs is "a god to drive the half-gods out. But waiting for a messiah is a long business and you get many fake ones. There is no record in the Bible of the number of fake messiahs that came before Our Lord, but the history of the last ten years of bullfighting would record little else."

Talking about a messiah of killers who makes one feel that he is taking Godlike attributes to himself is closer to diabolism than to Christianity, closer to the romantics' titanism, their rebellion against the gods and the laws of the universe. It is certainly not the reverential attitude. W. H. Auden observes that the romantic hero's catastrophe, his wound, is his claim to distinction – it makes him Somebody; he does not want to be rid of it or of his suffering, any more than the Ancient Mariner or Ahab or Hamlet does, "for who will he be then?" [27] The titan hero is obviously going to have to know how to take it, like Prometheus, since he is sure he will be punished by the powers that be for his rebellion (or his wish to rebel) against the way that things are: he *feels* like a threat to the universe (i.e., he wishes he were so powerful, a demigod).[28] Knowing that he will be punished does not stop him, however, any more than it stopped Prometheus from stealing the fire from heaven.

The emphasis in much of the criticism of *The Old Man and the Sea* is on its "classicism", on its rehandling of the theme of the tragic flaw of pride and exceeding one's limits, as evidenced by Santiago's telling himself that he violated his luck by going out too far (pp. 121, 127, 128, 133). Santiago may not be a rebel against the powers of the universe like Ahab, but he is a daring

[27] *The Enchafèd Flood: The Romantic Iconography of the Sea* (New York, Random House, 1950), pp. 111-114 (quotation from p. 112).
[28] Note the fearful similes as Jordan feels that his aggression is recoiling a hundredfold on his head (after blowing up the bridge): "He had the feeling of something that had started normally and had then brought great, outsized, giant repercussions. It was as though you had thrown a stone and the stone made a ripple and the ripple returned roaring and toppling as a tidal wave. Or as though you shouted and the echo came back in rolls and peals of thunder, and the thunder was deadly. Or as though you struck one man and he fell and as far as you could see other men rose up all armed and armored."

romantic voyager, a lone wolf, part of whose superiority lies in the fact that he does not fear going far out, unlike the owner of the boat that the boy works on – an obviously mediocre character (p. 14). His daring to go far out shows that he has *cojones* and is some more of his claim to hero status, like his being *El Campeón* for having beaten "the great negro from Cienfuegos who was the strongest man on the docks" at the "hand game" (p. 76). It is on a par with his being a "strange old man" (pp. 15, 73) for being able to take it and outlasting the fish with which he identifies himself: the fish also is "wonderful and strange" (p. 53). Recall that Cantwell has "strange" wicked eyes (Ch. xii) and Renata is "a strange girl" (Ch. xxx).[29]

Santiago identifies himself not only with the great fish but with the strange tough loggerhead turtles whose hearts go on beating even after they have been butchered: "I have such a heart too and my feet and hands are like theirs" (p. 41). The romantic wild-animal (or wild-bird) imagery serves also to glorify the heroes: the animals with which they identify themselves are superior to the ordinary variety of animals; they are dangerous, like the heroes. Thus the old man at the end of the story is dreaming once again of the lions playing on African beaches; they are all he dreams of any more (p. 27).[30] We keep hearing about Cantwell's wild-boar blood, and when he has a heart attack

[29] The word *strange* is obviously some of Hemingway's latter-day honorific terminology. Lillian Ross quotes Hemingway as calling himself "a strange old man" (p. 46). Renata loves Cantwell for learning fast about things he doesn't know (according to Hemingway in Ch. xvi of *Death in the Afternoon*, this is a sign of the great writer) and for making "lovely quick decisions" (Ch. x). She loves him also because "he had never been sad one waking morning of his life; attack or no attack" (Ch. xli). Jordan shares the same idea earlier: "All the best ones, when you thought it over, were gay. It was much better to be gay and it was a sign of something too. It was like having immortality while you were still alive" (Ch. i). Jackson, Cantwell's driver, is by contrast "one of those *sad* Americans" (Ch. vii), like another sad American – Robert Cohn. One must take it with a smile to be a hero.
[30] Robert O. Stephens points out in "Hemingway's Riddle of Kilimanjaro: Idea and Image", *American Literature*, XXXII (March 1960), 86-87, that in *Green Hills of Africa* Hemingway and the gun bearer M'Cola work out a ranking of the animals into noble and obscene (Ch. ii, iv). The rhinoceros and hyena are obscene (thus the hyena becomes a death

he rests (standing) against the concierge's desk "as lightly as a hawk rests" (Ch. xxiii). In *The Dangerous Summer*, Part I, Hemingway says, "Hawks always make me happy"; earlier he relates a ludicrous self-glorifying incident with a wolf:

We inspected the animals, the poultry and stables and the gun room and I went into the cage of a wolf which had been recently trapped on the place and played with him which pleased Antonio. The wolf looked healthy and the odds were all against his having hydrophobia so I figured all he can do is bite you so why not go in and see if you can work with him. The wolf was very nice and recognized someone who liked wolves.[31]

The hero group of *The Sun Also Rises* all identify themselves with the bulls, and when Jake explains that a bull is dangerous when he is detached from the herd, Bill says, "Don't you ever detach me from the herd, Mike" (Ch. xiii). Like the virile bulls, the heroes hate and bear down on the steers, who get gored for wanting to be friends while not being "one of us", like Robert Cohn. Such honorific imagery implicitly invites the reader to identify himself with the hero and his circle.

Being superior, the hero is one of Melville's *Isolatoes*, "not acknowledging the common continent of men, but each *Isolato* living on a separate continent of his own" (*Moby Dick*, Ch. xxvii). Nothwithstanding the "no man is an island" of Donne's devotion prefixed to *For Whom the Bell Tolls*, the romantic commonplace "every man is an island" is much closer to the state of affairs in Hemingway's work. And the world in which his heroes live is very much like that described in "Dover Beach": the world that seems "so various, so beautiful, so new, Hath really neither joy, nor love, nor light, Nor certitude, nor peace, nor help for pain" but is like "a darkling plain . . . Where ignorant armies clash by night" – where lovers must be true to each other with the more desperation to make up for all that is lacking, to exclude the hostile outside and find their little certitude by merging their identities (the women especially want to lose theirs).

---

symbol in "The Snows of Kilimanjaro"); the lion, leopard, kudu, and water buffalo are noble. Even the animal kingdom is divided into phony and hero.

[31] *Life*, September 5, 1960, pp. 97, 87.

They are two against the world, alone together, as Frederic Henry emphasizes:

We slept when we were tired and if we woke the other one woke too so one was not alone. Often a man wishes to be alone and a girl wishes to be alone too and if they love each other they are jealous of that in each other, but I can truly say we never felt that. We could feel alone when we were together, alone against the others. (Ch. xxxiv)

Frederic particularly likes taking down Catherine's hair: ". . . it would all come down and she would drop her head and we would both be inside of it, and it was the feeling of inside a tent or behind a falls" (Ch. xviii). Note the similarity of this intensely romantic imagery to the "good place" of "Big Two-Hearted River", the inside of the tent where Nick is isolated from the world, safe where "nothing could touch him" (Part I).

The isolation and individualism do not disappear from Hemingway in his supposed transformation of outlook in the 1930's. His heroes continue to be strangers in an alien world, just as they are so often foreigners "in another country" which they observe but do not belong to. They are lone tourists, isolated in time and space, spectators who ring themselves around with the protective personal code and the intense present moment, the something one finds alone on the Gulf Stream. They are Hemingway's version of the romantic hero, put in the particular 1920's terms in which he sees the twentieth century.

Romantic seems to me a more meaningful term with which to describe Hemingway than the increasingly fashionable *existentialist*. John Killinger's study of Hemingway and existentialism may serve to illustrate what I mean. According to Killinger, practically all existentialism is distinguished by the reduction of knowledge to "the very simplest facts", which he arbitrarily reduces to three: emphasis on the separate identity of the individual, emphasis on each man's choice of being either a "genuine individual" or just part of the crowd, and emphasis on the way of life one chooses – which becomes the measure of good and evil, good being to "exist authentically" (pp. 6, 10-12). He who asserts his individuality is the "authentic" man, possessing "the Godlike attribute of self-determination" (p. 11); he is also, by definition, a rebel against the established order, homeless, an *isolato*, outsider, wanderer, or stranger (p. 12). He exists in a state of anguish (Sartre's *l'angoisse*, Heidegger's *das Angst*), a somewhat mysterious term but a state which appears to result from his keen awareness of his impending annihilation, nothingness (Heidegger's *Nichts*, Sartre's *néant*, Unamuno's and Hemingway's *nada*).

The trouble with this description, to my mind, is a lack of historical perspective. There is no mention in the discussion of existentialism's distrust of systems, abstractions, and collective movements of all sorts (pp. 6-9) that emphasis on the individual is not peculiar to existentialism – that it is, in fact, typical of romanticism (which appears to me the spiritual forerunner of existentialism). Moreover, there is no consideration given to the anthropological fact that the very concept of individualism is a comparatively late development of Western civilization, that conformity to group mores is not a recent American or Western perversion but the larger part of man's history – especially in primitive or "natural" states of society – or that emphasis on the individual flourished historically during the roughly synchronous romantic and industrial revolutions, since which its implications are still being elaborated, argued, and studied.

The desirable and undesirable aspects of individualism versus group interests may be said to form one of the central concerns of our time and in our time to be, obviously, different than in any other, but they were also issues of prime importance for John Stuart Mill. The dilemma is not peculiarly contemporary, the concern just of a post-World-War II philosophical movement with headquarters in France. Nor is the question such a clear-cut matter of being an "authentic" individual on the one hand or a mere voiceless member of the crowd on the other (everyone thinks of himself as an individualist, more or less rugged; no one identifies himself with the mass man for long).

The emphasis on the individual, the semi-deification of the hero as the eternal rebel against convention, against the laws of society or those of nature, the presentation of the hero as an outsider, a lone and lonely man in a state of superiority but fear and cosmic anguish, all are thoroughly romantic in genesis. It is a "hard philosophy", in Killinger's words (p. 13), not just because of the modern breakdown in social and religious values and traditions which the individual must replace with his own values, nor because of its almost puritanical ethical severity (pp. 65-67), but because of the strain that it imposes on the hero to maintain his superhuman status. There becomes a right and a wrong way to everything he does, exactly as there is in the stern code of the Hemingway hero, who would no longer be the hero if he let himself go and behaved like other ordinary human beings.

Some of the dread of nothingness seems to be dread of being a nobody, just as the anguish seems to be in good part conscience money paid for an ego-gratifying wish to be god or demigod:

... in effect, of all the actions a man may take in order to create himself as he wills to be, there is not one which is not creative, at the same time, of an image of man such as he believes he ought to be. ... I am thus responsible for myself and for all men, and I am creating a certain image of man as I would have him to be. In fashioning myself I fashion man.

. . . .

The existentialist frankly states that man is in anguish. His meaning is as follows – When a man commits himself to anything, fully realising that he is not only choosing what he will be, but is thereby at the same time a legislator deciding for the whole of mankind – in such a moment a man cannot escape from the sense of complete and profound responsibility.[32]

The price for enjoying such a romantic wish is a sense of having the burden of the world on one's shoulders: ". . . from the instant of my upsurge into being, I carry the weight of the world by myself alone without anything or any person being able to lighten it." The reason for this anguish is not far to seek: "The best way to conceive of the fundamental project of human reality is to say that man is the being whose project is to be God." [33] Such

---

[32] Jean-Paul Sartre, *Existentialism and Humanism*, tr. Philip Mairet (London, Methuen and Co. Ltd., 1955), pp. 29-30.

[33] Jean-Paul Sartre, *Existentialism and Human Emotions*, tr. Bernard Frechtman and Hazel E. Barnes (New York, Philosophical Library, Inc., 1957), pp. 56-57, 63.

a view of human reality is common not just to existentialism but to romanticism.

Moreover, that part of the dread or melancholy (*Angst*) of the hero which arises from his realizing the intolerable limitations of selfhood and mortality is a dominant mood of romantic literature – not just the mood of contemporary existentialist writers nor of the elder waiter in Hemingway's "A Clean, Well-Lighted Place". These limitations and his impending annihilation are facts infinitely galling to the romantic hero.

The dislike of complication and desire for simplicity is not merely a reduction of superficials to fundamentals, elementals, or first things, as Killinger suggests. It is, I think, a desire for the simple and sure often seen in the romantic nostalgia for childhood. In a way, the rejection of complication is a rejection of the uncertainties of adulthood, when things are not so clear or sure.

It seems to me that such characteristics achieve more perspective when viewed against their historical flourishing in the romantic movement than when viewed as something peculiarly contemporary. It is true, naturally, that there are differences as well as likenesses in any modern handling of this outlook: the points of divergence between Hemingway and Byron are as significant as their similarities. The modern variations on the theme of romanticism are quite as important as the theme itself, but it is also important to identify the theme and not imagine that our times with the aid of the anachronistic Kierkegaard and Nietzsche made up both theme and variations.

By calling Hemingway romantic I do not intend merely adverse criticism (*romantic* being primarily a dyslogistic word for a sizable group of new critics). My wish is to show what general philosophical outlook he shares and to examine in particular his variations on it. Whether his occasional similarities to existentialist writers are close enough to warrant classifying him with them, I doubt, and I am suspicious of the apparent motives behind attempts to link him to a fashionable philosophy, since they seem intended to make him more "respectable" intellectually. No matter what it is called, Hemingway's value system must be assessed on its own merits or failings, without borrowed prestige, if we are ever to see his work in proportion or judge it fairly.

SELECTED BIBLIOGRAPHY

References, including first references, to Hemingway's work and others' fictional work are given whenever possibly by chapter numbers in the text or by titles of short stories or poems. References by page number to *The Old Man and the Sea* are given in the text. In all other cases, first references are given in footnotes and subsequent references in the text whenever possible.

Aldridge, John W., *After the Lost Generation: A Critical Study of the Writers of Two Wars* (New York, McGraw-Hill Book Co., Inc., 1951).

Allen, Charles A., "Ernest Hemingway's Clean, Well-Lighted Heroes", *The Pacific Spectator*, IX (Autumn 1955), 383-389.

Anderson, Charles R., "Hemingway's Other Style", *Modern Language Notes*, LXXVI (May 1961), 434-442.

Anderson, Sherwood, *Dark Laughter* (New York, Boni and Liveright, 1925).

——, *Letters of Sherwood Anderson*, ed. Howard Mumford Jones, with Walter B. Rideout (Boston, Little, Brown and Co., 1953).

Atkins, John, *The Art of Ernest Hemingway: His Work and Personality* (New York, Roy Publishers, 1953).

Auden, W. H., *The Enchafèd Flood: The Romantic Iconography of the Sea* (New York, Random House, 1950).

Backman, Melvin, "Hemingway: the Matador and the Crucified", *Modern Fiction Studies*, I (August 1955), 2-11.

Baker, Carlos, *Ernest Hemingway: A Life Story* (New York, Charles Scribner's Sons, 1969).

——, ed., *Ernest Hemingway: Critiques of Four Major Novels* (New York, Charles Scribner's Sons, 1962).

——, ed., *Hemingway and His Critics: An International Anthology* (New York, Hill and Wang, 1961).

——, *Hemingway: The Writer as Artist*, 3rd ed. (Princeton, Princeton University Press, 1963).

Baker, Sheridan, *Ernest Hemingway: An Introduction and Interpretation* (New York, Holt, Rinehart and Winston, 1967).

Bardacke, Theodore, "Hemingway's Women", in McCaffery, pp. 340-351.

Barea, Arturo, "Not Spain but Hemingway", *Horizon*, III (May 1941), 350-361.

Barnes, Lois L., "The Helpless Hero of Ernest Hemingway", *Science and Society*, XVII (Winter 1953), 1-25.

Bartlett, Phyllis, "Other Countries, Other Wenches", *Modern Fiction Studies*, III (Winter 1957-58), 345-349.

Beach, Joseph Warren, *American Fiction 1920-1940* (New York, The Macmillan Co., 1941).

——, "How Do You Like It Now, Gentlemen?", *The Sewanee Review*, LIX (Spring 1951), 311-328.

Beaver, Joseph, " 'Technique' in Hemingway", *College English*, XIV (March 1953), 325-328.

Bellow, Saul, "Hemingway and the Image of Man", *Partisan Review*, XX (May-June 1953), 338-342.

Benson, Jackson J., *Hemingway: The Writer's Art of Self-Defense* (Minneapolis, University of Minnesota Press, 1969).

Bishop, John Peale, "The Missing All", in McCaffery, pp. 292-307.

Brooks, Cleanth, Jr., and Robert Penn Warren, *Understanding Fiction* (New York, Appleton-Century-Crofts, Inc., 1943).

Burgum, Edwin Berry, "Ernest Hemingway and the Psychology of the Lost Generation", in McCaffery, pp. 308-328.

Burke, Kenneth, *Counter-Statement*, 2nd ed. (Los Altos, Calif., Hermes Publications, 1953).

——, *The Philosophy of Literary Form* (Baton Rouge, Louisiana State University Press, 1941).

——, *A Rhetoric of Motives* (New York, George Braziller, Inc., 1955).

Burnam, Tom, "Primitivism and Masculinity in the Work of Ernest Hemingway", *Modern Fiction Studies*, I (August 1955), 20-24.

Carroll, Latrobe, "Willa Sibert Cather", *The Bookman*, LIII (May 1921), 212-216.

Cather, Willa, *Not Under Forty* (New York, Alfred A. Knopf, 1936).

——, *One of Ours* (Boston, Houghton Mifflin Co., 1937).

——, *Willa Cather on Writing*, foreword by Stephen Tennant (New York, Alfred A. Knopf, 1949).

Colvert, James B., "Ernest Hemingway's Morality in Action", *American Literature*, XXVII (November 1955), 372-385.

Cowley, Malcolm, *Exile's Return: A Literary Odyssey of the 1920's*, rev. ed. (New York, The Viking Press, 1951).

——, "Hemingway: Work in Progress", *The New Republic*, October 20, 1937, pp. 305-306.

——, ed., The Viking Portable *Hemingway* (New York, The Viking Press, 1944).

Cummings, E. E., *The Enormous Room* (New York, The Modern Library, 1934).

Daniel, Robert, "Hemingway and His Heroes", *Queen's Quarterly*, LIV (Winter 1947-48), 471-485.

Dos Passos, John, *Manhattan Transfer* (Boston, Houghton Mifflin Co., 1925).

——, *Three Soldiers* (New York, The Modern Library, 1932).

Eastman, Max, "Bull in the Afternoon", in McCaffery, pp. 66-75.

Edel, Leon, "The Art of Evasion", *Folio*, XX (Spring 1955), 18-20.

Eliot, T. S., "Hamlet and His Problems", in *The Sacred Wood* (London, Methuen and Co. Ltd., 1950), pp. 95-103.

Fadiman, Clifton, "Ernest Hemingway: An American Byron", *The Nation*, CXXXVI (January 18, 1933), 63-64.

Farrell, James T., *"The Sun Also Rises"*, in McCaffery, pp. 221-225.

Faulkner, William, *Soldiers' Pay* (New York, Liveright, 1926).

Fenimore, Edward, "English and Spanish in 'For Whom the Bell Tolls' ", in McCaffery, pp. 205-220.

Fenton, Charles A., *The Apprenticeship of Ernest Hemingway: The Early Years* (New York, The Viking Press, 1958).

Fitzgerald, F. Scott, *The Beautiful and Damned* (London, The Grey Walls Press, 1954).

——, *This Side of Paradise* (New York, Charles Scribner's Sons, 1951).

Ford, Ford Madox, Introduction to *A Farewell to Arms* (New York, The Modern Library, 1932), pp. ix-xx.

Frohock, W. M., "Violence and Discipline", in McCaffery, pp. 262-291.

Fuchs, Daniel, "Ernest Hemingway, Literary Critic", *American Literature*, XXXVI (January 1965), 431-451.

Geismar, Maxwell, "Ernest Hemingway: You Could Always Come Back", in McCaffery, pp. 143-189.

Gerstenberger, Donna, *"The Waste Land* in *A Farewell to Arms"*, *Modern Language Notes*, LXXVI (January 1961), 24-25.

Goldhurst, William, *F. Scott Fitzgerald and His Contemporaries* (Cleveland, The World Publishing Co., 1963).

Graham, John, "Ernest Hemingway: The Meaning of Style", *Modern Fiction Studies*, VI (Winter 1960-61), 298-313.

Halliday, E. M., "Hemingway's Ambiguity: Symbolism and Irony", *American Literature*, XXVIII (March 1956), 1-22.

——, "Hemingway's Hero", *The University of Chicago Magazine*, XLV (May 1953), 10-14.

——, "Hemingway's Narrative Perspective", *The Sewanee Review*, LX (Spring 1952), 202-218.

Hemingway, Ernest, *Across the River and into the Trees* (New York, Charles Scribner's Sons, 1950).

——, *By-Line: Ernest Hemingway; Selected Articles and Dispatches of Four Decades*, ed. William White (New York, Charles Scribner's Sons, 1967).

——, *The Dangerous Summer*. Part I: *Life*, September 5, 1960, pp. 77-88, 91-92, 94, 96-100, 102, 104, 106, 109; Part II: *Life*, September 12, 1960, pp. 61-66, 68, 73, 75-76, 78-80, 82; Part III: *Life*, September 19, 1960, pp. 74-76, 78, 81-82, 84, 87-88, 90, 95-96.

——, *Death in the Afternoon* (New York, Charles Scribner's Sons, 1932).

——, "The Denunciation", *Esquire*, November 1938, pp. 39, 111-114.

——, *A Farewell to Arms* (New York, Charles Scribner's Sons, 1929).

——, *For Whom the Bell Tolls* (New York, Charles Scribner's Sons, 1940).

——, *Green Hills of Africa* (New York, Charles Scribner's Sons, 1935).

——, Introduction to *In Sicily* by Elio Vittorini, tr. Wilfrid David (New York, New Directions, 1949), pp. 7-8.

——, "Joseph Conrad", *the transatlantic review*, II (September 1924), 341-342.

——, ed., Introduction to *Men at War* (New York, Crown Publishers, 1942), pp. xi-xxxi.

——, "Monologue to the Maestro", *Esquire*, October 1935, pp. 21, 174A, 174B.

——, *A Moveable Feast* (New York, Charles Scribner's Sons, 1964).

——, *The Old Man and the Sea* (New York, Charles Scribner's Sons, 1952).

——, "Old Newsman Writes", *Esquire*, December 1934, pp. 25-26.

——, "On the Blue Water", *Esquire*, April 1936, pp. 31, 184-185.

——, "Pamplona Letter", *the transatlantic review*, II (September 1924), 300-302.

——, *The Short Stories of Ernest Hemingway* (New York, Charles Scribner's Sons, 1953).

——, *The Short Stories of Ernest Hemingway: The First Forty-Nine Stories and the Play "The Fifth Column"* (New York, The Modern Library, 1938).

——, *The Sun Also Rises* (New York, Charles Scribner's Sons, 1926).

——, *Three Stories and Ten Poems* (Paris, Contact Publishing Co., 1923).

——, *To Have and Have Not* (New York, Charles Scribner's Sons, 1937).

——, *The Torrents of Spring* (New York, Charles Scribner's Sons, 1926).

——, "A Visit with Hemignway: A Situation Report", *Look*, September 4, 1956, pp. 23-31.

Hemingway, Leicester, *My Brother, Ernest Hemingway* (Cleveland, The World Publishing Co., 1962).

Hemphill, George, "Hemingway and James", in McCaffery, pp. 329-339.

Hoffman, Frederick J., *The Modern Novel in America 1900-1950* (Chicago, Henry Regnery Co., 1951).

——, "No Beginning and No End: Hemingway and Death", *Essays in Criticism*, III (January 1953), 73-84.

——, *The Twenties: American Writing in the Postwar Decade* (New York, The Viking Press, 1955).

Hovey, Richard B., *Hemingway: The Inward Terrain* (Seattle, University of Washington Press, 1968).

Hulme, T. E., "Romanticism and Classicism", in *Critiques and Essays in Criticism 1920-1948*, ed. Robert Wooster Stallman (New York, The Ronald Press Co., 1949), pp. 3-16.

Joost, Nicholas, *Ernest Hemingway and the Little Magazines: The Paris Years* (Barre, Mass., Barre Publishers, 1968).

Kashkeen, J., "Ernest Hemingway: A Tragedy of Craftsmanship", in McCaffery, pp. 76-108.

Kauffmann, Stanley, "Double Feature", *The New Republic*, December 19, 1960, pp. 21-22.

——, "Hollywood and Hemingway", *The New Republic*, October 6, 1958, pp. 21-22.

Killinger, John, *Hemingway and the Dead Gods: A Study in Existentialism* (Lexington?, University of Kentucky Press, 1960).

Lair, Robert L., "Hemingway and Cézanne: An Indebtedness", *Modern Fiction Studies*, VI (Summer 1960), 165-168.

Levin, Harry, "Observations on the Style of Ernest Hemingway", in *Contexts of Criticism* (Cambridge, Mass., Harvard University Press, 1957), pp. 140-167.

Lewis, Robert W., Jr., *Hemingway on Love* (Austin, University of Texas Press, 1965).

Lewis, Wyndham, *Men Without Art* (London, Cassell and Co. Ltd., 1934).

Loeb, Harold, *The Way It Was* (New York, Criterion Books, Inc., 1959).

McCaffery, John K. M., ed., *Ernest Hemingway: The Man and His Work* (Cleveland, The World Publishing Co., 1951).

Madden, David, ed., *Tough Guy Writers of the Thirties* (Carbondale, Southern Illinois University Press, 1968).

Marinetti, F. T., "The New Futurist Manifesto: Wireless Imagination and Words at Liberty", tr. Arundel del Re, *Poetry and Drama*, I (September 1913), 319-326.

Mencken, H. L., *Prejudices: Fifth Series* (New York, Alfred A. Knopf, 1926).

Meyer, Karl E., "Just the Hard Facts: The Divorce of Journalism and Judgment", *The New Republic*, April 24, 1961, pp. 11-15.

Miles, Josephine, *Major Adjectives in English Poetry: From Wyatt to Auden*. University of California Publications in English, XII, No. 3, 305-426 (Berkeley, University of California Press, 1946).

Moynihan, William T., "The Martyrdom of Robert Jordan", *College English*, XXI (December 1959), 127-132.

O'Faolain, Sean, *The Vanishing Hero: Studies in Novelists of the Twenties* (London, Eyre and Spottiswoode, 1956).

Oldsey, Bern, "The Snows of Ernest Hemingway", *Wisconsin Studies in Contemporary Literature*, IV (Spring-Summer 1963), 172-198.

Oldsey, Bernard S., "Hemingway's Old Men", *Modern Fiction Studies*, I (August 1955), 31-35.

Partridge, Eric, *Shakespeare's Bawdy: A Literary and Psychological Essay and a Comprehensive Glossary*, rev. ed. (London, Routledge and Kegan Paul Ltd., 1955).

Plimpton, George, "Ernest Hemingway" (The Art of Fiction, XXI), *The Paris Review*, XVIII (Spring 1958), 60-89.

Pound, Ezra, "The Serious Artist", in *Literary Essays of Ezra Pound*, ed. T. S. Eliot (Norfolk, Conn., New Directions, 1954), pp. 41-57.

Remarque, Erich Maria, *All Quiet on the Western Front*, tr. A. W. Wheen (Boston, Little, Brown and Co., 1958).

Rosenfeld, Isaac, "A Farewell to Hemingway", *The Kenyon Review*, XIII (Winter 1951), 147-155.

Ross, Lillian, "How Do You Like It Now, Gentlemen?", *The New Yorker*, May 13, 1950, pp. 36-38, 40-46, 49-56.

Rovit, Earl, *Ernest Hemingway* (New York, Twayne Publishers, Inc., 1963).

Sanderson, Stewart, *Ernest Hemingway* (New York, Grove Press, Inc., 1961).

Sanford, Marcelline Hemingway, *At the Hemingways: A Family Portrait* (Boston, Atlantic-Little, Brown and Co., 1962).

Sartre, Jean-Paul, *Existentialism and Human Emotions*, tr. Bernard Frechtman and Hazel E. Barnes (New York, Philosophical Library, Inc., 1957).

——, *Existentialism and Humanism*, tr. Philip Mairet (London, Methuen and Co. Ltd., 1955).

Schorer, Mark, "The Background of a Style", *The Kenyon Review*, III (Winter 1941), 101-105.

——, "Technique as Discovery", in *Essays in Modern Literary Criticism*, ed. Ray B. West, Jr. (New York, Rinehart and Co., Inc., 1952), pp. 189-205.

Schreiber, Georges, *Portraits and Self-Portraits* (Boston, Houghton Mifflin Co., 1936).

Schwartz, Delmore, "Ernest Hemingway's Literary Situation", in McCaffery, pp. 114-129.

Scott, Arthur L., "In Defense of Robert Cohn", *College English*, XVIII (March 1957), 309-314.

Shockley, Martin Staples, "Hemingway's Moment of Truth", *The Colorado Quarterly*, V (Spring 1957), 380-388.

Skinner, Cornelia Otis, "For Whom the Gong Sounds", in *Soap Behind the Ears* (New York, Dodd, Mead and Co., 1942), pp. 89-96.

Spilka, Mark, "The Death of Love in *The Sun Also Rises*", in *Hemingway and His Critics*, ed. Baker, pp. 80-92.

Stein, Gertrude, *The Autobiography of Alice B. Toklas* (New York, The Literary Guild, 1933).

——, "Composition as Explanation", in *Selected Writings* of Gertrude Stein, ed. Carl Van Vechten (New York, Random House, 1946), pp. 453-461.

——, *Three Lives* (Norfolk, Conn., New Directions, 1933).

Stephens, Robert O., "Hemingway's Riddle of Kilimanjaro: Idea and Image", *American Literature*, XXXII (March 1960), 84-87.

Tillyard, E. M. W., *Poetry Direct and Oblique* (London, Chatto and Windus, 1948).

Trilling, Lionel, "An American in Spain", in *Ernest Hemingway: Critiques of Four Major Novels*, ed. Baker, pp. 78-81.

——, "Hemingway and His Critics", in *Hemingway and His Critics*, ed. Baker, pp. 61-70.

Warren, Robert Penn, "Hemingway", *The Kenyon Review*, IX (Winter 1947), 1-28.

Wasiolek, Edward, "Tolstoy's 'The Death of Ivan Ilyich' and Jamesian Fictional Imperatives", *Modern Fiction Studies*, VI (Winter 1960-61), 314-324.

Weeks, Robert P., ed., *Hemingway: A Collection of Critical Essays* (Englewood Cliffs, N. J., Prentice-Hall, Inc., 1962).

——, "Hemingway and the Spectatorial Attitude", *Western Humanities Review*, XI (Summer 1957), 277-281.

——, "Hemingway and the Uses of Isolation", *The University of Kansas City Review*, XXIV (December 1957), 119-125.

West, Ray B., Jr., "Ernest Hemingway: The Failure of Sensibility", in *Forms of Modern Fiction*, ed. William Van O'Connor (Minneapolis, The University of Minnesota Press, 1948), pp. 87-101.

Wilson, Edmund, "Hemingway: Gauge of Morale", in McCaffery, pp. 236-257.

——, *The Shores of Light: A Literary Chronicle of the Twenties and Thirties* (New York, Farrar, Straus and Young, Inc., 1952).

Wimsatt, W. K., Jr., with Monroe C. Beardsley, *The Verbal Icon: Studies in the Meaning of Poetry* (Lexington?, University of Kentucky Press, 1954).

Wolfe, Thomas, *The Letters of Thomas Wolfe*, ed. Elizabeth Nowell (New York, Charles Scribner's Sons, 1956).

Young, Philip, *Ernest Hemingway* (New York, Rinehart and Co., Inc., 1952).

——, *Ernest Hemingway: A Reconsideration* (New York, Harcourt, Brace and World, 1966).

——, "Our Hemingway Man", *The Kenyon Review*, XXVI (Autumn 1964), 676-707.

INDEX